Academically Adrift
Limited Learning on College Campuses

Richard Arum and Josipa Roksa

The University of Chicago Press
Chicago and London

The University of Chicago Press, Chicago 60637
The University of Chicago Press, Ltd., London
© 2011 by The University of Chicago
All rights reserved. Published 2011.
Printed in the United States of America

20 19 18 17 16 15 14 13 12 11   7 8 9 10

ISBN-13: 978-0-226-02855-2   (cloth)
ISBN-13: 978-0-226-02856-9   (paper)
ISBN-10: 0-226-02855-0   (cloth)
ISBN-10: 0-226-02856-9   (paper)

Library of Congress Cataloging-in-Publication Data
Arum, Richard.
    Academically adrift : limited learning on college campuses / Richard Arum and Josipa
Roksa.
        p.   cm.
    Includes bibliographical references and index.
    ISBN-13: 978-0-226-02855-2 (cloth : alk. paper)
    ISBN-10: 0-226-02855-0 (cloth : alk. paper)
    ISBN-13: 978-0-226-02856-9 (pbk. : alk. paper)
    ISBN-10: 0-226-02856-9 (pbk. : alk. paper) 1. Education, Higher—United States.
2. Learning—United States. 3. Critical thinking—Study and teaching (Higher)—
United States. 4. Reasoning—Study and teaching (Higher)—United States. I. Roksa,
Josipa. II. Title.
    LA227.4.A78 2001
    378.19'8—dc22
                                                                    2010031799

Academically Adrift

For our students

Contents

Acknowledgments

The research project that led to this book was organized by the Social Science Research Council (SSRC) as part of its collaborative partnership with the Pathways to College Network—an alliance of national organizations that advances college opportunity for underserved students by raising public awareness, supporting innovative research, and promoting evidence-based policies and practices across the K–12 and higher-education sectors. The initial conception and organizational impetus for this endeavor grew out of efforts led by former SSRC program director Sheri Ranis. Ann Coles, former director of the Pathways to College Network, provided critical assistance in gaining external support for this project. Other members of the Pathways to College Network leadership team, including Alma Peterson and Cheryl Blanco, also provided support for our efforts over the past several years. In addition, we are grateful to Michelle Cooper, Alisa Cunningham, and Lorelle Espinosa at the Institute for Higher Education Policy (IHEP), who have supported this project through their current leadership roles in the Pathways to College Network.

This research project was made possible by generous support from the Lumina Foundation for Education, the Ford Foundation, the Carnegie Corporation of New York, and the Teagle Foundation, as well as a 2007–8 Fulbright New Century Scholar "Higher Education in the 21st Century: Access and Equity" award.

The following foundation officers provided critical support and advice that has proven essential for the success of this project: Tina Gridiron Smith and Dewayne Matthews, as well as Jamie Merisotis and Susan Johnson (Lumina Foundation); Jorge Balan and Greg Andersen (Ford Foundation); Barbara Gombach (Carnegie Corporation of New York); and Donna Heiland and W. Robert Connor (Teagle Foundation). We are also profoundly grateful to Roger Benjamin, Alex Nemeth, Heather Kugelmass, Marc Chun, Esther Hong, James Padilla, and Stephen Klein at the Council for Aid to Education for technical collaboration in data collection that made this research possible. Moreover, we would like to express our deep gratitude to the administrators who coordinated site-based data collection and staff at the twenty-four institutions that supported the fieldwork required for this project, as well as to the students who volunteered and consented to participate in this research study.

The researchers are also appreciative of input from the project's advisory board: Pedro Reyes, professor and associate vice chancellor for academic planning and assessment, University of Texas; Myra Burnett, vice provost and associate professor of psychology, Spelman College; William (Bill) Trent, professor of educational policy studies, University of Illinois; and Meredith Phillips, associate professor of public policy and sociology, University of California at Los Angeles. The manuscript also benefited from insightful comments and suggestions received during presentations in diverse settings including the SSRC's Learning in Higher Education conference, organized with the support of the National Association of State University and Land Grant Colleges (Chicago, November 2008); the annual meeting of the American Educational Research Association (San Diego, April 2009); the annual meeting of the American Sociological Association (San Francisco, August 2009); the International Sociology Association's Research Committee on Social Stratification and Mobility (Florence, May 2008); New York University's Applied Psychology Colloquium; the University of Virginia Curry School of Education's Risk and Prevention Speaker Series; the Center for Research on Educational Opportunity, University of Notre Dame; the Department of Sociology at Memorial University, Canada; and the Collegiate Learning Assessment Spotlight Workshop.

Critical comments and recommendations for the project were provided by some of our close colleagues including Joan Malczewski, Mitchell Stevens, and Jonathan Zimmerman, as well as by students in the fall 2009 New York University doctoral seminar "Educational Research in the United States: Problems and Possibilities." We are grateful to our colleagues and students, as well as to the anonymous reviewers at the University of Chicago Press, for their constructive feedback.

The Social Science Research Council program coordinators for this project were Kim Pereira and Jeannie Kim, who provided full-time management of the Collegiate Learning Assessment longitudinal project study from fall 2007 to summer 2008 and from fall 2008 to summer 2010 respectively. Without their professional competence, dedication, and commitment, this research would not have been possible. Additional assistance was provided at the SSRC by Maria Diaz, Carmin Galts, Sujung Kang, Julie Kellogg, Abby Larson, Katherine Long, Jaclyn Rosamilia, and Nicky Stephenson. Melissa Velez served as a primary research assistant for the statistical analysis, and is coauthor of chapters 2 and 3 as well as the methodological appendix. Velez's statistical sophistication and sociological insights have been heavily drawn upon throughout this project. Research assistance was also provided by Daniel Potter, who coauthored chapters 2 and 4, and Jeannie Kim, who coauthored chapter 3. Potter and Kim made both technical and substantive contributions to the chapters they coauthored.

Dedicated staff at the University of Chicago Press skillfully led this book through the final revisions and publication process. We are particularly indebted to Elizabeth Branch Dyson for her feedback and guidance; her enthusiasm and belief in the importance of this project propelled us through the final months of writing. We would also like to thank Anne Summers Goldberg for her technical assistance and Renaldo Migaldi for his meticulous editorial work.

Finally, we would like to express our deepest personal gratitude to those who have lived with us and nourished us throughout this project. Shenandoah, best friend and confidant, provided much needed balance and a sense of humor along the way. Joan served as a personal and professional companion. Sydney, Eero, Luke, and Zora, through their dedication to their own schooling and their commitment to inhabit these colleges and universities in the future, served as inspirations.

While this research would not have been possible without the contributions from the individuals and institutions identified above, Richard Arum and Josipa Roksa are fully responsible for all findings presented, claims made, and opinions expressed in this book.

1

College Cultures and Student Learning

"Colleges and universities, for all the benefits they bring, accomplish far less for their students than they should," the former president of Harvard University, Derek Bok, recently lamented. Many students graduate college today, according to Bok, "without being able to write well enough to satisfy their employers . . . reason clearly or perform competently in analyzing complex, nontechnical problems."[1] While concern over undergraduate learning in this country has longstanding roots, in recent years increased attention has been focused on this issue not only by former Ivy League presidents, but also by policy makers, practitioners, and the public. Stakeholders in the higher education system have increasingly come to raise questions about the state of collegiate learning for a diverse set of reasons. Legislators—and privately, middle-class parents as well—increasingly have expressed worry over the value and returns to their investments in higher education. Business leaders have begun to ask whether graduates have acquired the necessary skills to ensure economic competitiveness. And increasingly, educators within the system itself have begun to raise their voices questioning whether organizational changes to colleges and universities in recent decades have undermined the core educational functions of these institutions.

These diverse concerns about the state of undergraduate education have served to draw attention to measuring whether students are actually developing the capacity for critical thinking and complex reasoning at college. In a rapidly changing economy and society, there is widespread agreement that these individual capacities are the foundation for effective democratic citizenship and economic productivity. "With all the controversy over the college curriculum," Derek Bok has commented, "it is impressive to find faculty members agreeing almost unanimously that teaching students to think critically is the principal aim of undergraduate education."[2] Institutional mission statements also echo this widespread commitment to developing students' critical thinking. They typically include a pledge, for example, that schools will work to challenge students to "think critically and intuitively," and to ensure that graduates will become adept at "critical, analytical, and logical thinking." These mission statements align with the idea that educational institutions serve to enhance students' human capital—knowledge, skills, and capacities that will be rewarded in the labor market. Economists Claudia Goldin and Lawrence Katz, for example, have recently argued that increased investment in U.S. higher education attainment is required for both economic growth and reduced economic inequality. Goldin and Katz's recommendations rest on the assumption that increased college graduation rates will likely have such desirable economic outcomes because the labor market values "the highly analytical individual who can think abstractly."[3] But what if increased educational attainment is not equivalent to enhanced individual capacity for critical thinking and complex reasoning?

While there has been a dearth of systematic longitudinal research on the topic, there are ample reasons to worry about the state of undergraduate learning in higher education. Policy makers and practitioners have increasingly become apprehensive about undergraduate education as there is growing evidence that individual and institutional interests and incentives are not closely aligned with a focus on undergraduate academic learning per se. While as social scientists we want to avoid the pitfalls of either propagating historically inaccurate sentimental accounts of a romantic collegiate past followed by a tragic "fall from grace" or, alternatively, scapegoating students, faculty, and colleges for the current state of affairs, it is imperative to provide a brief description of the historical, social, and institutional context in which the phenomenon under investigation manifests itself to illuminate its multifaceted dimensions.

Higher Education Context: Continuity and Change

Historians have noted that from the inception of U.S. colleges, many students often embraced a collegiate culture that had little to do with academic learning. While some students who used colleges to prepare for the ministry "avoided the hedonism and violence of their rowdy classmates" and focused on academic pursuits rather than extracurricular activities, the majority of students chose another path. For many students in past decades, college was a time when one "forged a peer consciousness sharply at odds with that of the faculty and of serious students." Undergraduates as a whole historically embraced a college life—complete with fraternities, clubs, and social activities—that was produced, shaped, and defined by a peer culture oriented to nonacademic endeavors.[4]

Sociologists have long cautioned about the detrimental effects of peer cultures on an individual's commitment to academic pursuits in general and student learning in particular.[5] Many students come to college not only poorly prepared by prior schooling for highly demanding academic tasks that ideally lie in front of them, but—more troubling still—they enter college with attitudes, norms, values, and behaviors that are often at odds with academic commitment. In recent cohorts of students, Barbara Schneider and David Stevenson have described the prevalence of "drifting dreamers" with "high ambitions, but no clear life plans for reaching them." These students "have limited knowledge about their chosen occupations, about educational requirements, or about future demand for these occupations."[6] They enter college, we believe, largely academically adrift.

While prior historical scholarship reminds us that U.S. undergraduates have long been devoted to pursuing social interests at college, there is emerging empirical evidence that suggests that college students' academic effort has dramatically declined in recent decades. Labor economists Philip Babcock and Mindy Marks, for example, have recently conducted critically important empirical work that meticulously examines data from twelve individual-level surveys of student time use from the 1920s to today. They have found that full-time college students through the early 1960s spent roughly forty hours per week on academic pursuits (i.e., combined studying and class time); at which point a steady decline ensued throughout the following decades. Today, full-time college students on average report spending only twenty-seven hours per week on academic activities—that is, less time than a typical high school student spends at school. Average time studying fell from twenty-five hours per week in 1961 to twenty hours per week in 1981 and thirteen hours per week in 2003. The trends are even more pronounced when Babcock and Marks identify the percentage of students who report studying more than twenty hours per week: in 1961, 67 percent of full-time college students reported this level of effort; by 1981, the percentage had dropped to 44 percent; today, only one in five full-time college students report devoting more than twenty hours per week on studying. Babcock and Marks carefully explored the extent to which changes in student effort simply reflect the fact that different types of individuals currently attend college and course taking patterns have changed. They found that such compositional explanations were inadequate: "Study time fell for students from all demographic subgroups, within race, gender, ability and family background, overall and within major, for students who worked in college and for those who did not, and at four-year colleges of every type, size, degree structure and level of selectivity."[7]

Students' lack of academic focus at today's colleges, however, has had little impact on their grade point averages and often only relatively modest effects on their progress towards degree completion as they have developed and acquired "the art of college management," in which success is achieved primarily not through hard work but through "controlling college by shaping schedules, taming professors and limiting workload."[8] Biostatistician Valen Johnson has taken advantage of unique data from Duke University on student course evaluations, grades, and enrollment decisions to demonstrate that students "preferentially enroll in classes (and subject areas) with instructors who grade leniently."[9] For example, an undergraduate in Mary Grigsby's recent study of collegiate culture at a Midwestern public university commented:

> I hate classes with a lot of reading that is tested on. Any class where a teacher is just gonna give us notes and a worksheet or something like that is better. Something that I can study and just learn from in five [minutes] I'll usually do pretty good in. Whereas, if I'm expected to read, you know, a hundred-and-fifty-page book and then write a three-page essay on it, you know, on a test let's say, I'll probably do worse on that test because I probably wouldn't have read the book. Maybe ask the kids, what's in this book? And I can draw my own conclusions, but I rarely actually do reading assignments or stuff like that, which is a mistake I'm sure, but it saves me a lot of time.

Grigsby's student not only saved a great deal of time with his approach to classes—hours that could be reapportioned to leisure pursuits—but also was able to do well by conventional standards of his grade point average and progress towards degree. The student observed: "You know I can get out of here with a 3.5 but it doesn't really matter if I don't remember any-thing . . . . It's one thing to get the grade in a class and it's another to actu-ally take something from it, you know."[10]

Students' ability to navigate academic course requirements with such modest levels of individual investment and cognitive effort points to a sec-ond set of social actors responsible for growing concern over undergradu-ate learning on today's campuses: the college professoriate. If one is to cast aspersions on student cultures that exist on college campuses today, one would do well to focus equal attention on the faculty cultures and orienta-tions that have flourished in U.S. higher education. Learning at college, after all, is an activity that ideally emerges from an interaction between faculty and students. "What students and teachers mean by 'taking' and 'teaching' courses is determined not by subject or levels alone, but also by the intentions of the participants," Arthur Powell and his colleagues observed two decades ago about U.S. high schools. In these settings, formal and informal "treaties" often emerged: where teaching was "perceived as an art of capturing audiences and entertaining them," and teachers and students "arrange deals or treaties that promote mutual goals or that keep the peace."[11] Higher education researcher George Kuh has extended this insight to colleges and universities, arguing that a "disengagement com-pact" has been struck on many contemporary campuses between faculty and students. This compact is described by Kuh as

> "I'll leave you alone if you leave me alone." That is, I won't make you work too hard (read a lot, write a lot) so that I won't have to grade as many papers or explain why you are not performing well. The existence of this bargain is suggested by the fact that at a relatively low level of effort, many students get decent grades—B's and sometimes better. There seems to be a break-down of shared responsibility for learning—on the part of faculty members who allow students to get by with far less than maximum effort, and on the part of students who are not taking full advantage of the resources institu-tions provide.[12]

If students are able to receive high marks and make steady progress towards their college degrees with such limited academic effort, must not faculty bare some responsibility for the low standards that exist in these settings?

When discussing the extent to which faculty are implicated in condon-ing and accommodating low levels of student commitment to academic coursework, it is important to acknowledge how varied faculty work lives are given the differentiated structure of U.S. higher education. In many lower-tier public colleges and universities that in recent years have faced growing resource constraints, traditional forms of faculty direct instruction have themselves been undermined by the replacement of full-time tenure track faculty with adjunct, graduate student, and other alternative forms of instruction. Recent government reports indicate that the percentage of full-time instructional faculty in degree-granting institutions declined from 78 percent in 1970 to 52 percent by 2005.[13] The changes in lower-tiered public institutions have often been even more pronounced. Full-time faculty in resource-poor institutions likely feel increasingly overwhelmed and demoralized by the growing institutional demands placed on them and their inability to identify sufficient resources to maintain traditional levels of support for undergraduate education.

In other settings where the costs of higher education have increased at roughly twice the rate of inflation for several decades and resources are therefore less constrained, faculty are nevertheless often distracted by institutional demands and individual incentives to devote increased attention to research productivity. Christopher Jencks and David Riesman, for example, astutely noted four decades ago that "large numbers of Ph.D.s now regard themselves almost as independent professionals like doctors or lawyers, responsible primarily to themselves and their colleagues rather than their employers, and committed to the advancement of knowledge rather than of any particular institutions."[14] Throughout the higher education system, faculty are increasingly expected to focus on producing scholarship rather than simply concentrating on teaching and institutional service. This faculty orientation is deep-seated, as graduate training programs that prepare the next generation of faculty are housed primarily at research universities and offer little focus or guidance on developing instructional skills. As Derek Bok observed, "in the eyes of most faculty members in research universities, teaching is an art that is either too simple to require formal preparation, too personal to be taught to others, or too innate to be conveyed to anyone lacking the necessary gift."[15]

Ernest Boyer's work in the late 1980s highlighted the changing "priorities of the professoriate" as well as the institutional diffusion of the university research model to faculty at institutions throughout the system. Boyer noted that while 21 percent of faculty in 1969 strongly agreed with the statement that "in my department it is difficult for a person to achieve tenure if he or she does not publish," two decades later the percentage of faculty agreeing with that statement had doubled to 42 percent.[16] By 1989, faculty at four-year colleges overwhelmingly reported that scholarship was more important than teaching for tenure decisions in their departments.

For example, in terms of the significance of teaching related assessments for tenure, only 13 percent of faculty at four-year colleges reported classroom observations as very important, 5 percent reported course syllabi as very important, 5 percent reported academic advisement as very important, and 9 percent reported student recommendations as very important. Interestingly, the only form of instructional assessment that more than one in eight faculty considered as critical for tenure was student course evaluations: 25 percent of four-year college faculty reported these instruments as very important for tenure decisions. To the extent that teaching mattered in tenure decisions at all, student satisfaction with courses was the primary measure that faculty considered relevant: a measure that partially encourages individual faculty to game the system by replacing rigorous and demanding classroom instruction with entertaining classroom activities, lower academic standards, and a generous distribution of high course marks. Research on course evaluations by Valen Johnson has convincingly demonstrated that "higher grades do lead to better course evaluations" and "student course evaluations are not very good indicators of how much students have learned."[17]

Faculty also reported in Boyer's study that institutional service within the university community was relatively inconsequential for tenure decisions: only 11 percent of faculty at four-year colleges reported this factor as being very important. While faculty widely reported that teaching and university service were generally not very important for tenure, 41 percent reported the number of publications as very important, 28 percent reported the reputation of the presses and journals publishing the books or articles as very important, 28 percent reported research grants as very important, and 29 percent reported recommendations from outside scholars (which are primarily based on evaluation of faculty members' published research records) as very important. The significance of external recommendations can be contrasted with recommendations from other faculty within the institution, which only 18 percent of four-year college faculty considered as very important.[18] For Boyer, what was particularly troubling about these findings was the fact that this faculty orientation had spread widely beyond the research university to a much larger set of otherwise institutionally diverse four-year colleges. Boyer worried that at many college campuses, "the focus had moved from the student to the professoriate, from general to specialized education, and from loyalty to the campus to loyalty to the profession."[19]

While some have argued, and indeed it is possible, that faculty research and teaching can be complementary, the empirical evidence unfortunately suggests that this tends not to be the case on most of today's campuses. In *What Matters in College?* Alexander Astin constructed two scales: one of the faculty's research orientation (defined primarily in terms of publication rate, time spent on research, and personal commitment to research and scholarship) and one of the faculty's student orientation (reflecting primarily the extent to which faculty believed that their colleagues were interested in and focused on student development). The two scales were strongly negatively correlated, and ironically, if not surprisingly, the faculty's student orientation was negatively related to salary compensation.[20] After examining a range of student outcomes from academic to affective, Astin concluded that "there is a significant institutional price to be paid, in terms of student development, for a very strong faculty emphasis on research."[21]

By the turn of the century, however, incentives for faculty throughout the four-year college system increasingly had come to emphasize and encourage professors to focus on pursuing their own scholarship and professional research interests. While recent faculty time-use studies have shown only modest changes in time devoted to research, teaching, and advisement (with the former two categories showing slight increases between the early 1970s and the early 1990s, and the latter category moderately declining), the time-use data does show that four-year college professors spend only limited time on preparing instruction, teaching classes, and advising students. On average, faculty spend approximately eleven hours per week on advisement and instructional preparation and delivery. The time-use data also indicates that faculty report directly engaging in research activities only from two hours per week in liberal arts colleges to five hours per week at research universities.[22] The remainder of time during a typical academic work week is consumed with a host of other professional and quasi-administrative functions including committee meetings, e-mail correspondence, review of professional manuscripts, and external consulting.

While some of these additional noninstructional obligations are mandated by the institutions that employ faculty—as in the university and department committee meetings that professors often complain about— many of these additional activities likely advance faculty careers, but are largely unrelated or only indirectly related to undergraduate instruction. Massy and Zemsky have referred to the process whereby faculty gain increased discretionary time to pursue professional and personal goals, while undergraduate education is devalued, as an "academic ratchet." Massy and Zemsky note:

Put simply, those hours not used for teaching courses, for grading papers, or for meeting with students become available for research and scholarship, for consulting and other professional activities, and in most research universities, for specialized teaching at the graduate level. Institutional rhetoric about the importance of teaching notwithstanding, we believe that the reductions in discretionary time associated with more and better teaching usually are not compensated by additional salary or other rewards, whereas success or failure with regard to other obligations carries significant rewards and penalties . . . Even when most faculty use their time to meet professional and institutional obligations, the academic ratchet still shifts output from undergraduate education toward research, scholarship, professional service, and similar activities—a process that we have termed "output creep."[23]

Christopher Jencks and David Riesman several decades earlier provided a similar account of faculty movement away from undergraduate instruction at research universities in *The Academic Revolution*. They noted that the availability of external funding gave successful researchers significant leverage over the colleges and universities that employed them:

Since the amount of research support has grown much faster than the number of competent researchers, talented men have been in very short supply and command rapidly rising salaries. They are also increasingly free to set their own working conditions. The result has been a rapid decline in teaching loads for productive scholars, an increase in the ratio of graduate to undergraduate students at the institutions where scholars are concentrated, the gradual elimination of unscholarly undergraduates from these institutions, and the parallel elimination of unscholarly faculty.[24]

In recent decades the allure of external funding for research has been greatly enhanced by the growth of commercial opportunities associated with research activities in higher education. Federal government legislation, such as the Bayh-Dole Act of 1980, allowed colleges and universities to patent discoveries that had been developed with federal research support and facilitated the growth of university collaborations "with the private sector in the development of the commercialization of new technologies."[25] Colleges and universities—institutions that, according to Derek Bok, share with compulsive gamblers the trait that "there is never enough money to satisfy their desires"—eagerly embraced these new opportunities to acquire new sources of funding.[26] Universities also engaged in these emerging corporate ventures to acquire the symbolic resources that the collaborations conferred. Sociologists Walter Powell and Jason Owen-Smith have astutely observed that "the commercialization of university-based knowledge signals the university's role as a driver of the economy. Such a lofty status has much more legitimacy and cachet, and makes it possible for universities, especially public universities, to boast their success in creating employment opportunities."[27]

Whether one focuses on "output creep" occurring as a result of an "academic ratchet" that individual faculty engage in to expand their professional discretionary time, on the "academic revolution" produced by the expanding power of the faculty researcher that Christopher Jencks and David Riesman described in the late 1960s, or on the "commercialization of higher education" following the Bayh-Dole Act of 1980 that Walter Powell and Jason Owen-Smith examined, one thing is clear: undergraduate education in many colleges and universities is only a limited component of a much broader set of faculty professional interests, and one that generally is not perceived as being significantly rewarded. And if there is any doubt that college professors are less likely than other individuals to focus on material incentives, recent surveys of students and faculty have found that faculty are more likely than students to report that being well off financially is an essential or a very important goal to them.[28] We do not believe, however, that financial incentives are primarily responsible for faculty commitment to research. Rather, we believe that given the transformation of higher education, one of the few remaining moral bases for academic life is a quasi-religious commitment to embracing research as a "vocational calling." As Anthony Kronman recently observed, "the equation of scholarly specialization with duty and honor . . . makes the development of one's place in the division of intellectual labor a spiritually meaningful goal and not just an economic or organizational necessity."[29] For many faculty, commitment to their own individual research programs is thus understood not as an act of self-aggrandizement or personal selfishness, but rather as a moral imperative that one must pursue and struggle to achieve regardless of institutional obstacles.

While faculty distracted by professional interests other than undergraduate instruction share responsibility for the current state of undergraduate learning occurring on U.S. campuses, it is worth emphasizing again that the professoriate respond to incentives established not only by their larger professional fields of scholarship, but also more specifically by higher-education institutions and the administrators who oversee the colleges and universities where they are employed. While many U.S. colleges follow governance policies that cede formal control over curriculum and instruction to the faculty as a whole, administrators have the institutional authority and responsibility to determine work loads and ensure that faculty are spending sufficient effort on undergraduate instruction as opposed to other legitimate professional activities (e.g., graduate instruction, academic scholarship, and professional service).

If faculty at U.S. colleges can be described as being distracted by professional interests other than undergraduate instruction, it is likely even more the case that contemporary higher education administrators experience institutional interests and incentives that focus their attention elsewhere. As former Harvard University President Derek Bok has noted:

> While (academic) leaders have considerable leverage and influence of their own, they are often reluctant to employ these assets for fear of arousing opposition from the faculty that could attract unfavorable publicity, worry potential donors, and even threaten their jobs. After all, success in increasing student learning is seldom rewarded, and its benefits are usually hard to demonstrate, far more so than success in lifting the SAT scores of the entering class or in raising the money to build new laboratories or libraries.[30]

We believe that administrators are likely even more distracted than faculty from a focus on undergraduate instruction due to the simple fact that their professional lives (with the possible exception of administrators working in the area of student services) tend to reduce and limit their amount of interpersonal contact with students. After all, faculty on average spend eleven hours per week on teaching and advisement activities that to some extent must remind them of the significance of student learning.

One empirical way to highlight the extent to which administrators have allowed higher-education institutions to drift away from an undergraduate instructional focus is to identify the staffing and employment changes that those institutions have implemented in recent decades. While administrators at colleges and universities with strong traditions of faculty governance can legitimately claim that curriculum and instruction are appropriately considered faculty matters and not administrative responsibilities, decisions around employment structure and staffing are universally considered to be under the purview of administrators. In colleges and universities across the country, not only have part-time instructors increasingly replaced full-time professors, but resources have increasingly been diverted towards nonacademic functions. Sociologist Gary Rhoades has documented that over the past three decades, "this group [of non-faculty

support professionals] has become the fastest growing category of professional employment in higher education."[31] While some of these individuals
have been hired for administrative functions such as human relations, accounting, and regulatory compliance, Rhoades has observed that the most
significant increase has occurred in the broad area of student services including admissions, financial aid, career placement, counseling, and academic services such as advising and tutoring that have been reassigned
to non-faculty professionals. These "managerial professionals," as Rhoades
has termed them, have come to comprise "nearly 30 percent of the professional positions on campus and more than three times the number of administrative positions." In related changes, the percentage of professional
employees in higher education comprised of faculty has decreased from
approximately two-thirds in 1970 to 53 percent by 2000.[32]

This internal transformation of higher education, while often focused on
elevating student services as broadly defined, has implicitly deemphasized
the role of faculty and faculty instruction per se at these institutions. The
nonacademic professionalization of higher education can also be observed
in appointments to college and university leadership positions, as well as
their compensation packages. While the vast majority of higher-education
leaders continue to emerge from earlier positions in the college professoriate, in recent decades individuals increasingly have been drawn from
nonacademic backgrounds and hired through a process dependent on professional search consultants. About one in seven college and university
presidents now comes from outside academia; the role of external professional search consultants in the selection process has grown from 12 percent in 1984 to more than half today.[33] In addition, administrative positions
in higher education have become increasingly well compensated.[34] On average, college and university presidents' compensation in the private sector
is approximately $500,000, with many making over a million dollars per
year. "When you have college presidents making $1 million, you're going
to have $800,000 provosts and $500,000 deans," Patrick M. Callan, president of the National Center for Public Policy and Higher Education has
noted. "It reflects a set of values that is not the way most Americans think
of higher education."[35] While there is nothing inherently wrong with well-
paid higher education administrative personnel, the nonacademic professionalization of higher education leadership, and the process whereby it
is identified, our concern here is simply about how these changes might
affect institutional attention to academic instruction. As the sociologist
Steven Brint has noted, "we know that the backgrounds of top executives
can influence the climate of the firms they lead . . . If this is true in corpo-

rations, is it not likely to be true a fortiori in colleges and universities?"[36] Arguably, shifts in the character of administrative leadership are associated with the phenomenon of colleges and universities today becoming much more interested in the fulfillment of nonacademic services and functions, while focusing less on traditional academic instruction.

Indeed, as sociologist Mitchell Stevens noted in his recent ethnography of a selective private residential college: "The College is an academic institution, and a justly proud one, but it also is proud of its twenty-eight varsity sports teams, its budding artists and musicians, its community service projects, diverse student body, spectacular campus, and loyal alumni."[37] Colleges and universities have secured their centrality in our society not only by providing credentials that "serve as ever more important cues about worker capability and character," but also by "making college life more athletic, more masculine, and more fun."[38] Colleges and universities are not just "sieves" that sort and train students, but also "incubators," "temples," and "hubs"—i.e., settings for the development of cultural dispositions, network formation, knowledge production, and institutional relationships.[39]

Changes in Institutional Functions and Identities

Traditionally, U.S. colleges and universities had embraced both academic and moral education as primary institutional functions and rationales. While Harvard historian Julie Reuben has shown how colleges and universities over time shifted the approach whereby moral education was inculcated in students—with "the religious stage, falling roughly between 1880 and 1910; the scientific, from about 1900 to 1920; and the humanistic and extracurricular, roughly 1915–1930"—these institutions defined their organizational missions in large part by embracing the responsibility of providing academic and moral guidance to young adults in their charge.[40] Following World War II, however, colleges and universities that were enrolling increasing numbers of students turned away from these functions and embraced more narrowly defined technocratic ends, such as the generation of scientific knowledge and the production of graduates to fill professional and managerial positions. Some observers have largely celebrated these organizational changes. For example, Clark Kerr, former chancellor at the University of California, Berkeley, observed that in these transformed institutions "there is less sense of purpose" but "there are more ways to excel. There are also more refuges of anonymity—both for the creative person and the drifter."[41] Other scholars, however, have lamented this transformation, worrying that U.S. higher education does not have "an adequate basis for establishing a consensus of moral values"—other than support for "diversity and mutual tolerance"—and thus is "in the midst of a moral crisis."[42]

Since the student rebellions of the 1960s, the extent to which collegiate life has embraced nonacademic pursuits has likely been aided and abetted by college administrators and staff who have "largely withdrawn from oversight of manners and morals."[43] While colleges once assumed a quasi-parental role and struggled with mixed success to ensure "the enforcement of academic and social rules," educators and administrators have grown "less certain than they once were as to what students *ought* to be or become, and are reluctant to go to the mat with the young for principles in which they themselves only half believe." Even if a consensus was reached on the definition of an appropriate and desirable code of student conduct, college administrators and faculty have often found it "politically expedient to avoid collective regulation of student behavior."[44] Although administrators in recent years on some college campuses have implemented policies to limit and control alcohol and drug use, in most secular colleges there has been little institutional responsibility taken for the moral development or social regulation of students. It is thus not particularly surprising that behaviors at odds with academic values, such as cheating on exams, have been demonstrated to have increased significantly in recent decades. In a longitudinal comparison of nine colleges, for example, college students who admitted that they copied from other students on tests or exams increased from 26 percent in 1963 to 52 percent in 1993. Rates of student cheating were particularly high in colleges that had no honor code governing student conduct.[45]

These developments are not unique to higher education; they have occurred concurrent with broad-based cultural changes in the relationship between youth and education. They occurred, for example, during an historic period where elementary and secondary students had begun to enjoy a wide range of new legal rights and entitlements that undermined students' sense of traditional forms of authority relationships in education.[46] Concurrently, legally mandated supplementary student services in special education programs increased dramatically, redefining earlier assumptions of individual and institutional responsibility for managing students' academic and social difficulties. Middle-class parents increasingly saw themselves less as collaborative partners with school authorities who were believed to possess legitimate authority in loco parentis and more as "advocates" for their children's educational needs. Educators became progressively more reluctant to require students to master certain forms of knowledge over other less culturally privileged ones. Students in K–12, and particularly in higher education, increasingly became defined as "consumers" and "clients." In this context, schools are expected not to provide quasi-parental guidance and social regulation, but instead to meet client needs through delivery of elaborate and ever-expanding services.

The effects of these broad-based cultural changes on higher education were enhanced by federal and state policies that shifted financial support from institutions to individuals. As higher-education researchers Sheila Slaughter and Larry Leslie have documented, in the early 1970s the federal government began formulating internal policy papers calling for "a freer play of market forces" that would "give individuals the general power of choice in the education marketplace" as well as specifying "levels and types of student support which will make most institutional aid programs unnecessary."[47] At the federal and state level, institutional aid programs were increasingly replaced by "high tuition–high aid policy through which government gave aid to students rather than institutions, thus making student consumers in the tertiary marketplace. Institutions competed with each other to attract students and their Pell grants."[48] Student aid was essentially structured as an educational voucher. While the G.I. Bill of 1944 provided portable scholarship support for veterans to use at accredited institutions, the higher-education reauthorization legislation passed in 1972 provided portable financial aid to large numbers of students who were defined as qualified based on income levels. In recent years, this market-based logic has only been further extended by federal policies that have facilitated the growth of college finance models that rely on tax credits and student loans.[49]

Personal financial investment in higher education has significantly grown with increases in the cost of higher education and an expanded reliance on private credit-based financing. Specifically, from 1978 to 2008, tuition and fees (not including room and board) increased from $9,903 to $25,143 in private four-year colleges and from $2,303 to $6,585 in public four-year colleges in constant 2008 dollars.[50] Family and student sources of financing also shifted, with the fastest-growing source of funding being private-sector loans. From 1997 to 2007, private-sector student loans in constant dollars increased almost seven times, from $2.5 billion to $17.6 billion.[51] Approximately 60 percent of students graduating four-year colleges have taken out student loans; from 2000 to 2007 the average student-loan debt per borrower increased 18 percent, from $19,300 to $22,700 in constant 2007 dollars.[52] In addition to student-loan debts, students during this period also increasingly used credit cards to support themselves and their educational expenses while in college. Undergraduates in their senior year in 2008 on average had $4,100 in credit card debt, with one-fifth of seniors carrying credit card balances greater than $7,000. Moreover, 30 percent of students reported putting tuition costs on their credit cards.[53] The assumption of significant debt during college became typical, as did the hours many students spent in paid employment while attempting to complete their degrees.

Social scientists are just beginning to explore the implications of this shift for how students are understanding and experiencing their college years. The increased debt burden could potentially serve to impose a new sense of self-discipline on students, and a refocused attention on academic activities. Alternatively, it might lead students to become distracted from their coursework by the importance of paid employment, or it might produce other unanticipated consequences. Full-time college students on average today spend five hours more per week working than in the early 1960s, although national data suggests that fewer than one in six full-time students at four-year colleges work more than twenty hours per week.[54] In terms of increased debt, an intriguing recent study of students at one selective southern Californian institution found that undergraduates had little worry about their ability to find high-paying jobs after college to repay their student loans. Students reported that they defined the purpose of these loans as serving not just as an investment in the future but also as a means to experience fully a collegiate life—a personal objective that included a commitment to a student culture characterized by frequent socializing, travel, and entertainment.[55] Regardless of how rising costs and increased reliance on loans affect student academic and social behavior, changes in the character of higher-education financing are potentially related to the deepening of consumerist orientations within higher education.

A market-based logic of education encourages students to focus on its instrumental value—that is, as a credential—and to ignore its academic meaning and moral character. The historical sociologist David Labaree has argued that "we have credentialism to thank for aversion to learning that, to a great extent, lies at the heart of our educational system."[56] Many students' lack of commitment to substantive academic learning is consistent with their definition of the situation: "It is only rational for students to try to acquire the greatest exchange value for the smallest investment of time and energy."[57] Faculty also do not have much incentive to challenge this emerging reward structure, as conflicts with students over these matters potentially can distract from research, lower teacher or course evaluations, and generate administrative problems associated with student resistance.

Private colleges and universities, of course, have always to some extent adopted market-based orientations and competed for students—just as students have competed for access to elite private education. In recent decades, however, as the market-based logic of higher education has been extended, public colleges and universities have begun to share more in common with their counterparts in the private sector. There are likely many positive consequences associated with defining students as consumers and clients as schools become more responsive to articulated individual student needs. Our point here, however, is that there is no guarantee that students will prioritize academic learning at the core of their institutional demands. There are many reasons instead to expect students as consumers to focus on receiving services that will allow them, as effortlessly and comfortably as possible, to attain valuable educational credentials that can be exchanged for later labor market success. As historical sociologist David Labaree has noted:

> The payoff for a particular credential is the same no matter how it was acquired, so it is rational behavior to try to strike a good bargain, to work at getting a diploma, like a car, at a substantial discount. The effect on education is to emphasize form over content—to promote an educational system that is willing to reward students for formal compliance with modest performance requirements rather than for demonstrating operational mastery of skills deemed politically and socially useful.[58]

While colleges and universities have always in part been businesses that have competed to attract students and cater to their individual needs, they also have traditionally seen themselves as enterprises with quasi-parental authority and the responsibility to define appropriate educational goals with regard to academic content, social behavior, and moral development. The balance between these competing institutional functions has noticeably shifted in recent decades.

Measuring Learning in Higher Education

Organizational inertia, the assumption that students are meeting the academic goals espoused in mission statements, and a lack of external pressure to demonstrate learning have all contributed to a failure systematically to measure and evaluate students' gains in higher education. The tide is shifting, however, as concerns about turning out productive workers and not wasting resources become paramount in an era of globalization and fiscal constraints. Learning in higher education was recently placed in the national spotlight by a report of the Secretary of Education's Commission on the Future of Higher Education entitled *A Test of Leadership*. Reminiscent of the critique in *A Nation at Risk* of elementary and secondary education in the 1980s, *A Test of Leadership* placed the responsibility for the nation's competitiveness in the global economy on the doorsteps of educational institutions. With respect to student performance, the commission noted that "the quality of student learning at U.S. colleges and universities is inadequate, and in some cases, declining."[59] Supporting this claim, it reported on sobering statistics from the National Assessment of Adult Literacy. Specifically, from 1992 to 2003 the percentage of college graduates judged proficient by various literacy measures was relatively low, and by two of those three indicators competency declined (prose, 40 to 31 percent; document, 37 to 25 percent; and quantitative, 31 percent at both time points).[60] While a debate has since ensued on the definition of proficiency, the commission nevertheless used the results from this study to urge improvement and increased accountability to monitor student learning in higher education.[61]

The commission also identified a lack of transparency and accountability with respect to institutional performance in general and student learning in particular. "Despite increased attention to student learning results by colleges and universities and accreditation agencies, parents and students have no solid evidence, comparable across institutions, of how much students learn in colleges or whether they learn more at one college than another," its report noted. "Similarly, policymakers need more comprehensive data to help them decide whether the national investment in higher education is paying off and how taxpayer dollars could be used more effectively."[62]

From our standpoint, the evidence of student and organizational cultures' inattention to learning and high levels of societal investment makes discussion of higher education's accountability both largely inevitable and in certain respects warranted. We are deeply skeptical, however, that *externally* imposed accountability systems will yield desirable changes in educational practices—for reasons that we will discuss in the concluding chapter of this book. More immediately, as social scientists we raise two additional core reservations regarding such endeavors. First, it is not clear that the state of knowledge in the field is adequate to the task. Specifically, as we will discuss in detail below, there is only a very limited tradition of social scientific efforts to measure learning rigorously across individuals and institutions in higher education, and even less of a scholarly research corpus that attempts to identify individual and institutional factors associated with improved postsecondary student performance. Given these limitations, it is doubtful that the implementation of an externally imposed accountability system would yield outcomes that would be either meaningful or productive.

Second, while the question of how much students in particular colleges are learning—or, whether they are learning anything associated with academic knowledge at all—is worth pondering at a societal and regulatory level, in terms of applied social science research designed to improve institutional policy and practice, it is the wrong question. Rather than asking whether students are learning anything at college and designing accountability regimes to address the absence of measurable gains at underperforming schools, we need first to identify the specific factors associated with variation in student learning across and within institutions. Such an empirical analysis requires that large numbers of students in multiple institutions are tracked over time as they progress through college. Longitudinal measurement of test score performance, coursework, institutional characteristics, social background, and college experience is needed to build our knowledge of the processes and mechanisms associated with student learning. Datasets of this character in elementary and secondary education have existed for several decades and have enabled researchers to address these questions adequately.

To date, however, longitudinal datasets with these features have not existed in the field of U.S. higher education. As social scientists we were tired of waiting on the U.S. government to muster the political will to overcome institutional resistance and begin collecting longitudinal data tracking student learning in higher education over time. Our frustration was so great that when an opportunity arose to join a group of innovative practitioners to collect independent data on this topic, we began building our own dataset that could for the first time systematically identify the relevant individual and institutional factors associated with student learning in higher education. Our research addresses the critical absence of similar studies by tracking students through a large and representative sample of higher-education institutions with objective measures of their learning as well as of their coursework, social background, and experience of life on today's college campuses.

The Determinants of College Learning dataset

Our research was made possible by a collaborative partnership with the Council for Aid to Education,[63] an organization that brought together lead-

ing national psychometricians at the end of the twentieth century to develop a state-of-the-art assessment instrument to measure undergraduate
learning, and twenty-four four-year colleges and universities that granted
us access to students who were scheduled to take the Collegiate Learning
Assessment (CLA) in their first semester (Fall 2005) and at the end of their
sophomore year (Spring 2007).[64] Students who consented to participate
in our study not only completed the CLA at multiple points in their college careers, but also responded to surveys on their social and educational
backgrounds and experiences. In addition, we collected course transcript
data and institutional information on high schools and colleges that the
students attended. The research in this book is based on longitudinal data
of 2,322 students enrolled across a diverse range of campuses. Colleges in
our sample include schools of varying size, selectivity, and missions. The
sample includes liberal arts colleges and large research institutions, as well
as a number of historically black colleges and universities (HBCUs) and
Hispanic-serving institutions (HSIs). The schools are dispersed nationally
across all four regions of the country. We refer to this multifaceted data as
the Determinants of College Learning (DCL) dataset.

Logistical and resource constraints required our reliance on participating institutions to implement appropriate random sampling and retention
strategies. We thoroughly investigated the extent to which students in our
sample were indeed representative of students from these institutions as
well as of U.S. higher education more broadly (this book's methodological appendix provides detailed comparisons with data from the Integrated
Postsecondary Education Data System and the Beginning Postsecondary
Students Longitudinal Study). On most measures, students in the DCL
dataset appeared reasonably representative of traditional-age undergraduates in four-year institutions, and the colleges and universities they attended resembled four-year institutions nationwide. The DCL students'
racial, ethnic, and family backgrounds as well as their English-language
backgrounds and high school grades also tracked well with national statistics. For example, 65 percent of DCL students had college-educated parents, as compared to 59 percent of a national sample of traditional-age
students in four-year institutions. Half of students in both the DCL and
national samples earned A or A− in high school. Moreover, the four-year
colleges and universities in the DCL sample have a proportion of white students and a level of academic preparation similar to those of four-year institutions in general. Indeed, the 25th and 75th SAT percentiles of entering
students at the DCL institutions and four-year institutions nationwide are
virtually identical. As a likely result of the voluntary participation required

in our study, however, our sample did have fewer men, as well as fewer students of lower scholastic ability as measured by standardized tests—for example, students' combined scores at the 25th percentile of the SAT were lower in our sample than at DCL institutions or four-year institutions nationwide. Consequently, we believe that any biases introduced into our analysis by the sampling procedures used are likely to be in the direction of leading us toward overestimating students' *positive* educational experiences and institutional success.

The Collegiate Learning Assessment

The Collegiate Learning Assessment (CLA) consists of three open-ended, as opposed to multiple-choice, assessment components: a performance task and two analytical writing tasks (i.e., to make an argument and to break an argument). According to its developers, the CLA was designed to assess "core outcomes espoused by all of higher education—critical thinking, analytical reasoning, problem solving and writing."[65] These *general skills* are "the broad competencies that are mentioned in college and university mission statements."[66] Rather than testing for *specific content knowledge* gained in particular courses or majors, the intent was to assess "the collective and cumulative result of what takes place or does not take place over the four to six years of undergraduate education in and out of the classroom."[67] The developers of the CLA argue that it assesses abilities distinct from those measured in general education tests such as the Scholastic Aptitude Test (SAT) and the American College Testing (ACT) program. "Consequently, an SAT prep course would not help a student on the CLA and instruction aimed at improving CLA scores is unlikely to have much impact on SAT or ACT scores."[68]

While the CLA as a whole is considered by some as state-of-the-art, the performance task component is its most well-developed and sophisticated part. Our analysis, which follows in this book, will focus on that component. The performance task allows students ninety minutes to respond to a writing prompt that is associated with a set of background documents. The testing materials, including the documents, are accessed through a computer. The Council for Aid to Education has published several examples of representative performance tasks that are worth describing here in detail.

The "DynaTech" performance task asks students to generate a memo advising an employer about the desirability of purchasing a type of airplane that has recently crashed. Students are informed: "You are the assistant to Pat Williams, the president of DynaTech, a company that makes precision electronic instruments and navigational equipment. Sally Evans, a member of DynaTech's sales force, recommended that DynaTech buy a small private plane (a SwiftAir 235) that she and other members of the sales force could use to visit customers. Pat was about to approve the purchase when there was an accident involving a SwiftAir 235." Students are provided with the following set of documents for this activity: newspaper articles about the accident, a federal accident report on in-flight breakups in single engine planes, Pat Williams's e-mail to her assistant and Sally Evans's e-mail to Pat Williams, charts on SwiftAir's performance characteristics, an article from *Amateur Pilot* magazine comparing SwiftAir 235 to similar planes, and pictures and descriptions of SwiftAir models 180 and 235. Students are then instructed to "prepare a memo that addresses several questions, including what data support or refute the claim that the type of wing on the SwiftAir 235 leads to more in-flight breakups, what other factors might have contributed to the accident and should be taken into account, and your overall recommendation about whether or not DynaTech should purchase the plane."[69]

A second performance task that the Council for Aid to Education has circulated is related to crime reduction. The test instructs students that "Jamie Eager is a candidate who is opposing Pat Stone for reelection. Eager critiques the mayor's solution to reducing crime by increasing the number of police officers. Eager proposes the city support a drug education program for addicts because, according to Eager, addicts are the major source of the city's crime problem." Students again are provided with a set of documents including newspaper articles, crime and drug statistics, research briefs, and internal administrative memos. The CLA requires that students should specifically address the following: "Mayor Pat Stone asks you to do two things: (1) evaluate the validity of Eager's proposal and (2) assess the validity of Eager's criticism of the mayor's plan to increase the number of officers." [70]

The Council for Aid to Education has also published a detailed scoring rubric on the criteria that it defines as critical thinking, analytical reasoning, and problem solving—including how well the student assesses the quality and relevance of evidence, analyzes and synthesizes data and information, draws conclusions from his or her analysis, and considers alternative perspectives. In addition, the scoring rubric with respect to written communication requires that the presentation is clear and concise, the structure of the argument is well-developed and effective, the work is persuasive, the written mechanics are proper and correct, and reader interest is maintained.[71]

The design of the prompts and the criteria applied for evaluation follow "a criterion sampling approach to measurement" that "assumes that the whole is greater than the sum of its parts and that complex tasks require an integration of abilities that cannot be captured when divided into and measured as individual components."[72] The philosophy behind the approach is to "sample tasks from the domain in which that person is to act, observe her performance, and infer competence and learning."[73] The CLA thus attempts to identify "real-world tasks that are holistic and drawn from life situations." Given that the performance tasks involve solving "complex, holistic, real-world problems," college institutions that attempt to "teach to the test" will be schools that teach students "to think critically, reason analytically, solve problems, and communicate clearly."[74]

The CLA has been lauded by many. For example, the Commission on the Future of Higher Education noted that it "promotes a culture of evidence-based assessment in higher education" and is "among the most comprehensive national efforts to measure how much students actually learn at different campuses."[75] The former program director of higher education for the Carnegie Corporation of New York, Daniel Fallon, noted that the CLA "rose from the field" as "the best creative thinking of the academic research and psychometric community" focused on measuring student learning in higher education.[76] Even testing skeptics, such as James Traub, have noted that the "C.L.A. is light years ahead of the fill-in-the-blanks format of most standardized tests."[77]

Nevertheless, the CLA also has its fair share of critics. The criticism falls into several broad categories. First, there are those who resist any increased encroachment of testing and assessment in education in general and higher education in particular. Resistance to standardized assessment of student learning in U.S. higher education has been historically broad and deep amongst educators. As Patrick Callan, president of the National Center for Public Policy and Higher Education, notes: "Higher education has deflected the idea for the past quarter-century by arguing the kinds of things we want undergraduate education to teach are not really measurable."[78] Resistance has been particularly pronounced at private colleges, which are not responsive to public officials. "Trying to create an uber-instrument . . . will be a grave disservice to the individuals, institutions, and the country," the president of the National Association of Independent Colleges and Universities, David Warren, has commented. "We will get a meaningless outcome at a great cost."[79]

These critics of increased standardized learning assessment argue that such efforts are also unnecessary given the successes of a U.S. higher education system that already inherently ensures accountability through market forces. As Princeton professor and former president of the American Council of Learned Societies, Stanley Katz, has noted: "the public is quite satisfied with what higher education is doing on the whole. This is a market system, and the customers are buying. We have by a considerable measure the finest system of higher education in the world. And if that's the case, this is an 'ain't broke, don't fix it' situation."[80] While we share Katz's sentimental attachment to a U.S. higher education system that has generously provided us with both training and employment, we are skeptical of most of the assumptions inherent in this argument. The "market" system for higher education in the U.S. is characterized by a limited number of selective institutions that share many features in common, that control access to scarce goods (i.e., prestigious credentials) and that are heavily subsidized by public sources of support such as college grant provisions, loan guarantees, tax exemptions, and research grants.

In recent decades, the U.S. higher education system has fallen behind many other countries in terms of the percentage of individuals it graduates.[81] Moreover, whether college students are more effectively educated in the U.S. than abroad is today an open empirical question, but will perhaps not remain so for much longer. The Organisation of Economic Cooperation and Development (OECD) is currently launching a feasibility study for the international Assessment of Higher Education Learning Outcomes (AHELO) that will parallel its earlier efforts that have successfully assessed academic performance of fifteen-year-olds from a comparative international perspective since 2000 with the Programme for International Student Assessment (PISA). The OECD efforts are designed to develop a "direct assessment of learning outcomes in higher education" that "could provide member governments with a powerful instrument to judge the effectiveness and international competitiveness of their higher education institutions, systems and policies in the light of other countries' performance, in ways that better reflect the multiple aims and contributions of tertiary education to society."[82] It is worth noting here that AHELO decided to embrace and adapt the CLA "to an international context with a view to provide a proof of concept" for its assessment of generic skills that "can be measured across diverse institutions, languages and cultures." In particular, students in multiple countries in 2016 "will complete an online assessment, using their critical skills along with data provided for each task. The questions are not specialized so that they can be answered by most undergraduates, whatever their field of study."[83]

A second line of criticism is not necessarily opposed to testing itself, but questions the validity of general, broad-based assessments that do not focus on the specific knowledge taught in particular courses and majors (e.g., life sciences, mathematics, physical sciences, and social sciences). Catherine Hoffman Breyer at the University of Washington, for example, has argued that "a standardized test, such as the CLA, with its focus on generic skills and knowledge, could not detect the specialized information and skills each student had worked to master."[84] In a similar fashion, Steve Chatman at the University of California at Berkeley's Center for Studies in Higher Education has asserted that "because of the differences in undergraduate experiences across majors within an institution, any attempt to capture an overall measure of performance across all of a college or university's students 'will necessarily be biased' by the makeup of its programs."[85] These critics are unclear, however, on why one should not consider a college's curricular composition itself to be an institutional policy associated with student learning or why one could not easily control for these differences when modeling results.

Third, skeptics of the CLA in the past have raised questions about the instrumental validity of the indicator. Some of these concerns, however, have now been addressed by a recent test validity study organized by the Fund for the Improvement of Postsecondary Education (FIPSE). This study brought together researchers from the Council for Aid to Education (CAE), the Educational Testing Service (ETS), and the American College Testing (ACT) program. It examined the instrumental construct validity of the CLA, the ACT's Collegiate Assessment of Academic Proficiency (CAAP) and the ETS's Measure of Academic Proficiency and Progress (MAPP) by administering all three tests in thirteen schools with more than 1,100 students participating. While CAAP and MAPP rely on a multiple choice format, score reliability with the CLA was high when considered at the aggregate school level (correlations of 0.75 to 0.84). In addition, at the individual level, correlations were higher across CLA open-ended and CAAP/MAPP multiple choice tests of critical thinking ($r = 0.53$) than CLA-CAAP/MAPP tests of different constructs ($r = 0.45$). While the results indicate that these tests should not be used as a basis to make institutional decisions about students as individuals (e.g., promotion or course placement), when aggregated in larger samples they can provide reliable estimates of institutional or group-level differences in performance on these tasks.[86]

Fourth, some higher-education practitioners have questioned not the CLA itself, but the modeling approach that the Council for Aid to Education and individual colleges and universities have used to identify institutional effects with this assessment instrument. CLA has generally been

used in a value-added framework, which entails comparing test scores of
enrolled freshmen and seniors at an institution in a given year, after controlling for student performance on a prior test such as the SAT or ACT.
These comparisons have not typically tracked specific students through
college, nor have they accounted for other non-school factors that might
be associated with differential rates of learning. Higher-education practitioners, such as Chancellor Howard Cohen of Purdue University Calumet,
has questioned whether one "can measure the 'value added' in college generally, when so much of the experience of students is beyond the control of
colleges."[87] If one longitudinally tracked students over time, however, and
adequately accounted for a full set of non-school factors—as we will do in
this project—even CLA critics such as Wheaton College Dean Gary N. Larson concede that the measurement approach would approximate a "gold
standard" for assessing student outcomes.[88]

Although there are significant methodological challenges to our project
(including issues of sampling, attrition, and selection that are discussed at
length in a methodological appendix), the study generates significant new
knowledge to guide future research, policy, and practice. While well short
of an experimental research "gold standard," descriptive findings based
on tracking many students enrolled in diverse institutions, with careful
longitudinal measurement of a wide range of factors and outcomes over
time, yields quite illuminating results on the nature and character of collegiate experiences and variation in student learning that can significantly
increase our understanding of the phenomenon.

Other Studies of Learning and Student Trajectories through College

In spite of the increasing attention of policy makers on measuring student
learning in higher education, and an extensive tradition of research on
academic performance in elementary and secondary education, efforts to
directly measure development of general cognitive skills in college have
been limited. Over the past decade the most widely used assessment of
student learning and personal development in higher education has been
the National Survey of Student Engagement (NSSE), which presents students with a questionnaire in multiple-choice format that gauges students'
self-assessment of their learning during college. Since the inception of the
NSSE in 2000, more than 1,300 colleges and universities in the United
States and Canada have used it to survey students about their learning.

It is unclear, however, whether students can accurately self-report an assessment of the degree to which they have actually learned general skills. As young adults, are they aware of what they do not know? If students cannot identify or define learning and critical thinking skills, how will they know whether they have obtained them? Self-reported assessments are also well known to be susceptible to inflated perceptions of one's own performance. For example, as the economists Robert Frank and Philip Cook have noted, "some 80 percent of us think we are better-than-average drivers" and "more than 90 percent of workers consider themselves more productive than their average colleague."[89] In addition, while George Kuh and others have used NSSE results to identify associations between self-reported student learning and self-reported college engagement, it has not yet been systematically demonstrated that all forms of college engagement are consistently associated with growth on objective measures of learning.

Instead of relying on students' self-reports of their cognitive gains, two large-scale national projects have aimed to measure student learning directly by relying on different modules of the CAAP, an assessment tool developed by the ACT program to measure general college skills including critical thinking, reading, and writing. The National Study of Student Learning (NSSL) followed approximately 4,000 students at twenty-three institutions through their first three years in college, beginning in the fall of 1992. While this project is no longer ongoing, it has provided important insights about the relationship between students' college experiences and their improvement in general skills such as reading, writing, and critical thinking. In 2006, Charles Blaich at the Center of Inquiry in the Liberal Arts at Wabash College launched the Wabash National Study of Liberal Arts Education. Starting with nineteen institutions, the study has since been expanded to include a diverse set of forty-nine institutions including liberal arts colleges, regional universities, research universities, and community colleges. Students participating in the study are surveyed and tested at their entry into higher education, at the end of their first year, and at the end of their senior year. This study assesses a range of college outcomes, from academic motivation and attitudes toward reading and writing to leadership, moral reasoning, and attitudes about diversity, as well as critical thinking (evaluated using the CAAP critical thinking test). Although the multiple-choice framework to assessing college learning can be criticized for its reductionist character, the Wabash and earlier NSSL studies are among the few large-scale efforts to assess how academic as well as nonacademic experiences are associated with student learning, and how those experiences are shaped by student backgrounds. By collecting information on students' demographic characteristics, pre-college attributes, and college experiences, as well as by conducting in-depth interviews with a subsample of students, the Wabash study in particular promises to provide crucial insights into factors shaping student development over four years of college.[90]

In addition to these studies, which directly measure students' experiences and performance during college, some studies have used standardized test scores, such as SAT and ACT pre-college measures and GRE post-college measures, to approximate a repeated indicator longitudinal assessment design.[91] Moreover, recent reports from the *Measuring Up* initiative have used professional exams and licensures as a proxy for learning. While these endeavors, which aim to approximate but not directly measure students' progress through college, present important steps in the measurement of student outcomes, they are limited to students who take specific tests, and thus miss a large proportion of students who do not pursue specific educational or occupational paths affected by graduate school or licensure exams immediately after college.

Although scant attention has been dedicated to measuring student learning with objective performance assessment across institutions and over time, several large projects have recently focused on tracking students through college and into the labor force. While ignoring the measurement and modeling of student learning, these endeavors provide useful models for thinking about student experiences and outcomes in higher education. William Bowen and Derek Bok in *The Shape of the River* examined outcomes of minority students admitted to selective colleges under race-sensitive policies relative to the outcomes of their white peers in the 1979 and 1989 entering freshmen cohorts. Non-white students at twenty-eight academically selective and predominantly private colleges "have, overall, performed very well" on a wide range of indications—including graduation rate, fields of study, advanced degree attainment, earnings, and civic engagement.[92] The one major exception to this pattern was observed in student academic outcomes measured by college grade point averages. Specifically, Bowen and Bok demonstrated that "black students with the same SAT scores as whites tend to earn lower grades."[93] James Shulman and William Bowen found in subsequent work that while college athletes graduate at relatively high rates from these selective college settings, their grades in college are lower than expected after controlling for prior preparation, and have been deteriorating over time.[94]

In more recent work, Douglas Massey and his colleagues have tracked a large number of students entering college in the fall of 1999 at a similar set of twenty-eight selective colleges and universities "essentially following the

cohort of freshmen entering Bowen and Bok's sample of schools as they became sophomores, juniors, and ultimately for most, graduating seniors."[95]
In a series of articles and books, Massey and his colleagues focused attention in particular on racial differences in student outcomes. In results similar to Bowen and Bok's earlier work, the lower grades of African-American
students were highlighted (net of extensive controls for social background
and academic preparation). Massey and his colleagues also identified the
extent to which African-American students faced greater economic pressures while at college, and the extent to which students regardless of race
who were engaged in many campus activities (other than membership in a
fraternity or sorority) earned higher grades.[96]

These endeavors provide invaluable information about students' experiences during their college years. However, they have failed to measure
student learning or link student experiences to growth in learning. Among
other outcomes, Bowen and Bok as well as Massey et al. report analyses of
college grades, the traditional and long-relied-upon method of measuring
learning in higher education. Grades are an effective way of measuring
student learning within a particular class, since most institutions have a
scaled grading system already in place. They are an unreliable comparative measure across classes or schools, however, since inconsistencies exist
across teachers within schools and there are discrepancies in scale and
grade definition between schools and over time as grade inflation has occurred. Although grades serve a valuable purpose within classrooms and
are worth collecting as a component of a larger evaluation strategy, on their
own they provide only a very limited and inadequate assessment of student learning.

Moreover, past endeavors examining college students' experiences and
outcomes have often focused on selective colleges and the experience of
non-white students attending these schools. While selective institutions
tend to garner much scholarly attention, most students do not have the
privilege of attending such schools. Students attending selective institutions differ from those attending the rest of higher education on a number
of individual characteristics as well as outcomes. The median SAT score for
institutions participating in the National Longitudinal Survey of Freshmen
(used by Massey at al.) was 1,243 and the majority of those students had
parents who had graduated from college, leading the authors to conclude
that "by any criteria, the twenty-eight institutions constitute an elite sample."[97] Similarly, students in the College and Beyond (C & B) dataset studied
by Bowen and Bok were more academically prepared than the national average and, not surprisingly, had much higher graduation rates: 85 percent

of C&B students graduated from the *same institution* within six years, compared to the national average of just over 50 percent.[98] Thus, knowing the patterns and consequences of specific activities at elite institutions does not necessarily extend to the majority of students who are attending nonselective colleges and universities. Questions about the growth in student learning over time and the patterns and consequences of different collegiate experiences on average U.S. campuses still remain to be answered.

Outline of our Presentation

In this book we will highlight four core "important lessons" from our research. First, in terms of undergraduate learning, four-year colleges and universities and students attending them are too often "academically adrift." While U.S. higher education is expected to accomplish many tasks, we draw on students' reports of their collegiate experiences to demonstrate that undergraduate learning is rarely adequately prioritized. Second, gains in student performance are disturbingly low; a pattern of limited learning is prevalent on contemporary college campuses. Third, individual learning in higher education is characterized by persistent and/or growing inequality. Fourth, while the overall level of learning is low, there is notable variation both within and across institutions that is associated with measurable differences in students' educational experiences.

In chapter 2 we continue to describe the 2,322 students in our study as they begin their college careers. We focus in particular on the extent to which they are improving their skills in critical thinking, complex reasoning, and writing as measured by the CLA during the first two years in college. Moreover, while inequalities in access persist, higher-education institutions today enroll an increasingly diverse set of students from a variety of backgrounds. We thus examine whether CLA performance at entry into higher education as well as gains over time vary across students from different social backgrounds, focusing in particular on different racial/ethnic groups and students from more or less educated families. This chapter reveals that American higher education is characterized by limited or no learning for a large proportion of students, and persistent or growing inequalities over time.

Chapter 3 examines how students navigate and experience contemporary college cultures. How distinctive are these cultures? Do students' academic attitudes, behaviors, and values simply reflect their divergent social backgrounds and academic abilities? Or do colleges differ in the extent to which they successfully promote student academic orientations and practices? We find disturbing evidence that many contemporary college academic programs are not particularly rigorous or demanding. Moreover, students rarely seem to focus on academic pursuits; many appear to be academically adrift in today's colleges and universities. We show, however, that colleges vary in the extent to which they support academically oriented student behaviors.

How are students' experiences in college related to their development of critical thinking, complex reasoning, and writing skills as measured by the CLA? We address this question in chapter 4, by exploring how academic and social integration—with the latter being promoted by many colleges to improve student retention—are related to student learning. The importance of rigorous coursework requirements, faculty expectations, and time spent studying is highlighted. In addition, we discuss whether student employment and extracurricular activities can become a distraction to student learning, as well as how various college majors and types of coursework are associated with improvement in CLA performance. While overall levels of learning are low, we identify specific experiences and higher-education contexts that are associated with improvement in critical thinking, complex reasoning, and writing skills during the first two years of college.

In our concluding chapter, we argue that the patterns identified in our study highlight the extent to which institutional reform is required in U.S. higher education. Specifically, while others have applied the metaphor of a river to the journey through college of today's students, our findings call attention to the fact that many undergraduate students are academically adrift on contemporary campuses. Educational reform requires improved measurement and understanding of the processes and factors associated with student learning. In an increasingly globalized competitive economy, the consequences of policy inattention are profound. Regardless of economic competitiveness, the future of a democratic society depends upon educating a generation of young adults who can think critically, reason deeply, and communicate effectively. Only with the individual mastery of such competencies can today's complex and competitive world be successfully understood and navigated by the next generation of college graduates.

2

Origins and Trajectories

Public and policy discussions of higher education over the course of the twentieth century have focused on one issue in particular: access. Massive expansion of higher education, led by the public sector, has created unprecedented opportunities for students to continue their education beyond high school.[1] Although institutional barriers and inequalities in access persist and concerns about affordability continue to mount, American higher education today educates more than eighteen million students in more than 4,300 degree-granting institutions.[2] Educational expectations have been on the rise, with more than 90 percent of high school students *expecting* to attend college.[3] And many are indeed crossing the threshold of higher education: more than 70 percent of recent high school graduates have enrolled in either a two-year or a four-year institution.[4] As Martin Trow has observed, higher education has been transformed from a privilege into an assumed right—and, for a growing proportion of young adults, into an expected obligation.[5]

Although growing proportions of high school graduates are entering higher education, many are not prepared for college-level work and many others have no clear plan for the future. Most American high schools have come to embrace a "college for all"

Daniel Potter and Melissa Velez coauthored this chapter.

mentality, encouraging students to proceed to higher education regardless of their academic performance. Consequently, high school students expect to enroll in college and complete bachelor's degrees, even when they are poorly prepared to do so judging from their grade point averages, high school rank, or courses taken.[6] In a survey of more than two thousand high school seniors in the Chicago metropolitan area, sociologist James Rosenbaum reported that almost half of the students in the sample (46 percent) agreed with the statement: "Even if I do not work hard in high school, I can still make my future plans come true."[7]

Students' ambitions are misaligned not only with their academic performance in high school, but also with the educational requirements of their expected occupations. In a recent study of American teenagers, Barbara Schneider and David Stevenson reported that only 44 percent of students had aligned ambitions, meaning that they expected to attain as much education as was typically required of their intended occupation.[8] Many students entering higher education today seem to understand that college education is important but have little specific information about or commitment to a particular vision of the future. One student in psychologist Jeffrey Arnett's study *Emerging Adulthood* summarized what many seemed to be experiencing upon entry into college: "I just wasn't ready. I wasn't really sure what I wanted to do."[9]

It is this unique point in time—when access to college is widespread, concerns about inadequate academic preparation are prevalent, and drifting through college without a clear sense of purpose is readily apparent—that serves as the historic context for our observations of the lives of students as they unfold at twenty-four four-year institutions. While sociologists have often focused on the top or the bottom of the educational hierarchy, we are describing college life as it is experienced by students attending typical four-year institutions (for a detailed discussion of the sample, see the methodological appendix). We begin our analysis by considering what these students bring to higher education, particularly in terms of academic preparation; what types of courses and activities they engage in; and, most importantly, how much they develop their skills in critical thinking, complex reasoning, and writing over their first two years in college. As policymakers champion increasing access and improving graduation rates, it is appropriate to ask: How much are students actually learning in contemporary higher education? The answer for many undergraduates, we have concluded, is not much.

Limited Learning

Teaching students to think critically and communicate effectively are espoused as the principal goals of higher education. From the Commission on the Future of Higher Education's recent report *A Test of Leadership* to the halls of Ivy League institutions, all corners of higher education endorse the importance of these skills. When promoting student exchange across the world, former Secretary of Education Margaret Spellings urged foreign students to take advantage of "the creativity and diversity of American higher education, *its focus on critical thinking*, and its unparalleled access to world-class research."[10] The American Association of University Professors agrees: ". . . critical thinking . . . is the hallmark of American education—an education designed to create thinking citizens for a free society."[11] Indeed, 99 percent of college faculty say that developing students' ability to think critically is a "very important" or "essential" goal of undergraduate education. Eighty-seven percent also claim that promoting students' ability to write effectively is "very important" or "essential."[12]

However, commitment to these skills appears more a matter of principle than practice, as the subsequent chapters in this book document. The end result is that many students are only minimally improving their skills in critical thinking, complex reasoning, and writing during their journeys through higher education. From their freshman entrance to the end of their sophomore year, students in our sample on average have improved these skills, as measured by the CLA, by only 0.18 standard deviation.[13] This translates into a seven percentile point gain, meaning that an average-scoring student in the fall of 2005 would score seven percentile points higher in the spring of 2007. Stated differently, freshmen who enter higher education at the 50th percentile would reach a level equivalent to the 57th percentile of an incoming freshman class by the end of their sophomore year. Three semesters of college education thus have a barely noticeable impact on students' skills in critical thinking, complex reasoning, and writing.

How do we know that a 0.18 standard deviation does not represent remarkable growth? There are no universal standards for learning in higher education, leaving open the question of how much learning is enough, or desirable, or even can reasonably be expected. The past provides one benchmark against which to compare the present. There is at least some evidence that college students improved their critical thinking skills much more in the past than they do today. Summarizing an extensive body of research, Pascarella and Terenzini estimated that seniors had a 0.50 standard deviation advantage over freshmen in the 1990s. In contrast, during the 1980s students developed their skills at twice the rate: seniors had an advantage over freshmen of one standard deviation.[14] While useful for demonstrating a decline in learning over time, standard deviations do not present an intuitive interpretation of student gains. Another way to assess the magnitude of learning during the first two years in college is to estimate how many students experience gains that fall below the level of statistical significance, or in other words are statistically not above zero. With a large sample of more than 2,300 students, we observe no statistically significant gains in critical thinking, complex reasoning, and writing skills for at least 45 percent of the students in our study.[15] An astounding proportion of students are progressing through higher education today without measurable gains in general skills as assessed by the CLA. While they may be acquiring subject-specific knowledge or greater self-awareness on their journeys through college, many students are not improving their skills in critical thinking, complex reasoning, and writing.

These disappointing results may lead some to dismiss the messenger and challenge the validity of the testing instrument: something must be wrong with how the CLA measures skills in critical thinking, complex reasoning, and writing; the CLA must be unable to capture the progress students make. While all educational assessments are inherently imperfect, the results reported here are not anomalous. There is growing evidence of meager progress made by students in higher education across a range of different assessment strategies. A recent endeavor led by educational researcher Charles Blaich, the Wabash National Study of Liberal Arts Education, reported equally discouraging findings. Using different (multiple choice) assessment instruments, and analyzing data for more than three thousand students from nineteen institutions, this study found that students have made no measurable improvement in critical thinking skills during their first year in college.[16] Low gains reported by the CLA are thus not simply an artifact of our measurement strategy, but a disconcerting reality.

But perhaps we are not following students long enough; perhaps students will make notable strides in the last two years of college, substantially improving their skills in critical thinking, complex reasoning, and writing by the time they graduate. While we are optimists at heart, there is plenty of reason for doubt. The Wabash National Study reported that students' academic motivation and interest in academic subject matter *declined* during their first year in college, leaving little hope that they would notably improve their academic skills in subsequent years.[17] And at least one study has indicated that most of the gains in general skills occur in the first two years of college.[18] Moreover, many indicators of good educational practice do not increase or become prevalent as students advance through higher education. Seniors do not spend much more time studying than freshmen. And while many freshmen report little academic demand in terms of writing, half of seniors report that they have not written a paper longer than twenty pages in their last year of college.[19] Similarly, approximately one-fifth of seniors, as well as freshmen, report coming to class "frequently" unprepared and indicate that their institutions give little emphasis to academic work.[20] Thus, in the most optimistic scenario, students will continue their meager progress, leading to less than impressive gains over the course of their enrollment in higher education. More realistically, students are likely to learn no more in the last two years than they did in the first two, leaving higher education just slightly more proficient in critical thinking, complex reasoning, and writing than when they entered. And as we are about to show, students are also likely to leave higher education as unequal, or more so, than when they entered.

Patterns of Inequality in CLA Performance

"We need to recognize that the most serious domestic problem in the United States today is the widening gap between the children of the rich and the children of the poor . . . . And education is the most powerful weapon we have to address that problem," said Lawrence Summers, former president of Harvard University, announcing that his institution would give full scholarships to low-income students.[21] This belief that education is a solution to social inequality—and many other social problems—is widespread. Ever since Horace Mann, a nineteenth-century American educational reformer, proclaimed that education was "the great equalizer of the conditions of men," schools have been charged with providing opportunities for all students and serving as a vehicle of social mobility.[22]

But there is also a much less sanguine view, in which education is believed to reproduce social inequality by "proportioning academic success to the amount of cultural capital bequeathed by the family." Students from upper-class families acquire "linguistic and cultural competence" and "familiarity with [the dominant, upper- and middle-class] culture." These skills and predispositions are in turn rewarded in school, granting children from more privileged families higher grades, better course placements, and other positive educational outcomes. Since schools expect but do not teach these cultural competencies, children from less advantaged families are left to fend for themselves, and in the process they typically reproduce their class location.[23]

To what extent do patterns of learning in higher education reflect the principles of social mobility or social reproduction? Students enter higher education unequal in a myriad of domains. Initial CLA performance tracks closely with family background: students from more educated families scored higher on the CLA when they entered college in the fall of 2005 (figure 2.1).[24] The gaps across different racial/ethnic groups were even more pronounced (figure 2.2). All racial/ethnic minority groups had lower levels of skill in critical thinking, complex reasoning, and writing, as measured by the CLA, when they first entered college than their white peers. The gap between African-American and white students was particularly stark: African-American students lagged almost one standard deviation (or 34 percentile points) behind their white peers when they entered college.[25]

Inequalities at the point of entry into higher education are not surprising, given the pervasive disparities in the K–12 system. The crucial question is what happens after students enter higher education: do colleges reproduce or reduce inequality in critical thinking, complex reasoning, and writing skills among students from different family backgrounds and racial/ethnic groups? With respect to parental education, the results point to a pattern of persistent inequality, with all groups of students experiencing similar gains in their CLA scores during their first two years of college. Consequently, the gaps in CLA performance across students from different family backgrounds are virtually the same at the end of the sophomore year as they were when students first entered college. Students whose parents

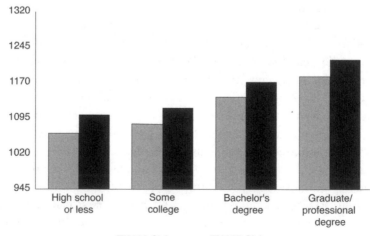

Figure 2.1. CLA scores from 2005 and 2007, by parental education (based on table A2.1)

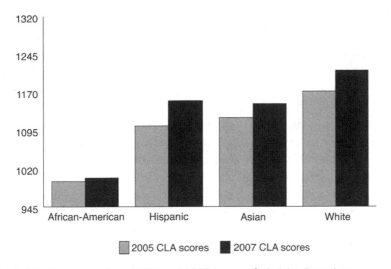

Figure 2.2. CLA scores from 2005 and 2007, by race/ethnicity (based on table A2.1)

had no college experience, for example, lagged 120 points behind those whose parents had graduate or professional degrees in 2005, and 116 points behind in 2007.[26] This pattern of persistent class inequality has previously been observed with respect to other outcomes, such as higher-education access and degree attainment.[27]

The patterns of racial/ethnic inequality are even more disconcerting. African-American students not only entered higher education with lower CLA scores than their white peers, they also gained less over time. During their first two years of college, white students gained 41 points while African-American students gained only 7 points. The gains of African-American students were thus only one-sixth those of the gains of white students. As a consequence, the gap between African-American and white students increased over time.[28] Other non-white racial/ethnic groups made progress similar to that of white students during their first two years of college, preserving inequalities observed at the point of entry into higher education.

Although students from less educated family backgrounds and from racial/ethnic minority groups continued to lag behind their more advantaged peers, women demonstrate the same level of critical thinking, complex reasoning, and writing skills as men. Indeed, gender represents one of the relatively few dimensions of stratification where a historically disadvantaged group managed to catch up—and in some instances move ahead of—the advantaged group. Trend statistics show a striking reversal of the gender gap in higher education. While women were underrepresented until the 1980s, they represent the majority of college entrants and bachelor's degree holders today.[29] Women and men demonstrated a similar level of skill in critical thinking, complex reasoning, and writing when they entered college, and this parity persisted on their journeys through higher education. Although it is not the focus of the remainder of this volume, gender parity in CLA performance is worthy of notice, as it stands out in contrast to the observed racial/ethnic and socioeconomic inequalities.

When students enter higher education academically disadvantaged, they remain unequal, or in some instances grow even further apart. Initial inequalities are thus largely preserved and, in the case of African-American students, even exacerbated. This pattern suggests that higher education in general reproduces social inequality. However, estimating the extent to which schools contribute to social stratification is a complicated matter, as students spend only a fraction of their time in the classroom, and inequality in educational outcomes is particularly sensitive to students' activities outside the classroom.[30] In subsequent chapters, we examine how students' activities inside and outside the classroom vary across different racial/ethnic and socioeconomic groups, as well as how these different activities contribute to inequality in CLA performance. But before we explore what students do once they enter higher education, we need to consider what they bring to college. How much do observed differences in CLA performance reflect students' academic experiences before entering college?

Inequality in Educational Experiences and Outcomes

By the time students enter higher education, they have eighteen years of experience behind them, much of which has been spent in formal schooling. Inequalities in schooling and family domains are apparent early in children's lives and persist or increase as they age. Annette Lareau's ethnography *Unequal Childhoods* provides an illuminating analysis of how family and schooling contexts interact to benefit some children more than others. Lareau proposes that parents from different class backgrounds engage in different styles of parenting, which are differentially rewarded in the educational system. Middle-class families engage in a "concerted cultivation" form of parenting, through which they "deliberately try to stimulate their children's development and foster their cognitive and social skills."[31] Through this process, children acquire skills, attitudes, and predispositions that are recognized and rewarded by mainstream institutions, such as schools. Middle-class parents not only transmit valuable cultural practices but also intervene directly in their children's education. Lareau provides a vivid example of this phenomenon with a description of the childhood of Stacey Marshall. Stacey's school had a gifted and talented program that provided students with an enriched and challenging curriculum. Stacey scored below the cutoff for the program. Working-class parents in this situation would likely have accepted the verdict of the school. Middle-class parents, in contrast, define their role vis-à-vis the school as that of serving as "advocates" for their children, and will thus marshal all available resources to ensure that their children have the most advantageous educational experiences possible. Stacey's mother challenged the school's bureaucracy, had Stacey tested privately, and subsequently achieved her daughter's admittance to the program.[32]

Interventions of middle-class parents and expectations of middle-class children that they can—and indeed have the "right" to—customize their educational experiences have become more consequential as schooling has become less proscriptive and more flexible and receptive to students' articulated needs, desires, and interests. One area that exemplifies this shift is tracking. The 1970s were characterized by the "unremarked revolution" in which formal tracking systems were largely abolished, shifting the decision-making about coursework from teachers and counselors to students. Instead of producing more equality, this shift simply transferred the responsibility: rather than being officially tracked by schools, students now track themselves. While children from all class backgrounds have high educational expectations, students from more advantaged family backgrounds are more likely to consistently select rigorous classes that place them on the path toward college.[33] Working-class children, in contrast, often fail to follow paths that are likely to lead to desired educational ends.

In a recent study of American adolescents, Schneider and Stevenson provide a vivid example of how students, particularly those from less advantaged backgrounds, can fail to realize their ambitions. A student named Rosa Lopez was passionate about becoming a physician. However, she had only a vague idea at best of what that entailed, and no concrete plans for achieving her goal. When asked about what education was required for a physician, she said: "I haven't really thought about it." In her junior year in high school, Rosa's academic performance began to slide and she failed to take many of the required courses for intended math and science majors. She dropped a science class for an art class, saying, "I wanted to have a fun class for the first time in my life."[34] Rosa was allowed to choose her own courses and make her own mistakes: decisions that did not provide her with proper academic preparation for her chosen career path.

A lack of knowledge and preparation for college among working-class students was also described by Annette Lareau in a follow-up with the children from *Unequal Childhoods*. A working-class teenager named Tara, for example, had to ask her counselor to calculate and interpret her high-school grade point average (GPA): "I had went to my counselor, his name was Mr. Bradley, and he did my GPA, like combined my averages, like add[ed] up all my grades . . . . I remember, it was close to a 3.5 or it was like 3.4. [I said] something like, 'Well, what's that?' He was like, 'That's a B.' So I knew I did good overall [in] high school." With little knowledge, little parental involvement, only one letter of recommendation, and a 690 combined SAT score, Tara did not get into any of the colleges she applied to, and was "taking a break from school."[35] As a result of complex home and school influences, fewer than 50 percent of high school graduates from families without college experience are regarded academically qualified for college as defined by recent government reports, compared to more than 80 percent of graduates with college-educated parents.[36]

Indeed, academic preparation, broadly defined, is one of the key factors contributing to lower educational outcomes of students from less socioeconomically advantaged families. Academic preparation can take numerous forms: being in a particular track with access to advanced placement (AP) courses, getting good grades, or performing well on standardized college admission tests (and knowing that one needs to take those tests in the first place). Regardless of the measures considered, students from less educated families perform worse on these benchmarks. Nineteen percent of students in our sample whose parents held graduate or professional degrees reported taking no AP courses. Twice as many students (37 percent) whose parents had not gone to college reported having no AP experience. Similarly, while only 13 percent of students whose parents had graduate or professional degrees were in the bottom quintile of the high school GPA distribution, almost three times as many students (35 percent) from families without college experience were in the bottom quintile (figure 2.3). Students in the top quintile essentially earned straight As (secondary school GPA higher than 3.96), while those in the bottom quintile earned mostly Bs or lower (secondary school GPA below 3.19).

The gaps among students from different family backgrounds are even more pronounced with respect to SAT/ACT scores.[37] The extent to which SAT/ACT scores measure academic preparation, experiences inside and

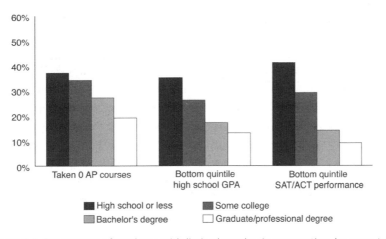

Figure 2.3. Percentage of students with limited academic preparation, by parental education (based on table A2.2)

outside elementary and secondary school classrooms, or student ability has been widely debated. Notwithstanding those debates, SAT/ACT scores are used by institutions as sorting mechanisms that aim to reflect students' scholastic aptitude and preparation for college-level work, and this renders them highly relevant for our study. We divided SAT/ACT scores into quintiles and compared students in the bottom, top, and middle (three) quintiles. The top quintile includes students who scored the equivalent of a combined verbal and math SAT score of 1,320 or higher; the bottom quintile is the equivalent of a combined SAT score lower than 990 points. Family background is closely related to SAT/ACT performance: the more educated the parents, the higher the students' scores. Only 9 percent of students whose parents held graduate or professional degrees scored in the bottom quintile. At the same time, almost five times as many students (41 percent) from families without any college experience were in the bottom quintile. These stark gaps in SAT/ACT scores likely reflect accumulated differences in the educational experiences of students from different family backgrounds over the four years of high school, and indeed over the twelve years of elementary and secondary schooling combined. SAT/ACT scores also tap into students' cultural repertoires and their "know-how." While Tara did not know her high school GPA or what it implied, Garrett, a middle-class student in Lareau's study, took the SAT multiple times and knew that he could "mix and match" (i.e., combine the best verbal and math scores).[38] Differences between more and less socioeconomically advantaged families are also becoming amplified by SAT/ACT prep classes, which can cost up to four thousand dollars for thirty-two hours of individualized instruction at Kaplan Test Prep and Admissions.[39] As Mark Ward, president of Kaplan's Pre-College Testing Programs, noted regarding students' participation in the SAT prep program: "Parents know that coaching helps, whether it's for baseball, ballet or the SAT's. They want their children to have an edge over their peer group."[40] But it is only middle- and upper-class parents who have the cultural and economic resources to give their children an edge in activities such as ballet or college admissions examinations that can be enhanced by "concerted cultivation" strategies.

Students from more educated families are thus leaving high school with stronger academic records, whether those reflect ability, the enhanced efficiency of the educational system, or the knowledge and means to shape the system to one's advantage. Regardless of the underlying mechanisms, students from less educated families enter higher education at a disadvantage. The gaps between students from different family backgrounds are noteworthy, given that we are examining a relatively privileged group of students: four-year college entrants. Many students from less educated family backgrounds tend to opt out of higher education or attend community colleges. But even when they enroll in four-year institutions, they have substantially weaker academic records than students from more educated families. And as we have seen in figure 2.1, these initial disadvantages are hard to overcome, as inequality in academic outcomes tends to persist over time.

Students from different racial/ethnic minority groups are also disadvantaged in the educational process, in part due to their less advantaged family backgrounds.[41] Socioeconomic differences have direct effects on educational success, as well as indirect influences through their relationship to test scores and other measures of academic preparation. However, students from different racial/ethnic groups differ not only in terms of their family backgrounds, but also along a number of other dimensions, such as the schools they attend.[42] Due to the historic and current patterns of residential racial segregation, a substantial proportion of racial/ethnic minority students attend predominantly non-white high schools. In our sample, more than one-third of Hispanic, African-American, and Asian students (41 percent, 38 percent, and 38 percent respectively) attended predominantly non-white high schools (i.e., high schools composed of 70 percent or more of racial/ethnic minority students), while only 2 percent of white students attended such schools.

Although the U.S. Supreme Court decision in *Brown v. Board of Education* struck down the "separate but equal" doctrine in 1954, many students in the United States have continued to attend segregated and unequal schools. James Coleman was among the first to use a large national dataset to provide systematic evidence of the negative consequences of racial segregation on academic outcomes of African-American students. Referred to as the "Coleman Report," his study illuminated how racial segregation shaped peer climates and impacted students' academic performance.[43] Ample subsequent research has linked racially segregated high schools to lower academic performance, in large part due to the association between segregation and poverty. Segregated African-American and Hispanic schools enroll high proportions of poor children, and this has consequences for peer climates, teacher quality, course offerings, and in the long run students' academic achievement.[44] Students in racially segregated schools also contend with a substantially greater amount of violence and social disorder, which has lasting consequences for their academic outcomes.[45]

Among four-year college entrants in our sample, there were no differences in AP course-taking between students attending predominantly white and non-white high schools.[46] However, students from high schools with high concentrations of non-white students were much less likely to be in the top quintile of the secondary school GPA distribution. Moreover, racial segregation has a particularly pronounced relationship to SAT/ACT. Previous studies have suggested that high school racial composition is related both to whether students have opportunities to learn the material included on the SAT/ACT and to whether they have opportunities to prepare for the test.[47] Consequently, only 8 percent of students who attended predominantly non-white high schools scored in the top quintile of the SAT/ACT distribution, while almost three times as many students (23 percent) from other high schools did so. As they entered college, students who attended predominantly non-white high schools had substantially lower levels of skill in critical thinking, complex reasoning, and writing as measured by the CLA. Moreover, the disadvantage of attending predominantly non-white high schools was not overcome once students entered higher education: the gap in CLA scores between students from different types of high schools remained stable over time (see tables A2.1 and A2.2 in methodological appendix).[48]

Another challenge faced by some racial/ethnic groups is their English-language competence. Immigrants constitute a large and growing student population in the United States. While immigrant students must overcome numerous challenges on the path toward educational success, one of them is familiarity with English.[49] Consideration of language is particularly relevant in a study that focuses on understanding students' critical thinking, complex reasoning, and writing skills, all of which rely to a lesser or greater extent on one's knowledge of English. We asked students whether English was the primary language spoken in the home when they were growing up. For 45 percent of Hispanic and 50 percent of Asian students, it was not. Students who varied on whether English language was spoken in the home did not report differential patterns of AP course-taking, nor did they report notable differences in high school GPAs or SAT/ACT performance. Once in higher education, students for whom English was not the primary language demonstrated only slightly lower skills in critical thinking, complex reasoning, and writing as measured by the CLA (see tables A2.1 and A2.2 in methodological appendix).[50]

Given the multiple and often overlapping disadvantages faced by racial/ethnic minority students, it is not surprising that they enter higher education less academically prepared than their white peers (figure 2.4). The disadvantage in academic preparation is particularly pronounced for African-American students. Although inequality in academic preparation is not surprising, the magnitude of the gaps is startling. Twenty-five percent of white students reported taking no AP courses in high school, but almost twice as many (45 percent) African-American students reported no AP experience. Other racial/ethnic groups were similar to white students in their AP course-taking, with Asian students being particularly inclined to take AP courses. With respect to high school GPA, white students clearly fared the best: only 11 percent were in the bottom quintile of the secondary

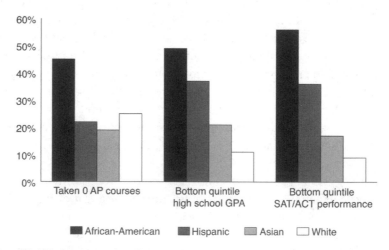

Figure 2.4. Percentage of students with limited academic preparation, by race/ethnicity (based on table A2.2)

school GPA distribution. In contrast, 49 percent of African-American students and 37 percent of Hispanic students had high school GPAs in the bottom quintile. While these gaps are troubling, the gaps in SAT/ACT scores are even more so. Only 9 percent of white students scored in the bottom quintile of the SAT/ACT distribution. In contrast, more than six times as many (59 percent) African-American students scored in the bottom quintile. Hispanic students faired only slightly better: 36 percent scored in the bottom quintile of the SAT/ACT distribution, four times the percentage of white students.

Weak academic preparation and particularly low SAT/ACT scores may not only hamper students' choices for entry into higher education but also shape their performance in college. Indeed, SAT/ACT performance and other measures of high school academic preparation are related to students' CLA scores (see table A2.1 in methodological appendix). Students with higher levels of academic preparation in high school demonstrate better skills in critical thinking, complex reasoning, and writing, as measured by the CLA, when they enter higher education. These patterns are particularly pronounced for the association between SAT/ACT performance and the CLA test: students in the top SAT/ACT quintile scored 1.5 standard deviations (or 43 percentile points) above students in the bottom SAT/ACT quintile when they entered college.

Understanding Inequality in Learning

Is inequality in learning over the first two years of college by race/ethnicity and family background, as measured by improvement in CLA scores, a reflection of differences in academic preparation? If we compared two students, both of whom took no AP classes, but one of whom had college-educated parents while the other one did not, would they improve at different rates on the CLA? Or if we compared an African-American student with a high GPA at a predominantly white high school to a white student with the same characteristics, would they have the same rate of change in CLA scores over the first two years of college? In general, if students had the same background characteristics and academic experiences, would we still observe gaps in CLA performance among students from different racial/ethnic and socioeconomic groups?

To answer this question, we begin by comparing 2007 CLA scores for different groups of students, controlling for their CLA performance in 2005. In other words, we are asking the question: What is the difference in 2007 scores between students from different family backgrounds *if* we adjust for their initial level of critical thinking, complex reasoning, and writing skills? We follow a convention from the sociological literature on K–12 achievement in referring to these estimates as growth. Researchers studying school sector differences, for example, have noted that "sector differences in senior test performance net of sophomore patterns reflect the impact of sector on *cognitive growth between the two administrations*, and in that sense, reveal how much of the 'added value' is attributable to school sector."[51] This approach presents an approximation of learning growth when data exits at only two points in time.[52] Thus, as we examine differences across groups in models that estimate 2007 CLA scores while controlling for students' performance at the point of entry into higher education, we adopt the rhetorical convention of simplifying the language around statistical "value-added" modeling to refer to these estimates as *growth* in learning during the first two years in college.

Figure 2.5 compares students whose parents had completed graduate or professional degrees with those whose parents had no college experience. The second half of the figure compares African-American and white students (complete results for students from different racial/ethnic and family background groups can be found in appendix table A2.3). The first set of bars indicates that students whose parents held graduate or professional degrees had a notable (almost 60-point) advantage in the 2007 CLA scores over students whose parents had no college experience, even after adjusting for their level of CLA-assessed skills when they entered college in the fall of 2005. The gap between African-American and white students

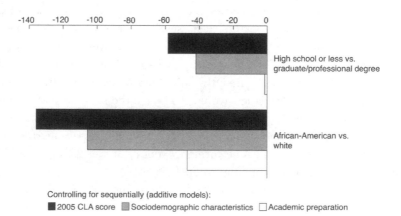

Figure 2.5. Predicted 2007 CLA score gaps by parental education and race, adjusted for specific characteristics (based on table A2.3)

is yet more pronounced. Even after considering initial performance, an average African-American student scored 136 points lower than an average white student at the end of the sophomore year.[53] What could help to explain these differences?

Students from different family backgrounds and racial/ethnic groups differ on a number of characteristics such as parental occupation, household composition, high schools attended, and academic preparation. If these factors are related to CLA growth, they may help to account for the observed gaps between different groups of students. Indeed, characteristics other than parental education and race/ethnicity are related to improvement in CLA scores (see table A2.3 in methodological appendix). For example, students who attended non-white high schools (with at least 70 percent racial/ethnic minority students) and those for whom English was not the primary language performed less well on the CLA at the end of their sophomore year, after adjusting for CLA performance at entry into higher education. Moreover, academic preparation has a strong relationship to CLA growth: students who had high GPAs and high SAT/ACT scores, and who took four or more AP courses, had notably higher growth in critical thinking, complex reasoning, and written communication during their first two years in college (i.e., they had higher 2007 CLA scores, after controlling for 2005 CLA scores).

To consider whether these other sociodemographic factors, particularly academic preparation, help to explain the gaps in CLA growth among students from different family backgrounds and racial/ethnic groups, we use a multivariate regression analysis to estimate the relationships of interests while holding other variables constant. In this approach, we statistically adjust estimates of family background and race/ethnicity for potential differences in other characteristics, producing estimates *as if* students from different family backgrounds and racial/ethnic groups were similar on other characteristics included in the model. Adjusting estimates for a range of sociodemographic and high school characteristics decreases by almost 30 percent the gap between students whose parents had no college experience and those whose parents completed graduate or professional degrees. A similar pattern is observed for the gap in CLA growth between African-American and white students: after adjustment for sociodemographic and high school characteristics, it decreases by slightly over 20 percent.[54] Differences in students' sociodemographic backgrounds and high schools attended thus help to explain some of the gaps in learning, but students from less educated families and African-American students continue to lag behind.

What about academic preparation? There are large differences in academic preparation, particularly SAT/ACT scores, between students from more and less educated families. What if we compared a student whose parents had high school diplomas to one whose parents held graduate or professional degrees, but statistically controlled for academic preparation (in addition to other sociodemographic and high school characteristics)? In this case there would be very little difference between the two. Equalizing students on academic preparation—including number of AP courses taken, high school GPA, and SAT/ACT performance—renders gaps between students from more and less educated families virtually nonexistent (and, statistically speaking, no longer significant). Academic preparation is thus a key factor that shapes differential rates of growth in critical thinking, complex reasoning, and writing skills among students from different family backgrounds during the first two years in college.

Academic preparation also plays an important role in understanding the gap in growth in CLA performance that exists between African-American and white students. After adjusting for academic preparation, the gap drops to approximately one-third of its original magnitude. Although this represents a notable reduction, a substantial gap remains. Even when we compare an African-American and a white student after controlling for differences in CLA performance at entry into higher education, a range of sociodemographic and high school characteristics, and academic preparation, the African-American student still scores 47 points lower than the white student at the end of the sophomore year.[55] Equalizing academic preparation between African-American and white students is thus a necessary but not sufficient condition for equalizing their growth in critical thinking, complex reasoning, and writing skills during the first two years in college.

These results offer at least some hope for reducing inequalities in higher education. Students from less educated families can do as well—in terms of growth in critical thinking, complex reasoning, and writing skills, as measured by the CLA—as those from more educated families, but they need better academic experiences in high school than they are currently receiving. Arguably, colleges also need to do more to compensate for the unequal starting points of students from different family backgrounds. This is even more the case for African-American students; equalizing their academic preparation would substantially reduce but not eliminate the gap with white students. This suggests that some of the African-American–white gap may be due to differential experiences in higher education.

Differences in Institutional Contexts

One way in which students' experiences in college may vary is the difference in types of institutions attended. The debate about whether educational institutions can make a difference is long-standing. Since the "Coleman Report," which is often misinterpreted as implying that school characteristics have little consequence for student learning, sociologists and economists have accumulated a voluminous body of research on school effects. On the one hand are the skeptics, claiming that schools have minimal, if any, consequences for inequality—echoing the classic work of Christopher Jencks and his colleagues, which claimed that "schools serve primarily as selection and certification agencies, whose job is to measure and label people, and only secondarily as socialization agencies, whose job is to change people."[56] In this view, where students go to college would have little relevance for their learning or for the gaps between different groups, after controlling for individual differences related to student selection into colleges in the first place.

On the other hand, persistent efforts to reform and improve schools rest on the belief that schools can indeed make a difference. And these efforts, we believe, are not a product of blind faith or completely misguided aspirations. Examination of graduation rates at four-year institutions, for example, shows that colleges graduate from less than 10 to almost 100 percent of their students within six years. This incredibly varied range is only partly related to student characteristics and school resources. Even after schools are equalized on a range of different factors, some schools have much higher graduation rates and some schools have much lower gaps in graduation rates across different groups of students. "These high-performers offer powerful evidence that our higher education system has the capacity for great improvement when it comes to maximizing the education and success for all."[57]

Even the "Coleman Report," which was skeptical about the ability of school resources to shape student learning, claimed that peers are highly consequential for student success. There are different ways of approximating peer climates, with one of the most common being institutional selectivity, measured by the SAT/ACT scores of the entering student body. Standardized test scores are among the principal metrics used to gauge individual academic aptitude, and in the aggregate they are an often-used index of a college's overall academic caliber.[58] Moreover, institutional selectivity is a particularly relevant characteristic in the context of this study, given the sizable correlation between students' SAT/ACT scores and their performance on the CLA. Being surrounded by peers who are well prepared for college-level work is likely to shape the climate of the institution as well as specific student experiences. Having high-performing students in the classroom can help improve achievement of all students, including those who have accumulated fewer skills before entering college.[59] We divided schools into three selectivity categories based on institutional reports of the combined SAT scores at the 25th percentile of the freshman incoming class. Highly selective colleges were defined as schools with students at the 25th percentile having combined verbal and math SAT scores higher than 1,150 (four schools with 25.2 percent of the overall sample fell into this category); less selective colleges were defined as schools with students at the 25th percentile having combined scores lower than 950 (six schools with 24.2 percent of the overall sample fell into this category).

Not surprisingly, students who were more academically prepared in high school attended more selective institutions (see table A2.4 in methodological appendix). While only 13 percent of students who had taken no AP classes attended highly selective institutions, four times as many students (53 percent) who had taken more than four AP classes did so. Similarly, students with higher secondary-school GPAs and higher SAT/ACT scores were more likely to attend highly selective institutions. The patterns across SAT/ACT groups are particularly pronounced. Virtually no student who scored in the bottom quintile of the SAT/ACT distribution attended a highly selective college. In contrast, two-thirds of students from the top quintile of the SAT distribution did so. While not surprising, these patterns show a strong sorting mechanism in higher education. Academically prepared students, whether defined on the basis of their high school AP courses, GPAs, or SAT/ACT scores, are attending institutions with higher concentrations of academically prepared students (at least as defined by average institutional SAT scores).

Moreover, environments with higher concentrations of academically able students are disproportionately inhabited by the traditionally more privileged groups (figure 2.6). Having parents who hold graduate or professional degrees is a distinct advantage for enrollment in highly selective institutions. Forty-four percent of students whose parents held graduate or professional degrees attended highly selective institutions. In contrast, only 8 percent of students whose parents had no college experience and 10 percent of those whose parents had some college experience enrolled in these institutions. Students across different racial/ethnic groups are relatively more equitably represented in the highly selective institutions, with

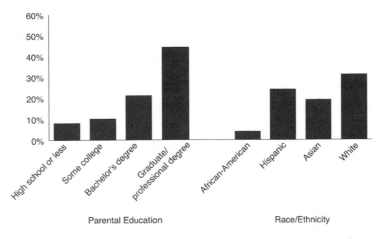

Figure 2.6. Percentage of students attending highly selective institutions, by parental education and race/ethnicity (based on table A2.4)

the exception of African-Americans. The majority of African-American students (66 percent) are enrolled in less selective institutions. No other racial/ethnic group has the majority of students in this category, and only 12 percent of white students attend these institutions. At the same time, only 4 percent of African-American students attend highly selective institutions, in comparison to 31 percent of white students. Success may thus be a product not simply of students' individual backgrounds or what they bring to higher education, but also of the context in which they are embedded. Given the patterns of institutional attendance, we can expect higher-education experiences to contribute to—or even exacerbate, as opposed to eliminate—the observed patterns of social inequality.

Higher Education in the Twenty-First Century

Impressive expansion of higher education over the course of the twentieth century has created unprecedented opportunities for access. Although inequalities in access—particularly to more selective institutions—persist, as do concerns about financial aid and affordability, students from all backgrounds and all levels of academic preparation are taking advantage of expanding opportunities and entering higher education. The success achieved in increasing access has not been paralleled in other areas of higher education. Graduation rates are stagnant or decreasing, and time to degree has been on the rise.[60] Among students starting at four-year institu-

tions, only 34 percent finish a bachelor's degree in four years and barely
two-thirds (64 percent) finish within six years.[61] Completion rates are even
more discouraging among students starting in community colleges.[62] These
patterns have recently placed degree completion on the national agenda,
thus fueling the growing questions about students' activities in higher education and institutional actions (or lack thereof) aimed at facilitating degree attainment.

But many students are not only failing to complete educational credentials; they are also not learning much, even when they persist through higher
education. In general, as we have shown, undergraduates are barely improving their CLA-measured skills in critical thinking, complex reasoning,
and writing during their first two years of college. Even more disturbingly,
almost half are demonstrating no appreciable gain in these skills between
the beginning of their freshman year and the end of their sophomore year.
In addition to limited growth, learning in higher education is also unequal.
Students from less educated families and racial/ethnic minority groups have
lower levels of skills in critical thinking, complex reasoning, and writing (as
measured by the CLA) as they enter college. These inequalities are largely
preserved—or, in the case of African-American students, exacerbated—as
students progress on their journeys through higher education.

Evidence of limited learning and persistent inequality should give pause
to the recent emphasis on "college for all" policies. State and federal policies
have increasingly been built around the premise of expanding postsecondary educational access until it becomes universal for future generations of
U.S. citizens. As President Barack Obama asserted in his first major speech
to Congress, "every American will need to get more than a high school
diploma," and "we will provide the support necessary for you to complete
college."[63] This ideological commitment virtually to unlimited educational
opportunity has been widely adopted and embraced throughout our education system. James Rosenbaum's research on high school counselors, for
example, provides an illuminating account of how a "college for all" ide-
ology has come to permeate schooling in this country. Rosenbaum notes
that whereas high school counselors once acted as "gatekeepers"—advising
certain students that, given their academic performance and interests, vocational programs were possibly a more appropriate choice than college—
counselors today "do not have to force students to make tough decisions;
they can encourage everyone to attend college."[64] According to Rosenbaum, "students get no concrete information about their best options from
the current situation or about the levels of achievement needed to reach

their goals." Instead, they receive "motivational platitudes" that emphasize a "warm, fuzzy approach" focused on "personal growth." Students are told: "to believe in themselves," "put forth more effort," or "establish themselves a little more as a person."[65] While some counselors work to steer students to more or less selective schools, in general they have become reluctant to provide information that might in any way discourage students from enrolling in college. For example, one counselor in Rosenbaum's study noted that although he believed a certain student was "not academically qualified . . . I've urged him to send in the application anyway. You know, there's no harm."[66] In recent decades, 30 percent of students with C grades in high school and 15 percent with grade point averages of C minus or lower have been admitted into four-year colleges.

Providing open and unlimited access to college might yield tangible benefits for students who otherwise might be denied these opportunities—as, sociologists Paul Attewell and David Lavin have demonstrated, occurred for individuals who were admitted to the City University of New York under an open admission policy.[67] However, only the most cynical policy analyst could advocate "college for all" without simultaneously demanding that once admitted into college, students would be compelled to demonstrate significant academic growth. Otherwise "college for all" becomes little more than a policy designed for warehousing students during the years when they would otherwise face an elevated risk of unemployment and criminal behavior.[68] The benefits of schooling solely associated with individuals attaining educational degrees and certificates that did not reflect improvement in academic performance—that is, the positive signaling function of educational attainment that sociologist Randall Collins referred to as "credentialing"—would, of course, also be significantly muted or indeed nonexistent once college education became universal.[69] Alternatively, as sociologists Samuel Lucas, Theodore Gerber, and others have argued, one would expect that increasingly universal access to college would lead to greater qualitative distinctions and inequality within higher education—whereby credentials from elite institutions and programs are differentially valued in relation to degrees attained elsewhere.[70] To be meaningful and consequential for students, our findings suggest, "college for all" policies require that higher-education institutions focus as much attention on monitoring and ensuring that undergraduate learning occurs as elementary and secondary school systems are currently being asked to undertake.

However, when higher-education institutions are faced with less-than-optimal outcomes, they often respond by looking back at K–12. "We can't beat colleges and universities up when retention rates are low and when people either fail or leave . . . . Many students who struggle in college lack the preparation and discipline to be there, but our society seems to assume that they belong in college nonetheless," claimed the former U.S. assistant secretary for postsecondary education, Diane Auer Jones.[71] It is fair to point out that a sizable proportion of students enter higher education unprepared for college-level work. For example, 17 percent of recent four-year college entrants took at least one remedial course during their first year.[72] And this percentage underestimates the need for remediation, as many students who are advised to take developmental courses do not do so.[73] Indeed, 40 percent of college faculty agree with the statement: "Most of the students I teach lack the *basic skills* for college level work."[74]

Some students are indeed entering college academically unprepared, partly because of the recent "college for all" policies, but this does not imply that what students do in higher education is irrelevant, or that institutions can or should do nothing to improve their outcomes. A number of studies have demonstrated differences in graduation rates across institutions, even for similar students.[75] Moreover, recent decreases in graduation rates seem driven primarily not by changes in students' academic preparation, but by declines in institutional resources, and especially by the distribution of students across institutions. Three-quarters of the decline in graduation rates is attributable to shifts in where students enroll in college.[76] While not ignoring that students enter higher education with differing levels of skills, these findings raise questions about what they are doing after entry, and how specific college experiences and contexts can shape their outcomes—including growth in critical thinking, complex reasoning, and writing skills.

Indeed, although overall CLA growth is quite limited, some students demonstrate notable gains. Students in the top 10 percent of the sample, for example, improve their CLA performance by more than 1.5 standard deviations from the fall of their freshman year to the end of their sophomore year. This would translate into a 43 percentile gain, indicating that if these freshmen entered higher education at the 50th percentile they would reach a level equivalent to the 93rd percentile of an incoming freshman class by the end of their sophomore year. Crucially, this category of high performers includes students from all family backgrounds and racial/ethnic groups, as well as students with different levels of academic preparation. This raises the question of what students are doing in higher education, particularly within specific institutional contexts, and how different experiences may be related to learning over the first two years in college. While the higher-education system as a whole is failing to improve many students' critical thinking, complex reasoning, and writing skills at desirable levels, what are the college experiences and contexts that facilitate student learning?

3

Pathways through Colleges Adrift

Undergraduate education is fundamentally a social experience. In a recent study of undergraduate student culture at a Midwestern public university, Mary Grigsby notes that 70 percent of students reported that social learning was more important than academics.[1] And while students did not completely disregard academics, they referred to it as "work" in contrast to social learning, which was regarded as "fun." The goal for students was to minimize the former and spend as much time as possible on the latter. One student aptly summarized the sentiments: "It [social life] shouldn't necessarily come at the expense of your studies (or) the overall goal of graduation, but if you're finding yourself where this is no longer enjoyable, then something is wrong. Take this time to have fun and enjoy your youth! Try not to take it too seriously."[2] Students' reports of their time use confirm these sentiments, indicating that students spend the majority of their out-of-class time on social and leisure activities, not studying.[3]

This emphasis on social life has also found its way into the major theories of student development and persistence in higher education. In an extensive study of student outcomes from academic success to personality, values, attitudes, and behaviors, higher-education researcher Alexander Astin in *What Matters in College?*

Jeannie Kim and Melissa Velez coauthored this chapter.

highlights the role of peers: "The student's peer group is the single most potent source of influence on growth and development during the undergraduate years."[4] Similarly, higher-education researcher Vincent Tinto's theory of student departure places an emphasis on the role of social (in addition to academic) integration for keeping students enrolled. "[Student departures] reflect the character of individual's social and intellectual experiences within the institution."[5]

While students may view peers as virtually all-important, social activities do not constitute the totality of college experiences. Another crucial actor in the journey through higher education is faculty. After emphasizing the importance of peers for college outcomes, Astin is quick to note that "next to the peer group, the faculty represents the most significant aspect of the student's undergraduate development."[6] It is faculty, within classrooms and beyond, who shape not only students' overall development but also their commitment to continuing their education: "Classrooms are central to the process of retention and the activities that occur therein are critical to the process through which students come to participate in the intellectual life of the institutions."[7] What faculty members do, and in particular whether they facilitate academic integration of students, is crucial for student development and persistence.

Moreover, peers and faculty members, together with institutional leadership, combine to produce specific college climates. Prominent models of student success in higher education place institutions at the center of their analyses. Students bring specific characteristics with them to higher education (often referred to as "inputs"). However, it is how those inputs interact with, and are channeled within, specific institutional contexts that explains student outcomes. Schools can go a long way in creating social and intellectual communities that will keep students engaged and help them to persist on their journeys through higher education.[8] "Institutions influence the quality of student effort via their capacity to involve students with other members of the institution in the learning process."[9] Student-focused institutions facilitate student development in many areas including critical thinking, analytical and problem-solving skills, and writing.[10] These recent studies of higher education are reminiscent of James Coleman's work from the 1950s. Studying high schools in northern Illinois, he showed that while students in general were more focused on their peers than on their teachers, schools could adopt institutional policies that served to promote organizational climates conducive to academic growth. Indeed, some schools did a much better job of promoting academically oriented peer cultures than others.[11]

Students thus enter college and university settings that are comprised of distinct peer cultures and institutional climates which potentially serve to develop and shape student outcomes. In this chapter we turn our attention to understanding the academic, social, and financial character of students' college experiences today. We explore the extent to which students are academically focused during their first two years of college and are asked to apply themselves to demanding curricular tasks. We examine questions such as: What is the character of the relationships between students and their professors? What are students' experiences with formal coursework? How do students perceive their peers and the institutional cultures at the colleges they attend? What sort of financial burdens do these students face as they attempt to navigate the first two years of campus life?

In exploring the academic, social, and financial dimensions of students' college experiences, we pay particular attention to two sources of variation. First, we examine the extent to which students' social background, high school context, and academic preparation are associated with different collegiate experiences. Second, we identify the extent to which students' academic, social, and financial realities vary across college campuses. Given that we only have two dozen higher-education institutions in the sample, our exploration of specific institutional factors associated with differences across colleges will be limited. Nevertheless, we will show in general the extent to which student experiences vary among colleges, and in addition, highlight how college selectivity is related to student college experiences.

Academic Engagement and Instructional Climates

As students make their way through college, there are multiple pathways, experiences, and mechanisms that are likely associated with variation in the types and depth of learning that occur there. Some students, for example, might spend hours engaged with new forms of media, embracing "friendship-driven" or "interest-driven" pursuits. Proponents of the educational value of these new media forms, such as Mizuko Ito and her colleagues, have claimed that these technologically-assisted informal activities "allow for a degree of freedom and autonomy for youth that is less apparent in a classroom setting. Youth respect one another's authority online, and they are often more motivated to learn from peers than from adults. Their efforts are also largely self-directed, and the outcome emerges through exploration, in contrast to classroom learning that is oriented toward set, predefined goals."[12]

Spending time surfing the internet in a dorm room "geeking out" on "interest-driven" pursuits, sitting on a quad and philosophically pondering one's place in the universe, or simply hanging out at a neighborhood bar enjoying the camaraderie of friends are all activities likely to lead to social learning, creative insights, and potentially individual growth. We are skeptical, however, that many of these activities are also likely to be closely associated with academic learning as measured by traditional forms of assessment.

For students to show improvement on objective measures of critical thinking, complex reasoning, and written communication—such as the CLA performance task we examine in this study—one would expect that students' engagement with traditional forms of academic interaction and instruction would be paramount. In order for students to learn though traditional instructional mechanisms while at college, they would need to be academically engaged with their faculty and classes. We therefore focus our analysis on the degree to which their academic and instructional experiences vary across and within the colleges they attend. To what extent do students' college experiences differ with respect to faculty interaction, academic requirements associated with their classes, types of courses taken, and credits and grades received?

Faculty interaction

One way that students can potentially be affected by the colleges they attend is through direct, positive interactions with their professors both within and outside of the classroom. Loren Pope, for example, in the popular trade book *Colleges That Change Lives* provides portraitures of forty colleges that have "outperformed most of the Ivies and their clones."[13] These schools focus "on the student, not the faculty," and their professors are asserted to be deeply involved in student lives: "There is not only a mentor relationship in class, but professors become hiking companions, intramural teammates, dinner companions, and friends."[14] Pope presents a student's account of the learning environment at one of these "exemplary" colleges as follows:

> The environment here is very conducive to trying new things. Every day, a
> new event, interaction or activity contributes to this influence. Just yester-
> day a professor stopped me walking back from class and recommended a
> book she'd been reading that reminded her of me. Tomorrow I'm going to
> have lunch with her to discuss topics from the book and talk with her about

possible research projects at the Biodiversity Station in Ecuador, where I will be working as part of my study-abroad experience. The professors are friends here. I have a class with four students and we sit down and talk with the professor as equals. It's a collaborative learning experience that can't be beat.[15]

According to Pope, students in these exceptional colleges also are provided early mentoring directly with faculty advisors. For example, at one of the colleges profiled, Pope notes, "all first-year students are personally matched with veteran faculty to help them make sound course choices. And if someone needs help, he or she gets it."[16]

While the student's account of a learning environment in one of Pope's exemplary colleges is uplifting, alternative perspectives of campus environments have also been vividly represented in prior research studies. For example, Tim Clydesdale in *The First Year Out: Understanding American Teens after High School* provides the following college freshman's assessment of his professor:

> Not at all understanding about student problems and concerns . . . . If you missed class, he didn't like you 'cause you were "giving up." If you "didn't care about his class," then you "didn't care about academics." He came at it with the attitude that "my class and your academics are the most important things in the world right now." And even if you have family members dying, even if you're sick, it doesn't matter . . . . It made me feel like, you know, he didn't care about the students. All he cared about were the numbers, which bothered me a lot.[17]

The two accounts from Pope and Clydesdale of student impressions illustrate well that students differ in their experiences, perceptions, and judgment of college faculty.

In our study we surveyed students at the end of their sophomore year to get a sense of their impressions of faculty and to ascertain how often they had interacted with faculty outside of class. In terms of impressions, we asked students whether they agreed or disagreed (on a seven-point scale) with the following assessments of their professors:[18]

- *Faculty members at my institution are approachable, helpful, and understanding.*
- *Faculty members at my institution hold students to high standards.*
- *Faculty members at my institution have high expectations for students like me.*

Students' perceptions of faculty were associated with individual social background along various dimensions (see table A3.1 in methodological appendix). White students, relative to students from other racial/ethnic backgrounds, were more likely to find professors approachable, helpful, and understanding as well as to perceive that faculty held high standards and expectations. Students from families with more highly educated parents were also more likely to have positive assessments of their professors. In addition, students' prior academic preparation was associated with perceptions of faculty. The greater the prior academic preparation of students, the more likely students were to describe their interactions with faculty in positive terms.

While differences in student perceptions of faculty reported on numerical scales are difficult to digest, we turn to the more concrete measure of actual student-faculty contact outside of the classroom during their second year of college. Students could potentially meet with a faculty member outside of class for many reasons. Ideally, as in the earlier description reported in Pope's account of an exemplary college, the interaction could involve extensions of classroom intellectual exchange and academic mentoring. In addition, it could involve discussion of course selection or involvement in extracurricular activities, such as involvement in faculty research projects or participation in college clubs. On average, students reported that during the previous semester they had met with faculty outside of class on three to four occasions—that is, approximately once per month.

We focus our presentation here, however, not on these typical students who are interacting with faculty outside of classrooms on a monthly basis, nor on the 31 percent of students in our sample who reported that they had met with a faculty member outside of the classroom once or twice during the previous semester, but rather on the 9 percent of students who in the previous semester reported *never* having met with a faculty member outside of class. Given their lack of faculty engagement, these students are potentially at elevated risk of limited academic achievement and noncompletion.[19] Moreover, these students are not unique to our sample; among recent entrants into four-year institutions, 17 percent have never met with a faculty member outside of class to discuss academic matters during their first year at the school, and 19 percent report that they had never met with an academic advisor.[20]

Students' social background is related to the risk of falling into the category of having never met with a faculty member. White students were least likely not to have had any contact outside of the classroom, whereas Asian students were twice as likely to fall into this category (14 percent compared to 7 percent). Students from families with lower levels of parental education were also more likely to not have met with faculty. Only five percent of students with parents who had graduate or professional degrees had never met with faculty, compared to 14 percent of students with parents who had ended their education at the high school level. Prior research has shown that differences across socioeconomic and racial/ethnic groups extend to more nuanced questions about types of faculty interactions (e.g., working on research projects, discussing class assignments, visiting informally); different groups thus seem not only to engage more or less with faculty, but also do so in varied ways, which is an important area for future investigation.[21]

Figure 3.1 identifies the percentage of students who had no contact with faculty outside of the classroom the prior semester, based on their initial academic preparation (measured by prior SAT/ACT scores) and the overall selectivity of the college (measured by the SAT scores of entering freshmen). As detailed in the previous chapter, we separate each of these two test-based measures into three categories. For student preparation, we identify the top quintile, bottom quintile, and middle (three) quintiles of students on these precollegiate standardized tests; and for college selectivity, we divided schools into selectivity categories based on institutional reports of the combined SAT scores at the 25th percentile of the freshman incoming class.

Students who entered college with lower initial academic ability were more likely to report having had no contact with faculty outside of class. Twelve percent of students in the bottom quintile of prior SAT/ACT performance had not met with a faculty member outside of class during the prior semester, relative to five percent of students in the top quintile. Some of these differences were likely due to variation in student motivation and interest. It is worth noting, however, that student decisions about whether to approach faculty outside of the classroom occur in specific institutional contexts. Whereas in the past decade, elementary and secondary educators have come under increased pressure to close the achievement gap between high- and low-achieving students (particularly with respect to race/ethnicity), discussion of the responsibility of college faculty to address similar gaps has been virtually absent or ignored. Instead, college faculty too often face institutional incentives to ignore students of low ability and to focus their efforts, when they are not engaged in their own research endeavors, on the most gifted and talented students they encounter. At a time when elementary and secondary institutions are focused on increasing the standards and educational attainment of traditionally underachieving groups

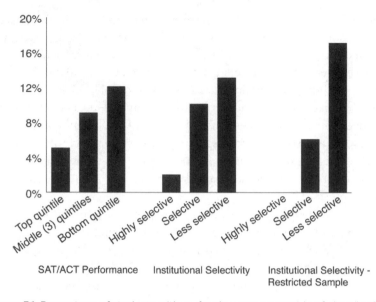

Figure 3.1. Percentage of students with no faculty contact outside of class, by SAT/ACT performance and institutional selectivity (based on table A3.1)

of students, it has been largely business as usual for many higher-education institutions that have long been accustomed to focusing on the "talented tenth" of high-achieving students.[22]

In the statistical analysis presented in our methodological appendix, we demonstrate that differences across schools in the likelihood that a student will have no contact with a faculty member are pronounced even *after* we control (i.e., adjust statistical estimates) for a large number of individual-level factors that might be underlying these institutional-level differences, such as academic preparation and sociodemographic characteristics.[23] While students' academic preparation at the individual level tracks well with the likelihood of the absence of faculty contact, this relationship is even stronger at the institutional level. At highly selective colleges, only 2 percent of students reported that they had failed to have any contact with faculty outside of classrooms the prior semester; at selective colleges this increased to 10 percent, and at less selective colleges to 13 percent. We find that institutional-level differences are responsible for as much explained variation in this outcome as all the wide-ranging individual-level factors we considered combined. Twenty-nine percent of the variation across colleges is accounted for by considering the extensive list of individual-level differences; an additional 22 percent is accounted for by our institutional-level selectivity measure, and 49 percent is due to other factors we have not modeled (e.g., college type, instructional resources, institutional setting).

The results on the right-hand side of figure 3.1 illustrate the role of institutional differences in the likelihood that student will have no contact with a faculty member in a more intuitive way. We restrict the analysis to a sample of 622 students who all shared a set of similar background characteristics: they were white students who had attended public high school, had parents who graduated from college, and were in the three middle quintiles of student SAT/ACT performance (i.e., combined verbal and math scores between 990 and 1320). Students with these specific characteristics attended colleges with different levels of selectivity in sufficient numbers to permit the identification of empirical differences. Of the 126 students with these characteristics who attended highly selective colleges, not one reported that they had failed to have contact with a faculty member outside of the classroom the prior semester. Students with these characteristics attending selective colleges had a 6-percent probability of having no faculty contact. At less selective colleges, the number of students with such characteristics who had not met with a faculty member outside the classroom the prior semester increased to 17 percent.

Peer climates

As students' perception and experience of college faculty vary, so too does their exposure to peer climates conducive to academic learning. Studies have repeatedly demonstrated that peer interaction is strongly associated with the academic decisions that students make in schools. Sociologists Mark Davies and Denise Kandel, for example, have noted that "the encouragement of one's parents and the plans of one's peers appear to shape ambitions more directly and with greater impact than any other source."[24] Peer influence is thought particularly potent because it is based on a sense of trust that exists between peers.[25] Peer influence manifests itself through a "conformity based on personal commitment and choice," and thus differs from authority-based influence exercised by parents or other adult figures.[26] With student orientations focused on collegiate social experience, something about which faculty and parents have less knowledge, students have a tendency to "adopt behaviors that are judged appropriate by their peers."[27] In considering influences on student learning, it is thus important to acknowledge and take into account the potential role of peer interactions. Specifically, in our project we queried students during their sophomore year on the following items:[28]

- *Students at my institutions have high academic aspirations.*
- *Students at my institution help each other succeed.*
- *Students at my institution work hard to succeed academically.*

In addition, we measured the proportion of time students spent studying with peers as opposed to the time they spent studying on their own.

Unlike the case for student evaluations of faculty, we found few racial/ethnic differences for student assessments of peers (see table A3.2 in methodological appendix). One exception to this pattern was Hispanic students, who reported lower levels of peer support (i.e., students helping each other succeed) than white students. Similarly, students whose home language was not English reported lower levels of peer support than students from English-speaking homes. Variation in students' reports of peer climates was more pronounced with respect to family background. Students in our sample whose parents had greater levels of educational attainment reported higher levels of peer academic aspirations and support.[29]

On two of the three measures of peer climates, we found pronounced differences across institutions. After controlling for individual-level differences in academic preparation and social background, we found that 25 percent of variation in students' reports of peer aspirations and 22 percent of variation in reports of peer support occurred across colleges. Institutional differences were approximately twice as powerful a determinant of students' reports of peers on these two measures than all of the other examined individual-level student characteristics combined.[30] When considering the measure of student reports of peer aspirations, students attending highly selective colleges had reports that were significantly higher than students attending less selective colleges.

In examining peer interactions specifically related to studying, we found only one notable difference: students who entered college with higher academic aptitude spent proportionally less time studying with their peers than students who came in with less prior demonstrated ability. Students in the top quintile of SAT/ACT performance studied with peers only 25 percent of their time at college, while students in the bottom quintile of SAT/ACT performance spent 31 percent of their time studying with peers. This difference in patterns of studying with and without peers is possibly associated with institutional practices that have recently encouraged students to attend peer study groups designed to support learning and enhance collegiate social integration and retention. Whether students need encouragement for enhancing collegiate social involvement, however, is unclear. Rebekah Nathan, for example, found in her investigation of undergraduate student culture that the majority of students surveyed viewed "social activities and interpersonal relationships as the main context for learning."[31] Setting aside the value of study groups for social integration and college retention, the effect of peer studying on academic learning has not yet received adequate attention in prior research.

Homework and course requirements

Students' perceptions of faculty and lack of regular contact with their professors outside of the classroom can perhaps be dismissed by some as no great cause for concern. After all, undergraduates are young adults and one could argue that they should take individual responsibility for their own learning. As long as students are applying themselves to their coursework and the academic demands of their professors are rigorous and challenging, collegiate learning is likely to occur at appropriate rates. We thus turn our analysis to the following questions: How hard are students working in college? And what sort of curricular expectations do professors have for students during their second year in college?

Consistent with other studies, we find that students are not spending a great deal of time outside of the classroom on their coursework: on average, they report spending only 12 hours per week studying (complete findings on homework and course requirements are reported in appendix table A3.3).[32] Even more alarming, 37 percent of students reported spending less than five hours per week preparing for their courses. The limited number of hours students spend studying is consistent with the emergence of a college student culture focused on social life and strategic management of work requirements. "For most of them, the important part of college is getting the degree in the end and the fun they have along the way, the friends they make, and the things they learn about themselves in peer relationships," Mary Grigsby notes in her recent study of undergraduate student culture at a Midwestern public university.[33] These students were highly social, with academics "not a central focus" of their collegiate self-definition. Bob, a student in Grigsby's study who lived in a house off campus with friends and aspired to work on a ski and rescue team, noted that "[the worst thing about school] is going to class, but I enjoy the other aspects of being at college. I meet new people and just going out and having fun and being free . . . . It's fun to go to bars, fun to party, but actually I enjoy

playing basketball, enjoy doing other sports and stuff. Oh, I watch television, clean around the house, mow the yard." Students often embraced a
"credentialist-collegiate orientation" that focused on earning a degree with
as little effort as possible. Academic "success" was achieved through "controlling college by shaping schedules, taming professors and limiting workload."[34] According to this researcher, "a common way to regulate workload
is simply to restrict the amount of time and effort one spends on a course
by doing no more than is necessary."[35]

Although low overall, the hours spent preparing for courses varied with
social and academic background. African-American students reported
studying two hours per week less than white students. Students with a parent who had attained an advanced graduate or professional degree studied
two more hours per week than students from families where neither parent
had any post-secondary education. Students from non-English language
homes spent slightly more time on their college homework. In terms of
prior academic preparation, students in the top quintile of SAT performance spent three-and-a-half hours more per week on their homework
than students in the bottom quintile. As we noted above, students in the
top SAT/ACT quintile relative to students in the bottom quintile also spent
a greater portion of this time studying alone rather than with peers.

College context was also strongly related to the amount of time students devoted to their homework. Differences across colleges were almost
as large a source of variation in hours spent studying as all the social and
academic background variables we examined combined.[36] In terms of differences across colleges, net of students' social and academic backgrounds,
the selectivity of entering class (measured by the SAT/ACT score reported
for a student at the 25th percentile) explained 49 percent of institutional
variation. Students who attended highly selective colleges spent almost
five hours more per week studying than students who attended less selective colleges. Once again, institutional differences in student behavior
were prominent even after controlling for individual-level characteristics.

While the amount of time students spend studying outside of class is
influenced by a wide variety of factors that educators can only partially
control, we turn our attention now to the question of what course assignments students were actually being asked by their professors to undertake.
Educators have much greater control over course assignments as well as,
arguably, a professional responsibility to define them adequately. We focus
our analysis on two specific questions we asked students in our study: How
many times during the prior semester they took a class where they "wrote
more than 20 pages over the course of the semester" and how many times

they took a class where they "read more than 40 pages per week." To simplify our presentation, we will focus on those students who either did or did not report having taken *any* courses that met these modest requirements.

Fifty percent of students in our sample reported that they had not taken a single course during the prior semester that required more than twenty pages of writing, and one-third had not taken one that required even forty pages of reading per week. Combining these two indicators, we found that a quarter of the students in the sample had not taken any courses that required either of these two requirements, and that only 42 percent had experienced *both* a reading and writing requirement of this character during the prior semester. If students are not being asked by their professors to read and write on a regular basis in their coursework, it is hard to imagine how they will improve their capacity to master performance tasks—such as the CLA—that involve critical thinking, complex reasoning, and writing.

One might suspect that our focus on sophomores had led to these low levels of engagement with reading and writing, and that virtually no student would still be in this category by the end of their college career. Unfortunately, that is not the case. A national survey of approximately three hundred thousand college freshmen and seniors in 587 four-year colleges and universities found that while 83 percent of freshmen reported that they had *not* written a paper during the current academic year that was twenty or more pages long, 51 percent of college seniors had not done so either. Even at the top 10 percent of schools in this study, 33 percent of college seniors reported that they had not written a paper of this length during their last year in college.[37]

Social background was closely associated with the extent to which students were enrolled in courses with rigorous academic requirements. African-American students were particularly likely to enroll in courses that did not require at least twenty pages of writing for the semester or forty pages of reading per week. Consequently, they were almost one-third less likely to take courses with *both* of these requirements than white students (32 percent compared to 46 percent, respectively). Similarly, students from families with parents who had ended their schooling in high school were twice as likely as students with a parent who had a graduate or professional degree to have not had a course requiring either twenty pages of writing or forty pages of reading per week (35 percent compared to 16 percent, respectively). Students who attended high schools where non-white students were concentrated were more likely not to have taken courses with these requirements (34 percent compared to 24 percent). Moreover, students who scored in the top quintile of SAT/ACT performance were almost three times less likely than students in the bottom quintile of the SAT/ ACT distribution to have had no courses the prior semester with significant writing and reading requirements (13 percent relative to 36 percent, respectively).

While academic preparation and social background are associated with academic requirements of courses, figure 3.2 demonstrates that differences across colleges are also pronounced. Specifically, while 71 percent of students at highly selective colleges took at least one course with more than twenty pages of writing assigned the prior semester, only 46 percent of students at selective colleges and 39 percent in less selective colleges experienced this curricular demand. The extent to which these writing assignments were asked of students varied as much across institutions as in response to the combined set of all other individual academic and social factors that we explored. The overall selectivity of the entering college class accounted for half of the institutional-level differences, while the individual-level academic and social variables accounted for only 2 percent of differences across institutions.

Pronounced institutional differences are also apparent for student exposure to courses that required more than forty pages of reading per week. At highly selective colleges, 92 percent of students reported at least one course with this requirement. Only 62 percent of students at selective colleges

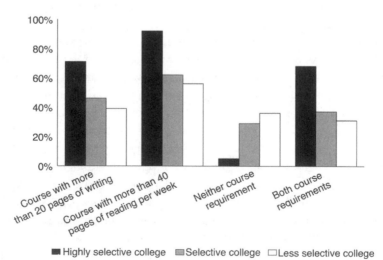

Figure 3.2. Reading and writing course requirements, by institutional selectivity (based on table A3.3)

and 56 percent of students at less selective colleges took a course requiring at least forty pages of reading per week. In highly selective colleges, 68 percent of students had experienced *both* reading and writing requirements in the prior semester, compared to only 37 percent at selective colleges and 31 percent in less selective colleges. An association between the college selectivity of the entering class and students' failure to take a course with *either* reading or writing requirement the prior semester was even more pronounced. Students at highly selective colleges were more than six times less likely to experience this fate than otherwise: only 5 percent of students at highly selective colleges lacked either of these curricular demands, compared to 29 percent of students at selective colleges and 36 percent of students at less selective colleges. If students are taking courses without significant reading and writing requirements, it is probably unreasonable to expect them to develop skills to improve on performance tasks that require critical thinking, complex reasoning, and written communication.

Courses taken

College students' exposure to a rigorous curriculum that is aligned with the development of skills in complex reasoning, critical thinking, and written communication is largely determined by the courses they take. Some courses are mandated by a college's "general education" or "distribution" requirements. Others, for students with less academic preparation, are required by college for remediation purposes. A large portion of coursework is typically chosen by students on the basis of individual preferences reflected in their choices of electives and fields of study.

During the first two years of college, many students have a good deal of their coursework taken up by general education and distribution requirements. Although there was some variation, the schools in our sample had relatively similar subject area requirements in terms of the mandated core curriculum. One of the few noteworthy differences across institutions was that more highly selective colleges provided greater specificity in outlining their general education curricula and providing identification of which classes would fulfill those requirements. The lack of detail offered in some of the less selective schools' general education descriptions is possibly an indication of how flexible those institutions are in accepting varied coursework as adequate towards fulfilling core requirements.

Past scholarship has demonstrated that student attitudes towards these required courses are, not surprisingly, mixed. On the one hand, three-quarters of students report on national surveys that general education coursework "add[s] to the enrichment of other courses I have taken" and "helps prepare me for lifelong learning."[38] Ernest Boyer, president of the Carnegie Foundation for the Advancement of Teaching, noted in his seminal work on the undergraduate experience in the late 1980s that one student reported that the core curriculum "stretched my mind. Without these general education requirements I would not have read important books."[39] On the other hand, Boyer also noted that most undergraduates perceive general education courses as something to "get out of the way."[40] In a similar fashion Mary Grigsby, in her study of student perceptions of college life, notes that many students find these courses burdensome and express frustration over "'jumping through the hoops' of general education requirements."[41]

In addition to general education requirements, students with inadequate prior academic training are required by many colleges to take remedial college coursework, particularly in English and mathematics. Depending on the college, students are often required to enroll at nearby community colleges for these classes. Although these courses are required for students with limited academic preparation, students often do not receive college course credit for their completion, nor do they always appear on four-year college transcripts. Research has been mixed on the effectiveness of these courses.[42]

While some coursework is prescribed, the U.S. higher education system as a whole is noted for the extent to which it affords eighteen-year-olds a great deal of latitude in choosing their coursework. In recent decades student preferences have shifted, with incoming students increasingly expressing interest in acquiring skills to "become well off financially" and decreasing interest in developing a "meaningful philosophy of life."[43] These changing preferences have led to a "dramatic flight from the arts and sciences" as the proportion of Bachelors of Arts degrees awarded to students who concentrated in these subject areas (i.e., humanities, social sciences, mathematics, physical sciences, biological sciences, and psychology) plummeted from 47 percent of all BA degrees in 1968 to 26 percent in 1986.[44] By the end of the century, the traditional liberal arts subject areas had recovered some of this lost ground, but the majority of bachelors' degrees conferred were still in occupationally related majors such as business, education, social work, communication, health, computer science, and engineering—an area that sociologist Steven Brint has dubbed the new "practical arts" core of the modern university.[45]

Quantitative social scientists have often been willing to assume that rational student deliberation and calculation underlie these changing college enrollment patterns. For example, economists of higher education William Bowen and Sarah Turner have noted: "Some students elect fields of study for reasons that are strictly intellectual; others may be influenced by job prospects, broad social and political trends, family background and parental pressures, and the curricular options made available by colleges and universities. An exhaustive analysis would require examination of all variables influencing the perceived returns (noneconomic as well as economic) related to investments by students and educational institutions of time and other resources in various fields of study."[46] While there is something reassuring about a model of student behavior that relies on rational decision-making aligned with "perceived returns" and student preferences, other scholarship that has been more attentive to student voices has highlighted a much less deliberate and clear decision-making process at work on today's college campuses.

Psychologist William Damon, for example, has noted in his recent work on youth transitions that a growing number of adolescents lack a sense of purpose. Rather than embracing a deliberately chosen path to attain a set of valued goals, college students and other adolescents are argued increasingly to exist in prolonged states of "directionless drift." According to Damon, "their delay is characterized more by indecision than by motivated reflection, more by confusion than by the pursuit of clear goals, more by ambivalence than by determination."[47] Damon describes in detail one of his interview respondents: Tommy, an eighteen-year-old from Pennsylvania who "expressed absolutely no sense of purpose" as a freshman at college:

> Tommy's indifference applied to his everyday decisions as well as his broader reflections. On the issue of choosing his academic program, he said, "I don't know what I'm going to take next term. They make you pick some courses. I'll just say 'what the hell' and flip a coin or something." On the question of aspirations, Tommy was quite comfortable with having none: "I don't really have goals for my future. What's the big deal about that? It would be fun to travel. I'd like that, especially if I could get someone to pay for it."[48]

While Tommy's lack of ambition is perhaps anomalous—for example, 81 percent of students in our study planned to attain a graduate degree following the completion of college, with 39 percent expecting this at a doctorate or professional degree level—his lack of direction is prevalent in a current generation of youth that has been described by contemporary sociologists as "motivated but directionless."

Rather than choosing courses that are closely aligned with well-articulated developmental or occupational goals, more mundane factors appear to influence course choices of "motivated but directionless" college students.[49] In Rebekah Nathan's *My Freshman Year*, for example, students provided the following set of course recommendations:

> "Take Professor Jones, the man to see when you need an 'A.'"
> "Don't take 302 with Smith because you can't understand what he wants you to know and he doesn't give As."
> "I loved 101. It was sooo fun! And sooo easy!"
> "Need to boost your GPA? Take 242."
> "145 sucks. Never *take* it. You do three times the amount of work for the same credits and lower grades."
> "Sign up for 235. The course is boring but it's easy as hell, and there's tons of extra credit."
> "Take 298, it's sooo easy."[50]

One of the students in Tim Clydesdale's longitudinal study of recent graduates from a New Jersey high school expressed a similar orientation at a "Public Ivy" residential college:

> It really isn't much different than high school, other than my professors are like doctors instead of just like regular people . . . . It's just like going to a high school class. You sit down, you listen to them lecture, and that's about it. I mean, it's really boring . . . . I hate learning; I hate sitting in classes and everything. I just do it for grades . . . . I've never had a class where I was really interested and into it. I just . . . did the work so I could get an "A" pretty much.[51]

Students in these studies are choosing courses to minimize short-term investments of individual commitment required to obtain high course marks—not making deliberate rational calculations about courses' "perceived returns" aligned with long-term personal goals. Decisions are indeed based on personal preferences, but student perspectives are often exceedingly myopic and focused on short-term gains, understood as increased freedom from strenuous academic effort.

In our sample, when inspecting grades reported on college transcripts, we found that on average students were academically evaluated as relatively successful by the instructors of the courses they had chosen (see table A3.4 in methodological appendix). The average collegiate grade point average of students was 3.2. Students with more highly educated parents had higher grades at college, as did students with higher SAT/ACT performance. Male students, African-American and Hispanic students, and students from high schools with 70 percent or more non-white students had lower grade point averages on their college transcripts than their peers. Interestingly, students in our study attending highly selective colleges had significantly higher grades than those attending other colleges. National research has highlighted the extent to which grade inflation is rampant not only throughout higher education, but particularly at elite colleges and universities. For example in 1997, the median GPA at Princeton was 3.42 and the proportion of course grades that were A or A-minuses was 45 percent at Duke, 44 percent at Dartmouth, and 46 percent at Harvard.[52] Valen Johnson quotes a Dartmouth professor explaining these high grades by noting that faculty at the college

> . . . began systematically to inflate grades, so that our graduates would have more A's to wave around. But, if you prefer to be accurate, you would say that we simply recognized and began to follow the trend toward national standards, national reputations, and national comparison groups. No longer do most of us on the faculty just compare one Dartmouth student with another; we take into account the vast pool of college students nationwide, all five million of them. That is, we imagine our students at a mythical Average U., and give the grades they would get there.[53]

Examining patterns of course concentration, we find that despite the reported "flight from the arts and sciences," students in our sample—likely primarily because of general education and distribution requirements— are still taking a large portion of their first- and second-year coursework in science, mathematics, humanities, and social science subject areas. For the sample as a whole, 24 percent of coursework over the first two years of college was in science and mathematics, 48 percent was in the humanities and social sciences (fields of study that, according to recent research on grade inflation, typically have courses that offer students higher grades).[54] Students on average took 16 percent of coursework in the "practical arts" (i.e., business, education, social work, engineering, computer science, communications, and health fields); 12 percent of coursework was devoted to other subjects that included courses on their transcripts in areas as diverse as golf, tennis, and "ultimate Frisbee." It is worth noting here that many of the courses in the traditional humanities and social sciences disciplines were in areas that were also quite varied. For example, 402 of the courses on student transcripts had the terms race, gender, or sex in their titles (an average of one course on 19.4 percent of student transcripts); 278 had the words cinema, film, or movie in their course titles (an average of 13.4 percent of transcripts); and 107 had the term sexuality in their titles (an average of 5.2 percent of transcripts).

There were few racial differences in the broad patterns of course concentration over the first two years of college.[55] The one exception to this was Asian students, who took a significantly higher percentage of coursework in science and mathematics than white students, and a lower percentage in the fields of education and social work. In terms of social background, students with parents who had attended graduate or professional school had higher levels of course concentration in the humanities and social sciences. Students from families that did not speak English at home were less likely to enroll in courses in the areas of education and social work, communications, or health. Students who attended high schools with 70 percent or greater concentrations of non-white students had a higher concentration of coursework in mathematics and sciences than otherwise— possibly reflecting the likelihood that they were focusing on institutionally mandated remedial or basic mathematics requirements. Students with higher academic preparation measured by prior SAT/ACT performance took more courses in humanities and social sciences and fewer courses in education, social work, and communications, relative to students with lower demonstrated ability. We also found pronounced well-known gender differences in course concentration patterns. Female students, relative to male students, took fewer courses in business, engineering, computer sciences, and science and mathematics; and higher levels of courses in education and social work, health, and humanities and social sciences.

In addition to these individual-level differences, students' course-taking patterns varied across institutions. Students attending highly selective colleges relative to students enrolled in less selective colleges took less communication coursework and significantly higher levels of coursework in the humanities and social sciences. For most of the subject areas examined, institutional differences across colleges were associated with more variation in student choices than all the individual-level factors combined. For example, the individual-level factors explained 15 percent of the variance in the percentage of humanities and social sciences coursework, but adding the college where the student was enrolled to the individual-level model increased the explained variance to 31 percent.[56]

Students have diverse reasons for taking various patterns of courses. What concern us primarily here are not the factors underlying these choices, but rather the consequences for the extent to which students are exposed to rigorous and challenging curriculum aligned with developing their capacity for critical thinking, complex reasoning, and writing. Specifically, we identified the extent to which students who concentrated in different areas of study (defined as course concentrations one standard deviation higher than average for the subject area) varied on the curricular experiences that were examined earlier in this chapter (i.e., times met with faculty, hours devoted to studying, and enrollment in courses with more than twenty pages of writing per semester or forty pages of reading per week). Our definition of subject-area course concentrator does not exclude the possibility that students can concentrate in more than one subject area. In our sample, 21.1 percent of students did not concentrate their coursework in any of our broadly defined subject areas during the first two years of college, 69.4 percent of students concentrated in one area, 9.4 percent concentrated in two areas, and only two students in our sample concentrated in three areas.

Figure 3.3 identifies differences in students' reports of faculty contact outside of class the prior semester, and the number of hours students devoted to studying per week based on their course concentration choices in the broad areas identified (for detailed results, see table A3.5 in methodological appendix). Students who were math and science course concentrators reported higher contact with their faculty outside of the classroom than other students; students who concentrated in health-related

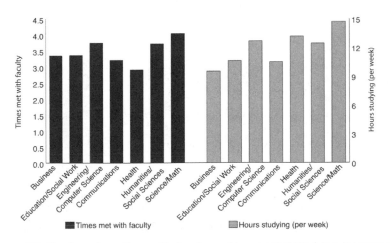

Figure 3.3. Number of meetings with faculty and hours spent studying, by course subject concentration (based on table A3.5)

coursework reported the lowest level of faculty contact outside of the classroom. Students concentrating in science and mathematics reported studying on average 14.7 hours per week, those who concentrated in business reported 9.6 hours per week, those concentrating in education and social work 10.6 hours per week, and those concentrating in communications 10.5 hours per week. Whether these differences were due to styles of instruction, course requirements, or selection effects associated with differences in the type of students choosing these various tracks is impossible to determine from these initial findings.

When we examine the reported course requirements by course concentration patterns in figure 3.4, however, troubling differences in curricular expectations were evident. Sixty-eight percent of students concentrating in humanities and social sciences reported taking at least one course requiring more than twenty pages of writing during the previous semester, and 88 percent reported taking at least one course requiring more than forty pages of reading per week. Moreover, 64 percent of students concentrating in humanities and social sciences reported both types of requirements, and only 8 percent experienced neither requirement. Students concentrating in science and mathematics, the other fields associated with the traditional liberal-arts core, reported relatively low likelihood of taking courses

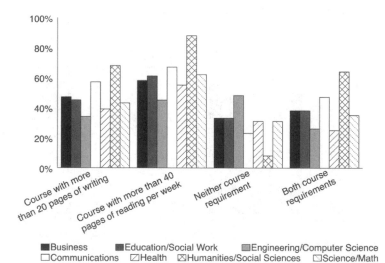

Figure 3.4. Reading and writing course requirements, by course subject concentration (based on table A3.5)

requiring more than twenty pages of writing, or of experiencing both (reading and writing) requirements.

Course concentrators in three of the four "practical arts" subject areas also reported fewer of the curricular requirements examined. Students concentrating in business coursework reported lower levels of reading requirements and higher frequency of having experienced neither the reading nor the writing requirement. Students concentrating in education and social work reported lower exposure to the writing requirement and, like students with concentrated business coursework, higher likelihood of experiencing neither the reading nor the writing requirements. Finally, students with course concentrations in engineering and computer sciences less frequently reported taking courses with either the reading or the writing requirement, and thus were more likely to report having experienced neither one. Given these differences in curricular requirements associated with coursework patterns, it is likely that students' choices in coursework, even broadly conceptualized and measured, will have significant consequences for the development of their capacity to perform tasks—such as the Collegiate Learning Assessment—that require skills in critical thinking, complex reasoning, and writing.

Student College Life

The widespread growth of higher education has held forth the promise of greater career opportunities for the current generation of students than for any previous generation. Yet, according to a study conducted by psychologist William Damon, "only about one in five young people in the 12–22 year age range express a clear vision of where they want to go, what they want to accomplish in life, and why."[57] Other recent studies on the lives of college students and their perceptions of purpose provide further evidence of this trend. In a recent study, sociologist Mary Grigsby found that students widely embraced cultural scripts of college life depicted in popular movies such as *Animal House* (1978) and *National Lampoon's Van Wilder* (2002) that "give the impression that a hedonistic collegiate culture is dominant."[58] These media depictions of college life provide students with normative frames of reference that define nonacademic collegiate behaviors and orientations as widely practiced, acceptable, and institutionally tolerated. This observation has been confirmed by anthropologist Rebekah Nathan, who enrolled as a freshman at her university in order to research undergraduate college culture. Nathan observed "how little intellectual life seemed to matter in college."[59] The patterns of student life, housing, clubs, organizations, Greek life, and other activities embraced by students have potential implications for how and what they learn in college.

There has been an abundance of research, for example, supporting the positive effects on educational outcomes of on-campus housing. Sociologists Stephanie Clemons, David McKelfresh, and James Banning claim that dormitories are critical to first-year success as well as for college persistence, due to the availability and easy accessibility of support.[60] These findings are reinforced by similar results reported by educational researchers George Kuh, Ernest Pascarella, and Patrick Terenzini.[61] The dormitory is often the place where students make their first social contacts in college, and the reported individual growth they experience by living on campus has been argued by others to have both social and academic dimensions. Higher-education researchers have claimed that engaging in dormitory life, although without explicit academic structures, might not only help students grow socially but also help them develop in a way that will improve their performance on tasks such as the ones that are assessed by the CLA.[62]

Listening to student voices in today's colleges, however, leads us to be skeptical of these claims. In Rebekah Nathan's research at a predominantly residential state university, students reported individual orientations that emphasized social rather than academic pursuits. As one student noted: "Honestly, I feel like nothing I've learned in the classroom will help me do what I want to do in the end. I think it's the people I meet, the friends I make, that really matter."[63] Given these student attitudes, we question whether those who find themselves on a trajectory of success are more likely to live on campus than others. In addition, dorm residence often is simply a proxy for social background and academic orientation, as Grigsby notes: "The living arrangements that students make after freshman year usually are influenced by their economic situation and reflect their goals and orientations toward academics and social life upon entering college. The choices they make throughout college are shaped by this beginning, both the economic and cultural resources they have, and the orientations towards academics and social life with which they enter college are central in shaping how they make meaning of college and how they choose to use it."[64]

Not all universities provide student housing throughout their college years, and not all students can afford to live on campus. There are individual as well as institutional differences, which likely combine to determine collegiate residential choices (see table A3.6 in methodological appendix). In our sample, a greater percentage of students whose parents had a higher level of education lived on campus during the spring of their sophomore year. Moreover, while on average 70 percent of students lived on campus, 99 percent of the students attending highly selective colleges and almost 90 percent of students entering college with higher initial academic performance lived on campus. Even after controlling for initial academic ability and other social background factors, the differences across colleges in the prevalence of dormitory residence for students in their sophomore year were pronounced.

Notable variation across institutions is also evident in the extent to which participation in Greek life is accessible and encouraged. In addition, Greek participation is related to individual characteristics. Students whose parents had higher levels of education spent more hours in fraternities and sororities. In contrast, African-American and Hispanic students spent far fewer hours involved in fraternities and sororities than did other groups. Students in Nathan's study who were more reluctant to become entangled in the Greek system expressed concerns over personal limitation and loss of individuality by joining.

> Students' greatest objections to the Greek system were its steep demands—
> that it required so much time ("I can't give up that many nights a week
> to one organization") and so many resources ("Why should I pay all that
> money to a fraternity to have friends when I can make friends for free?"), all
> of them mandatory ("I don't want people telling me what to do and where
> I have to be all the time"; "I'm an individual, not a group person"). Yet, the
> one student in ten who did join a fraternity or sorority was, according to
> 2003 surveys conducted by the Office of Student Life, much less likely to
> drop out of school and much more likely to report the highest level of satis-
> faction with campus life.[65]

The community students often find in Greek affiliation may lead to greater social integration associated with higher persistence in college.

In addition to Greek life, the students in our sample spent an average of approximately four hours per week in student clubs. However, not all students were equally involved: students from more educated families spent more hours involved in such clubs, as did those who were more academically prepared. Class differences may emerge in part because participation in collegiate culture costs money.[66] Moreover, while middle-class students perceive extracurricular activities as an opportunity to "meet other 'outgo-ing' and 'social' people—an important goal of their college experience," that is not the case for working-class students. As Patty, a working-class student in a recent study of college experiences conducted by Jenny Stu-ber, stated, "I don't do group activities; I don't do anything. I go to class, go to work, do my homework. Otherwise, leave me alone. I don't want to be on campus if I don't have to be."[67] This reluctance to engage in college life in part seems to reflect cultural differences in what students bring to college, and their familiarity and comfort with middle-class culture. Patty had attended a small rural high school, where she participated in theater and student government. When she entered college, she faced a different social context: "The people here are more like, I don't want to say sophisti-cated, but different than me. They seem more cultured. Did you ever have classes with people who like put sentences together and you're like 'How did you come up with that? Did you plan what you were going to say?' I sometimes feel like that, to be quite honest. Sometimes I feel like I don't measure up."[68]

While different groups of students in our sample were more or less likely to participate in college clubs, all students were equally likely to re-port volunteering. The absence of gaps in volunteering experiences across students may appear encouraging. However, the overall participation rate is quite low: students in our sample spent on average just over two hours a week volunteering. Moreover, almost 50 percent of students reported no volunteering experience over the course of the previous semester. Commu-nity service involvement generally decreases in transition from high school to college, for various reasons including financial limitations, time man-agement, and prioritizing academic and other campus activities.[69] Since volunteering is found to have positive effects on student outcomes in prior research, many colleges today are aiming to encourage service learning and incorporate volunteering into curricular requirements.[70]

Overall, both institutional and individual characteristics shape students' life in college. Although individual-level characteristics are a powerful determinant of many social choices, differing campus cultures influence which options are available or are more widely embraced. Various aspects of college life may help students to grow socially, something many stu-dents are increasingly stressing as the true purpose and developmental goal of college. These activities also potentially help students (particularly those who tend to be more advantaged) remain in college even when they do not embrace academic learning or find it particularly meaningful or worthwhile.

Financial Challenges

While college attendance has become more commonplace, college costs have increased over time, with current estimates approximating on average nearly half of median family income.[71] The majority of college students today require some sort of financial assistance, whether it is in the form of loans, scholarships, or grants. Given that student learning occurs in both an institutional and financial context, we highlight here how financial realities affect student life and, potentially, student learning.

Most students work in some form during their years in college. Sixty-five percent of students in our sample reported working in either on-campus or off-campus jobs (see table A3.7 in methodological appendix).[72] Although there are few differences across students in whether they are working or not, notable differences are revealed in the number of hours dedicated to the labor market. African-American and Hispanic students reported working more hours per week than white students. Moreover, students who came from less educated families invested more time in their jobs. Figure 3.5 shows that in addition to working longer hours, students from traditionally disadvantaged groups also relied extensively on different forms of financial assistance. African-American students and students from families without college experience were more likely to rely on grants to cover their college costs than their more advantaged peers. However, these groups were also covering a substantial portion of their college costs with loans. African-American students reported that 27 percent of their college costs were covered by loans, compared to 20 percent by white and 14 percent by Asian students. Students whose parents did not attend college reported that 24 of their college costs were covered by loans, compared to 16 percent of students whose parents held advanced degrees.

While grants and scholarships were awarded more often to disadvantaged youth in our sample, the needs of these students are often greater than the resources that are either available or accessible to them. Many low-income students likely to qualify for financial aid tend not to take advantage of aid programs.[73] Moreover, even among students who receive aid, the remaining tuition that low-income students often pay equals nearly half of their family income, while the amount higher-income students pay equals about one-tenth of their average family income.[74] Recent decades have seen an increasing reliance of students on loans for financing their college education. Previous studies have revealed "evidence that this shift toward loans has negative consequences for college access and retention for minority and low-income students."[75] The mounting debt and the

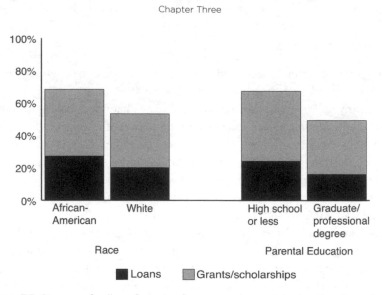

Figure 3.5. Sources of college financing, by race and parental education (based on table A3.7)

anticipated costs that must be paid back can potentially discourage continued enrollment or prevent graduation, particularly for students who are unsure of the extent to which they can exchange their college degrees for success in the labor market.

While we have so far portrayed a somber picture of students struggling to pay for their college education, there is another reality on college campuses: students work and borrow in order to support a particular lifestyle. Only slightly over one-third (37 percent) of students in our sample reported that they were working to pay college tuition. Another 6 percent, comprised mostly of disadvantaged groups of students, worked to send money home. However, that leaves the majority of students working for other reasons. We can anticipate that loans are similarly only partially used to cover tuition costs. Sociologists Steven Brint and Matthew Baron Rotondi interviewed students concerning their perspectives on the value of a college education and its relationship to debt. They argued that "students no longer think of student loans as a burden to be avoided or discharged quickly, but rather as a means of freedom, which opens up rather than limits behavioral options and particularly opportunities to enjoy 'the full college experience.'"[76] Today's students "do not view debt exclusively as an investment, but also as a vehicle for consumption."[77]

The culture and institutional practices of different colleges are likely to influence the various ways in which students are funding their education and balancing school and work. In our data, however, individual-level factors outweighed institutional differences across campuses in terms of accounting for differences in students' financial experiences. Brint and Rotondi's research, which has highlighted how pervasively students embrace cultural expectations of personally fulfilling collegiate life at one particular institution, is therefore likely to be broadly generalizable across college campuses. Brint and Rotondi found that

> for most of those interviewed, quality-of-life was at the heart of the full college experience . . . . Another student said that instead of taking out loans, ". . . I could have lived at home and commuted, but . . . that would take up a lot more time, and I don't want to take up that much time going in between school and the college experience . . . ." Altogether, among the respondents who answered this question, a sizable majority of the respondents said that taking out loans had "improved the quality" of their time in college.[78]

Recent survey results have further revealed that many students fail to consider the true meaning and long-term consequences of debt: "At the cognitive level, more than 90 percent of the students responded that 'Saving' was 'Very Important' or 'Important' at 'this stage of your life' whereas at the behavioral level only one-tenth reported that they sought to respond by 'hav[ing] a monthly budget.'"[79] Financial literacy, apparently, is not a cognitive competency developed at many colleges today, as "a near majority could provide no information about any of the following: the total amount they owed, the length of time they had to repay their loans, when their repayment began, or what their monthly repayment amount would be."[80] This lack of information makes students poorly positioned to make rational calculations about educational investment, as is made clear by the following retrospective student account portrayed by Anya Kamenetz in *Generation Debt*:

> I qualified for $5,000 in loans each semester for two semesters. The funny thing is, I only needed about $1,000 to cover the actual schooling. The rest of the money they included was for expenses. Since I had none living at home with Mom, I got it into my young, uneducated brain that I could use the money to move out of her house and become independent . . . I don't need to tell you what a mistake that was . . . or what easy prey I was for all

the credit companies . . . . I am now 31 years old and still in debt from those days . . . . What started out as $10,000 in student loans and about $2,000 in credit card debt has ballooned to a total of $33,000.[81]

Many students have come to believe that they "should enjoy their college social life since they will obtain a great job and salary after graduation."[82] This stems from their expectation that they will be employed soon after graduation and that all they need to secure that employment is a college degree—an assumption that has proven problematic for a cohort that was set to graduate from college into the severe economic recession of 2009. Considering that students often did not know which careers they would be pursuing by the time they graduated, however, it was neither practical nor realistic for many of them to make educational investment decisions based upon their expected salaries. These limitations to rational educational decision-making exist for many students regardless of the fact that many economists have been willing to assume analytical models based on students who act as "adolescent econometricians" when making choices about educational investments.[83] In addition, these financial opportunities, limitations, and circumstances potentially play a significant role in facilitating or hindering students' focus on the learning process.

Pathways Adrift

This comprehensive portraiture of the academic, social, and financial experiences of the collegiate class of 2009 provides vivid testimony of the extent to which many students have been left academically adrift on today's campuses. The typical student meets with faculty outside of the classroom only once per month, with 9 percent of students never meeting with faculty outside the classroom during the previous semester. Although 85 percent of students have achieved a B-minus grade point average or higher, and 55 percent have attained a B-plus grade point average or higher, the average student studies less than two hours per day. Moreover, half of students have not taken a single course that required more than twenty pages of writing, and approximately one-third have not taken any courses that required more than forty pages of reading per week during the prior semester.

While the life of a typical college student may not be conducive to academic pursuits, there is much variation across both students and institutions. Students' academic attitudes, behaviors, and values were related to their social background and academic preparation. In addition, college settings varied notably in the extent to which they successfully promoted student academic orientations and practices. In highly selective colleges, students were significantly more likely to meet with faculty outside of the classroom, to spend more hours studying, and to take courses with greater reading and writing requirements. Institutional contexts mattered over and above the individual-level differences, such as prior academic preparation and social background, that students brought to campus.

Many of the students in our study, who focused in only a limited way on academic pursuits, were quite active in other ways at college. They spent much time in various extracurricular endeavors including clubs, fraternities and sororities, and volunteering. Moreover, nearly two-thirds of our sample was working while in college, and if working, students on average devoted thirteen hours per week to such activities—an hour more than this subset of employed students spent preparing for classes. Even when students were studying, more than a quarter of that time was spent studying with peers.

The financial and social experiences of the students in our sample suggest that they are relatively hard-working and motivated. As a college class, they deserve and have earned our sympathy. Unfortunately their inflated ambitions and high aspirations have not institutionally been met by equivalently high academic demands from their professors, nor have many of them found a sense of academic purpose or academic commitment at contemporary colleges. Instead, many of the students in our study appear to be academically adrift. In the next chapter we explore the consequences of this lack of academic focus on student learning, and we seek to identify activities and experiences that facilitate the development of students' skills in critical thinking, complex reasoning, and writing.

4

Channeling Students' Energies toward Learning

The portrayal of higher education emerging from the preceding pages is one of an institution focused more on social than academic experiences. Students spend very little time studying, and professors rarely demand much from them in terms of reading and writing. But perhaps that is inconsequential. Many students enter higher education academically unprepared, and some would argue that no degree of studying, reading, or writing would notably improve their critical thinking, complex reasoning, and writing skills.[1] Indeed, this is a popular understanding of the role of school in students' lives. Students enter school—whether it is kindergarten or college—with preexisting differences. These differences combine to give some students advantages in their ability to absorb new academic material and develop academic skills relative to their peers. From this perspective, colleges operate primarily as sorting mechanisms. The education system is viewed as "a very complicated 'sieve,' which sifts 'the good' from 'the bad' future citizens, 'the able' from the 'the dull,' 'those fitted for the high positions' from those 'unfitted.'"[2]

This view of schooling as a mechanism that primarily works to reproduce, exacerbate, and certify preexisting individual-level

Daniel Potter coauthored this chapter.

differences is widely shared and embraced throughout American society. A recent national Gallup public opinion poll found that 80 percent of Americans believed that the achievement gap between white students and African-American and Hispanic students was mostly related not to the quality of schooling received, but to other factors.[3] These views are also often espoused by the most elite members of our society. Justice Antonin Scalia, for example, recently provided a similar account of schooling when explaining to a law student at American University—an institution ranked forty-fifth nationally in *U.S. News and World Report*—why the individual was highly unlikely to gain a prestigious clerkship at the U.S. Supreme Court. "I'm going to be picking from the law schools that basically are the hardest to get into," Scalia commented. "They admit the best and the brightest, and they may not teach very well, but you can't make a sow's ear out of a silk purse. If they come in the best and the brightest, they're probably going to leave the best and the brightest."[4]

This line of reasoning would imply that students' activities and experiences in higher education as well as institutional programs and practices are largely, if not entirely, inconsequential. We believe, however, that this view is overly cynical and inconsistent with prior research which demonstrates that students' actions and institutional contexts shape educational outcomes. Research on graduation rates, for example, has time and again demonstrated that degree completion varies across institutions, even after controlling for student characteristics—implying that schools indeed make a difference.[5] Numerous studies emanating from the National Survey of Student Engagement have shown that what students do in higher education, as well as whether higher education institutions facilitate student engagement, has consequences for a range of student outcomes from satisfaction and personal development to persistence and grades.[6] As Pascarella and Terenzini concluded, "the impact of college is largely determined by individual effort and involvement in the academic, interpersonal, and extracurricular offerings on a campus . . . ."[7] The previous chapter has demonstrated notable variation in student experiences, which vary not only across students but also across institutions. How are different college experiences related to development of students' skills in critical thinking, complex reasoning, and writing? And more importantly, are specific academic and social activities associated with learning, after we adjust for what students bring to higher education? Regardless of who walks through the doors of higher education, can institutions shape students' experiences in ways that facilitate learning?[8]

Academic and Social Climates

Entering college entails exposure to specific academic and social environments where faculty and students hold particular beliefs and expectations of themselves and others. Having faculty members who are perceived by students as being approachable and having high standards and expectations is associated with greater learning (see table A4.1 in methodological appendix).[9] Students' perceptions of these faculty attributes are related: faculty members who have high expectations also tend to have high standards and are approachable.[10] If we consider all three of these faculty attributes simultaneously, high expectations stand out as the only relevant factor, and are thus a particularly salient aspect of educational experience which is associated with students' learning. A prominent sociological tradition of status attainment over the past forty years has highlighted how expectations of significant others, including teachers, are important for facilitating students' educational success.[11] This still holds true on college campuses today: when faculty have high expectations, students learn more.

Moreover, having demanding faculty who include reading and writing requirements in their courses (i.e., when faculty require that students both read more than forty pages a week and write more than twenty pages over the course of a semester) is associated with improvement in students' critical thinking, complex reasoning, and writing skills. As Alexander Astin noted in his extensive review of student outcomes in higher education, students "learn what they study."[12] When students are asked to read and write in their courses, when academic coursework is challenging, and when higher-order thinking is included in the coursework, students perform better on tests measuring skills such as critical thinking and writing.[13] Similarly, the CLA performance task, which we are relying upon to measure learning, asks students to read, synthesize information, and write a coherent argument. If students are not practicing these skills in the classroom, they will not perform well or improve on such tasks over time. Unfortunately, as we have seen in the previous chapter, too few students have challenging academic experiences: one-quarter of students were not asked in any of their classes to either read more than forty pages a week or write more than twenty pages over the course of a semester, and another 25 percent were asked only to read but not to write at these levels.

While these results fit with conventional wisdom on what is required to encourage learning, they could reflect specific student characteristics instead of faculty requirements and expectations. As we have seen in the previous chapter, faculty expectations and demands are related to student attributes. Students who come from more advantaged social backgrounds and are better academically prepared have a more positive view of their professors. Consequently, some of the differences in CLA growth among students who report different reading and writing requirements or various levels of faculty expectations are explained by variation in student characteristics. However, even after we control (i.e., statistically adjust estimates) for a range of individual attributes, including academic preparation, students who report that faculty have high expectations and that they took classes where they had to read more than forty pages a week and had to write more than twenty pages over the course of the semester still improved their skills significantly more than did students lacking those experiences.

A skeptical reader could still propose that these results are an artifact of selectivity or some other institutional characteristic. This would imply that the observed differences are a product not of faculty attitudes and actions, but of some other unobserved institutional differences. To attend to this concern, we conducted an additional analysis that controls for institutions attended. This approach effectively adjusts the analysis for institutional differences that occur across schools. This would include selectivity and other characteristics such as location, public/private control, institutional type (e.g., Carnegie classification), and the like. Figure 4.1 presents the results from these final models.

Even after we have adjusted students' CLA scores for a host of individual and institutional differences, faculty expectations continue to be related to student learning. Students who reported that faculty had high expectations scored twenty-seven points higher on the CLA in 2007 than those who reported that professors had low expectations. A medium level of expectations was also associated with more learning, but not enough to differ significantly from students whose faculty had low expectations. Similarly, when students were asked to read and write at the level assessed, they performed better on the CLA. Doing one or the other (taking classes that required either reading more than forty pages a week or writing more than twenty pages over the course of a semester) was not adequate. The combination of reading and writing in coursework was necessary to improve students' performance on tasks requiring critical thinking, complex reasoning, and writing skills in their first two years of college. While the magnitude of these differences may not appear large, it is quite notable considering that over the time period examined, students on average improved their CLA performance by only thirty-four points. In this context,

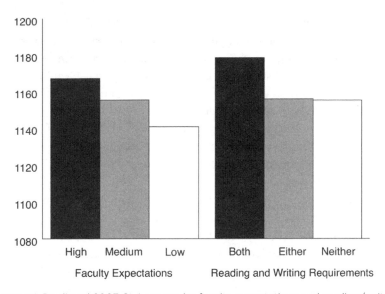

Figure 4.1. Predicted 2007 CLA scores, by faculty expectations and reading/writing course requirements (based on table A4.1, fixed-effects model).

a twenty-seven-point gap for faculty expectations and a twenty-three-point gap for reading/writing requirements are remarkable.[14]

While students' reports of faculty expectations and reading/writing requirements are associated with improvement in their critical thinking, complex reasoning, and writing skills, interaction with faculty outside the classroom was less important. We asked students how frequently they met with a faculty member outside of class during the previous semester, but this form of academic engagement was not related to learning during the first two years in college. This finding seems to contradict a long tradition of research in higher education that emphasizes the importance of interaction with faculty for students' development and academic achievement.[15] It is possible that our measure is not adequately nuanced; students could be meeting with faculty for a number of reasons. For example, they could be meeting with faculty because they are not doing well in a class or because they are working on a collaborative research project. Findings from prior research are suggestive of the type of faculty interaction outside of the classroom that is currently prevalent: while 95 percent of college seniors in a large national sample reported having discussed "grades or assignments" with an instructor, 29 percent reported that they had *never* discussed ideas from their readings or classes with faculty members outside of class during their last year in college. Intellectual engagement with faculty is even lower for younger students: 42 percent of first-year students have not discussed ideas from their readings or classes with faculty members outside of class.[16] The rare occasions of intellectual exchange may be quite fruitful, but the more common discussions of grades may not be particularly beneficial for students' cognitive growth.

It is also possible that this null finding of interaction with faculty is a recent trend reflecting an increasing reliance on adjunct and graduate instructors, particularly for general requirement courses in the first two years of college. Among students entering four-year institutions in the 2003–04 academic year, almost 50 percent reported taking classes with graduate student instructors during their first year.[17] Indeed, another recent study reported no relationship between student-faculty interaction and objective measures of critical thinking and writing skills.[18] The nature of instruction and interaction with faculty members in higher education may be changing in a manner such that we have to reevaluate the meaning and consequences of "meeting with faculty" for students' cognitive skills, and for student development in general.

Moreover, our student-reported measures of peer climates did not play much of a role in facilitating student learning. Participants' rating of the extent to which students at their institution have high expectations, help each other, and work hard to succeed were not related to development of students' critical thinking, complex reasoning, and writing skills during their first two years in college.[19] This does not mean that peers are irrelevant, as other measures such as studying with peers and spending time in fraternities/sororities will be shown below to be consequential for learning. Other aspects of peer interactions not examined in this study may also be related to students' cognitive development.[20]

Investing Time in Learning

Faculty may have high expectations and may require students to read and write reasonable amounts in their courses, but are students investing their time in ways conductive to learning? Time is the ultimate scarce resource. There are only twenty-four hours in a day, and time spent in one activity is time not spent in another. Symptomatic of this century's technological and social developments, college students are trying to overcome this fact by multitasking, saving precious minutes by doing two or more tasks at the same time. For example, students rarely walk on campus anymore without their eyes glued to Blackberries or iPhones. And to the chagrin of their instructors, students are often checking their Facebook and Twitter accounts while—or instead of—taking notes in class. Indeed, in a recent study, students reported that they spend on average between 125 (white students) and 131 (African-American students) hours on various activities Monday through Friday, even though the school/work week has only 120 hours. The same holds for the weekend, when 48 hours get stretched to between 52 hours for white students and 57 hours for African-American students.[21]

Simply said, there is too much to do and too little time. And since there is too much to do, academic demands have to compete with many other, arguably more enticing, alternatives. As figure 4.2 shows, today's college students dedicate a very small proportion of their time to academic pursuits. Students in our sample reported spending on average fifteen hours per week attending classes and labs. The rest of the time was divided between studying and myriad other activities. Studying is far from the focus of students' "free time" (i.e., time outside of class): only twelve hours a week are spent studying. Combining the hours spent studying with the hours spent in classes and labs, students in our sample spent less than one-fifth (16 percent) of their reported time each week on academic pursuits. Even if we focus only on the school/work week and assume that all academic activities occur within 120 hours between Monday and Friday, students would still be spending only 23 percent of their time on class and studying. This is not an anomaly—even at selective institutions, where one would expect students to spend more time on academic pursuits, other researchers have found that students spend only approximately 30 percent of their time from Monday to Friday attending classes and labs or studying.[22]

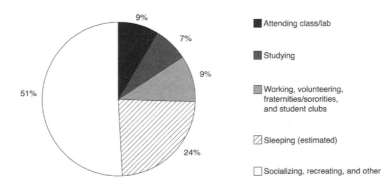

Figure 4.2. Student time use (percentages based on 168 hours—i.e., full seven-day week).

In addition to attending classes and studying, students are spending time working, volunteering, and participating in college clubs, fraternities, and sororities. If we presume that students are sleeping eight hours a night, which is a generous assumption given their tardiness and at times disheveled physical appearance in early morning classes, that leaves 85 hours a week for other activities—which is more than the combined amount of time students spend studying, attending classes, and participating in all of the activities we asked about. What is this additional time spent on? It seems to be spent mostly on socializing and recreation. A recent study of University of California undergraduates reported that while students spent thirteen hours a week studying, they also spent twelve hours socializing with friends, eleven hours using computers for fun, six hours watching television, six hours exercising, five hours on hobbies, and three hours on other forms of entertainment. Students were thus spending on average 43 hours per week outside the classroom on these activities—that is, over three times more hours than the time they spent studying.[23] National samples produce similarly disconcerting findings, showing that while one-third of students report spending less than six hours per week studying, two-thirds report spending six or more hours socializing with friends.[24] This is even though when students first enter higher education, they expect to spend much more time preparing for classes than socializing: as entering freshmen they anticipate spending 18 hours preparing for class and 12 hours relaxing and socializing.[25]

Given that students are spending very little time studying or attending classes, in both absolute and relative terms, we should not be surprised that on average they are not learning much. Other than the obvious lack of focus on academic matters, how is students' allocation of time related to their development of critical thinking, complex reasoning, and writing skills, as measured by the CLA?[26] We initially divided students' free time (i.e., time outside of class) into two categories: studying and extracurricular activities (including working, volunteering, participating in clubs and fraternities/sororities). The more time students spend in extracurricular activities, the smaller their gains on the CLA, controlling for the number of hours they spend studying (see table A4.2 in methodological appendix). At the same time, the more time students spend studying, the larger their improvement on the CLA (controlling for the number of hours they spend participating in extracurricular activities). Other studies have also noted that scarce hours spent studying are precious: in addition to having a positive association with grades, "studying and doing homework has stronger and more widespread positive effects [on a range of academic, cognitive, and affective outcomes in higher education] than almost any other involvement or environmental measure."[27]

However, students who spend various amounts of time studying or participating in extracurricular activities may differ on a range of other individual attributes. The observed consequences of time use for CLA growth may thus emerge from differences in student characteristics rather than from the activities themselves. When we adjust our estimates for students' background characteristics, including their academic preparation, the association between hours spent studying and CLA growth diminishes notably while the association between hours spent on extracurricular activities and CLA growth remains virtually unchanged. This implies that students who study more or fewer hours differ from each other in ways that explain their differential performance on the CLA. Although the implication is partly true, the story about studying is more nuanced, as the consequences of studying depend on the specific context in which the activity occurs—an issue we turn to next.[28]

A summary measure of the number of hours students spend studying and participating in other activities can provide a useful overview of time use, but it can also be misleading if specific activities have unique relationships to learning.[29] Prominent models of student success in higher education emphasize the importance of academic and social integration.[30] Thus, extracurricular activities that facilitate social integration are expected to be positively related to student outcomes, while those that pull students away from the campus community are expected to have negative consequences. A frequently given illustration of these processes is the contrast between employment on and off campus. Employment on campus is generally seen as enhancing student involvement and integration into the college community. Employment off campus, in contrast, is perceived as inhibiting students' integration and involvement. Thus, previous studies tend to find that on-campus employment is associated with more positive student outcomes than off-campus work.[31] Following this line of reasoning, activities that take students away from campus, such as volunteering and off-campus work, should be less beneficial than activities that keep students in contact with their peers, such as working on campus and spending time in student clubs, fraternities, or sororities.

To consider these propositions, we examine the number of hours invested in each activity, including studying with peers and studying alone, working on and off campus, volunteering, and spending time in student clubs, fraternities, and sororities. We could examine one activity at a time, and if we did, the relationships between each activity and CLA growth would be stronger and more likely to maintain statistical significance across models. However, our interest is less in considering how much specific activities matter on their own than in understanding how students' use of time as a whole is related to learning. We thus present an analysis that simultaneously considers the number of hours students spend in each of these activities.

A notable finding emerges with respect to the amount of time students spend studying (see table A4.2 in methodological appendix). There is a positive association between learning and time spent studying alone, but a negative association between learning and time spent studying with peers. Thus, the more time students spend studying alone, the more they improve their CLA performance. In contrast, the more time students spend studying with peers, the smaller their improvement on the CLA. One possible response to these findings is that they are simply an artifact of student differences: the argument would be that students who study alone and those who study with peers differ from each other, which explains the observed patterns of results for different modes of studying. While differences in students' social and academic backgrounds are associated with those different modes, such an association does not explain the relationship between studying and CLA growth.[32]

Adjusting CLA scores for student attributes, including academic preparation, does not alter the association between studying with peers and learning. Nor does adjusting for institutions attended make much of a difference. Hours spent studying alone are more sensitive to individual and institutional controls. For example, students' academic preparation and the selectivity of institutions attended are much more strongly related to the amount of time students spend studying alone than they are to the time spent studying with peers (with more academically prepared students and those attending more selective institutions spending more time studying alone). However, even after adjusting CLA scores for individual and institutional differences, hours spent studying alone continue to have a strong relationship to learning. Figure 4.3 graphically illustrates the results of this final analysis. All hours spent studying are thus not the same: studying alone is beneficial, but studying with peers is not.

These results deserve further discussion, considering an ever-growing emphasis in higher education on institutional support and promotion of study groups and collaborative learning models to enhance student engagement and retention. Today, two-thirds of students in four-year institutions report participating in study groups in their first year in college, and 14 percent do so often.[33] While lecturing has been used traditionally as the

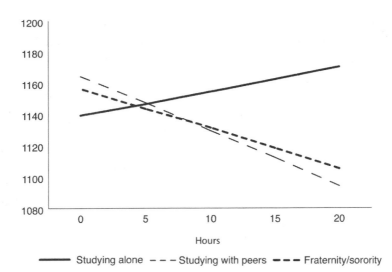

Figure 4.3. Predicted 2007 CLA scores, by hours spent on selected student activities (based on table A4.2, fixed-effects model)

predominant mode of instruction, recent decades have seen an increasing shift toward more student-centered approaches, including discussion and students working in small groups. This shift toward more student-centered approaches has been grounded in a broader movement aiming to transform undergraduate education from a focus on faculty teaching to an emphasis on student learning.[34] Encouraging greater reliance on active and collaborative learning in STEM fields (science, technology, engineering, and mathematics), the National Science Foundation noted that undergraduate education "must put greater emphasis on active, collaborative learning; focus on the processes of inquiry and discovery; and rekindle the unique curiosity, the sense of wonder, with which every child is born."[35] This argument was buttressed by research that reported improved academic achievement as well as engagement and interpersonal relationships from student participation in collaborative learning experiences.[36]

However, while the vision and potential of collaborative learning are enticing, the reality of implementation is much more challenging. As a recent study aptly titled *Grouping in the Dark* noted: "The conditions for group learning in higher education settings rarely meet the standards advocated by cooperative learning scholars. Few faculty have either extensive experience working in groups themselves or formal training about how to manage groups."[37] Given the challenges of group work and faculty misgivings, some have offered advice to faculty about keeping students on task and eliminating free riders.[38] But if faculty members find it challenging to produce a true collaborative learning environment, what happens when students get together to study? Can we expect that they will create the necessary conditions for learning, or does studying in this context become more of a social experience and an excuse for "hanging out" with peers?

The research is largely silent on this point. Previous studies specifically evaluating collaborative learning approaches largely examine students' experiences within classrooms. Moreover, collaborative learning strategies have been promoted heavily by the National Science Foundation and others in the science fields. It is possible that in those fields, which tend to have structured assignments and exams, study groups outside of class are advantageous. Whether this approach can be extended to getting together at Starbucks to discuss Durkheim's notion of social solidarity or the prevailing theories of social stratification remains to be determined. We are not questioning the possibility of students having enlightening theoretical discussions outside of the classroom and learning from their peers, but our results caution against the overarching emphasis on peer studying, until we know more about how and under what conditions those experiences occur and are able to enhance student learning.

As all hours spent studying are not the same, hours spent working differ also. Considering the context of work (on campus versus off campus) is important for understanding the consequences of work for learning (see table A4.2 in methodological appendix).[39] The amount of time students spend working on campus is positively related to improvement in CLA scores, although at a diminishing rate. If we predict the 2007 CLA score for an average student (i.e., a student at the mean of all individual characteristics and activities), student performance increases with on-campus employment until students reach approximately ten hours. If students dedicate more than ten hours to on-campus employment, additional hours no longer lead to improvement in CLA performance. The amount of time students spend working off campus, however, has a negative relationship to learning: the more hours students spend working off campus, even at modest levels, the lower their improvement on the CLA.[40] Part of the relationship between employment and learning is explained by individual characteristics: students who invest various amounts of time in employment on and off campus differ from each other. After we control for student characteristics, the relationship between employment and CLA performance decreases by approximately one-half. The association further diminishes after we control for institutions attended by students. This implies that both individual and institutional differences are important for understanding the consequences of student employment for learning.[41]

While working off campus can take students away from their peers and thus potentially hinder social integration, an activity that brings students together but has negative consequences for learning is participation in fraternities and sororities. As figure 4.3 shows, the more time students spend in fraternities and sororities, the lower their CLA performance. This pattern holds even after we adjust CLA performance for individual student attributes and for institutions attended. This finding is consistent with a number of recent studies cautioning about the influence of fraternities and sororities on higher-education outcomes. Although students who participate in sororities and fraternities self-report higher levels of college satisfaction, campus involvement, and cognitive development, previous studies using objective measures of learning reveal negative associations between fraternity or sorority membership and cognitive outcomes.[42] Negative association of fraternity or sorority membership with learning does not preclude the existence of positive student experiences in these contexts; however, it highlights the importance of considering a range of different outcomes, including standardized objective measure of learning, in addition to students' reports of their engagement and growth.[43]

While the presented results show that it matters how students spend their time, they also pose challenges to the prominent theories in higher education that emphasize the importance of social integration for student success. Patterns for on- versus off-campus employment initially support the social integration argument. However, employment is no longer consequential for learning after we control for student characteristics and institutions attended. Other activities that would pull students away from campus, such as volunteering, appear to have a negative relationship to learning. But again, those negative relationships are explained by student characteristics and institutions attended. Participating in student clubs on campus is not related to learning. And when students engage with their peers, either by studying with them or participating in fraternities and sororities, negative consequences for learning occur. Measures of social integration thus either have no relationship or a negative relationship to learning. Different forms of social integration, including studying with peers and participating in fraternities and sororities, may have some positive consequences for integration and persistence; however, they are not the most appropriate mechanisms for fostering learning.

As is the case for all observational studies, there is a possibility that the reported effects of student activities are not causal but reflect self-selection. Presented analyses control for the 2005 CLA performance as well as for a range of student characteristics and experiences and institutions attended. Nonetheless, it is possible that different types of students spend time in fraternities and sororities as well as studying with peers, and thus that the observed negative relationships are not a consequence of participation in those activities per se but of students' selection into them. We are not able to eliminate that explanation given our data, but only to establish that there is a relationship between specific forms of student engagement and cognitive growth. However, even if these relationships are partially due to self-selection, the findings suggest the need to think more thoroughly about different ways through which all students, even those not necessarily inclined toward learning, can benefit from higher education and develop their cognitive skills.

Fields of Study

Students do not only decide how to spend their time; they also make decisions about focusing their studies in specific subject areas. Although previous research has reported mixed results for the relationship between college major and cognitive development, our findings point to some noteworthy patterns.[44] To examine the relationship between fields of study and CLA performance, figure 4.4 reports the predicted 2007 CLA scores across college majors (adjusted for the 2005 CLA scores).[45] Two categories of majors stand out in the figure: social science/humanities and science/mathematics. Students in those fields of study have higher predicted CLA scores than students in other college majors. More specifically, students in those two categories perform higher (statistically speaking) on the CLA, after adjusting for 2005 CLA scores, than students majoring in either business or education/social work, which have the lowest predicted 2007 CLA performance. The other fields fall in between those two extremes.

What helps students in social science/humanities and science/mathematics majors improve their CLA scores more than business majors (which serve as a comparison category in our analyses)? The previous chapter suggested that students may face different reading/writing requirements and spend different amounts of time studying across fields. To consider how much those factors help to explain the observed gaps in learning, figure 4.5 reports gaps between business majors and each of the following categories: social science/humanities, science/math, engineering/computer science, and health. Those fields are chosen for illustration because they demonstrated gains in the CLA significantly higher than those for business majors

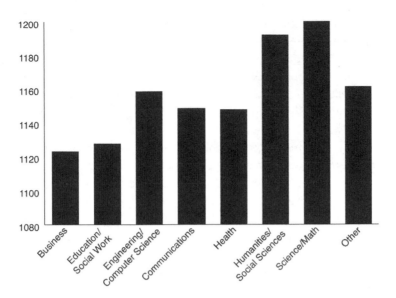

Figure 4.4. Predicted 2007 CLA scores, by college major (based on table A4.3, controlling for 2005 CLA scores)

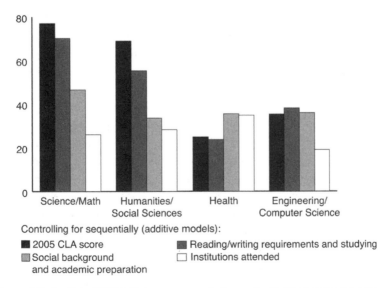

Controlling for sequentially (additive models):
■ 2005 CLA score
■ Social background and academic preparation
■ Reading/writing requirements and studying
□ Institutions attended

Figure 4.5. Predicted 2007 CLA score gaps between business majors and other fields (based on table A4.3)

(or marginally significantly higher gains than those for students majoring in engineering/computer science and health).

Science/mathematics majors scored 77 points higher than business majors on the 2007 CLA, while social science/humanities majors scored 69 points higher (after adjusting for the 2005 CLA scores). Those initial differences are represented in figure 4.5 by the black bars. Subsequent bars represent changes in these gaps after considering different explanations. We begin by examining whether reading/writing requirements (if students reported reading more than forty pages per week and writing more than twenty pages in a class over the course of a semester) and study patterns (amount of time spent studying alone and with peers) help us to understand these differences. After considering these two sets of factors, the gap between science/mathematics and business majors decreased by almost 10 percent and the gap between social science/humanities and business majors decreased by 20 percent. Thus, whether and how students study, as well as what demands they face from faculty, help to explain at least some of the gaps in CLA growth between students majoring in different fields.

In addition to reading/writing requirements and study patterns, students' social backgrounds and academic preparation also play an important role in helping us understand learning gaps across majors. Statistically adjusting our estimates for social background and academic preparation substantially decreases the gaps between science/mathematics and business majors as well as between social studies/humanities and business majors. This implies that science/mathematics and social studies/humanities majors are advantaged with respect to social background and/or academic preparation, which helps to explain their higher performance on the CLA. Indeed, while business majors in our sample have an average SAT/ACT score of 1092, science/mathematics majors scored on average 1207 and social studies/humanities majors scored on average 1200. Similarly, while less than 30 percent of business majors have parents with graduate or professional degrees, more than 40 percent of both science/mathematics and social studies/humanities majors come from homes with those educational credentials. Interestingly, the gap between health and business majors increases after controlling for social background and academic preparation, while the gap between engineering/computer science majors and business majors does not change. The increase in the gap between health and business majors implies that health majors are less socially advantaged and/or academically prepared than are business majors. Once we adjust for these factors, the higher performance of students majoring in health fields is revealed.

Finally, for more technically oriented fields (science/mathematics and engineering/computer science), where students go to school matters. Adjusting for institutions attended substantially decreases the gaps in CLA performance between science/mathematics and business majors, as well as between engineering/computer science and business majors. Considering institutions is enough not only to decrease the gaps across those fields of study, but also to render them not statistically significant. Thus, once we consider where students go to school (in addition to their social background, academic preparation, reading/writing requirements, and study patterns), there are no differences in CLA growth between science/mathematics and business majors or between engineering/computer science and business majors. Institutions once again are shown to play an important role in fostering student learning, above and beyond a range of student characteristics and experiences.

The differences in CLA growth that exist across fields, even after statistical adjustments for individual characteristics and institutions attended, suggest the existence of other factors that also vary across majors and may be worthy of consideration. One of these is educational expectations. If students in certain fields expect to pursue further education, particularly in the form of doctorate or professional degrees, they may work harder in college, in anticipation of needing skills such as critical thinking and writing to continue their educational journeys. Indeed, relatively few students in business and education/social service fields (14 and 16 percent, respectively) expect to pursue doctoral or professional degrees. Students majoring in health, social science/humanities, and science/math, in contrast, are much more likely to state that they expect to pursue doctorate or professional degrees (46 percent, 49 percent, and 73 percent respectively). Although these differences in expectations match the observed differences in CLA growth, the inclusion of educational expectations in the final model does not alter the reported findings. This is because educational expectations, while a strong predictor of CLA growth on their own, do not have a strong relationship to CLA growth after we consider other student characteristics, especially academic preparation. Including academic preparation in the model decreases the coefficient for educational expectations by more than one-half, and renders it not statistically significant.

While students choose specific fields of study, previous research also suggests that faculty engage in distinct practices across fields. Faculty members in different disciplines value specific domains of knowledge and forms of interaction. Consequently, they structure courses, interact with students, and emphasize and reward distinct interests, abilities, and competencies.[46] They also differentially encourage specific educational practices such as faculty-student contact or engagement in active learning, and they are more or less likely to communicate high expectations to students.[47] In other words, faculty in different fields create distinct socializing environments which foster development of specific skills, attitudes, and values.[48] Perhaps as a product of these socializing experiences (and individual selection into fields), students exhibit different "cultures of engagement." Students in social science and humanities demonstrate engagement by talking to professors outside of class, contributing to class discussion, and asking questions in lectures. Students in science and engineering fields, on the other hand, place higher value on quantitative skills and classes that help to solve problems, and they engage much more with peers (by studying together and helping each other understand course material).[49]

Given these findings, it may not be surprising that students in some fields perform higher on the CLA than others. The CLA measures a specific set of skills—namely critical thinking, complex reasoning, and writing—that is far from the totality of learning or the full repertoire of skills acquired in higher education. As students both select and are socialized into specific ways of knowing and thinking, they will perform well on the CLA to the extent that their disciplines emphasize the skills assessed. Moreover, some fields may be focusing more on oral than written communication, and thus while students may be acquiring critical thinking skills, they may not demonstrate them as readily in the written format. And even when students in certain fields do not perform as well on the CLA, this does not mean that they are not gaining valuable skills in other areas. In part, this is why there are certification requirements in fields such as education and health that require students to demonstrate knowledge in an occupationally specific domain.

It would be easy to conclude that students in different fields focus on different sets of skills, only some of which are captured by the CLA, thus leading to the observed differences in CLA performance. However, faculty members across subjects overwhelmingly agree that critical thinking, complex reasoning, and writing are key skills to be taught in higher education. One could hardly argue that we would not want teachers who are educating our children, or business majors who might be responsible for approving home mortgage loans, to develop the capacity to think critically or reason analytically. Moreover, health majors perform significantly higher on the CLA than do business majors, although both are applied fields. Differences across fields may become more pronounced as students immerse themselves more deeply into their chosen majors in the second two years of college. However, presented findings at least raise the question about the extent to which, despite the importance and value of specific skills for different fields, general skills such as critical thinking, complex reasoning, and writing could and should be developed across the undergraduate curriculum.

Financing College Education and Learning

Financing higher education is a persistent worry for students, parents, and policymakers. Given the high and rising costs of college, the decreasing availability of adequate grant support, and an increasing reliance on loans, not to mention the current economic crisis, the question of how to pay for college is a constant source of discussion and concern. The research community has participated in this dialogue by aiming to understand whether certain sources of funding are related to student outcomes, namely persistence and degree attainment. Much of the debate has focused on the role of financial aid, including merit versus need-based aid, in facilitating degree completion. Although many articles have been published on the topic, it is difficult to ascertain the true effects of financial aid because students who receive different types of aid often differ on a number of important but hard-to-measure characteristics. A large-scale experimental study currently conducted by Sara Goldrick-Rab and Douglas Harris at the University of Wisconsin–Madison is poised to provide some more definitive insights into the consequences of financial aid for student outcomes in the near future.

Notwithstanding the debates about causality, which we cannot engage given the observational nature of our study, we explored the relationship between sources of funding (namely grants/scholarships and loans) and students' performance on the CLA. We asked students to indicate the percentages of their college costs that were covered by grants, scholarships, and loans. The results indicate that grants/scholarships have a positive association with learning while loans have no relationship. Figure 4.6 reports the predicted 2007 CLA scores for hypothetical students covering between 0 and 100 percent of their college costs with grants/scholarships or loans. These predictions are adjusted for 2005 CLA scores as well as a range of individual characteristics and institutions attended. Students with higher proportions of college costs covered with grants/scholarships have higher predicted 2007 CLA scores. Comparing students at the extreme, a student who covered all of his or her college costs with grants/scholarships would score 45 points higher on the 2007 CLA than a student who received no

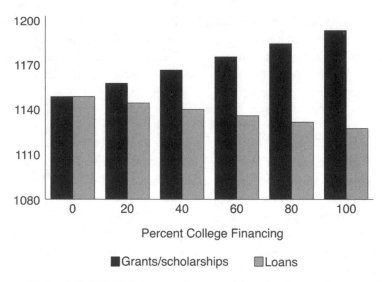

Figure 4.6. Predicted 2007 CLA scores, by percentage of college costs covered by grants/scholarships and loans (based on table A4.4, fixed-effects model; relationship between CLA scores and loans not statistically significant)

grants or scholarships. There is no relationship between the proportion of college costs covered with loans and CLA performance. While the gray bars in figure 4.6 slope slightly downward, this trend is relatively weak (approximately half the size of the trend for grants/scholarships) and not statistically significant.

One way in which different sources of funding could be related to student outcomes is through their relationship to other activities, particularly work. Financial aid packages are often constructed to include employment components, whether through the federal work-study program or various institutional programs. Students who request and are eligible for financial assistance may thus have specific employment obligations included in their financial aid packages. Moreover, since financial aid rarely meets the full cost of attending college, students may seek to work additional hours to cover the difference. College students may also work in order to avoid borrowing. Our analyses reveal that sources of funding are indeed related to hours worked on and off campus. The higher the proportion of college costs covered through grants/scholarships, the more time students spend working on campus and the less time they spend working off campus. In contrast, the higher the proportion of college costs covered through loans, the more time students spend working off campus. Financing college education through loans is positively related to working on campus as well, but that relationship is weaker than the relationship between grants/scholarships and working on campus.[50]

Relationships between students' estimates of college funding sources and hours worked, however, are relatively weak in our sample. Moreover, different forms of employment and different college funding strategies are related to students' social background and academic preparation. When we include on- and off-campus employment in the analysis in addition to other individual-level characteristics, the relationship between grants/scholarships and CLA growth on the one hand and loans and CLA growth on the other does not change notably (see table A4.4 in methodological appendix). In the final analysis, after statistically adjusting estimates for individual characteristics and institutions attended, employment during college does not appear to be related to CLA growth. The percentage of college costs covered through grants/scholarships, however, continues to have a positive association with students' learning. While not definitive, these findings point to an area deserving further investigation. Previous research has focused on examining the relationship between financial aid and persistence/attainment; our analyses suggest that learning is another outcome worthy of examination.

Gaps in CLA Growth between African-American and White Students

Having shown that specific student experiences facilitate learning in higher education, we return to the concern regarding differences in CLA growth between African-American and white students. In chapter 2, we carefully examined differences in learning gains across different groups of students, focusing in particular on students from different family backgrounds and racial/ethnic groups. Results showed that differences in the social contexts in which students grew up and their academic preparation explained the gaps in CLA growth between students from more and less educated families. However, those factors were not adequate to account for the gap in learning between African-American and white students. Although African-American students on average were more likely to attend schools that had 70 percent or more minority students, took fewer advanced placement courses, and performed less well on college admission tests, these differences only partially explained their lower rate of progress on skills measured by the CLA during the first two years of college. If factors prior to college entry could not explain the gap, could experiences during college provide some insights into the differential growth rates between these two groups?

The first bar in figure 4.7 reports the gap in 2007 CLA scores between African-American and white students, statistically adjusted for students' sociodemographic and high school characteristics, academic preparation, and skills at entry into higher education (i.e., 2005 CLA scores). Even after these adjustments, African-American students scored 47 points lower on the CLA at the end of their sophomore year than did white students. Next, we include students' college experiences in analysis, which slightly increases the gap in learning between African-American and white students. This pattern emerges through a complex combination of differential experiences. The primary factors driving the increase in the gap between African-American and white students are hours spent in fraternities, percent of college cost covered by grants and scholarships, and college major. These are areas in which African-American students have more positive educational experiences—that is, experiences more conducive to learning. They spent fewer hours on average in fraternities and sororities, had a higher proportion of their college costs covered by grants and scholarships, and were more likely to major in some fields with higher growth in learning (such as health). These positive experiences are partly countered by exposure to contexts less conducive to learning. For example, African-American students reported lower faculty expectations and demands—less than a third of African-American students had taken classes that required

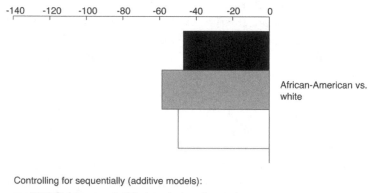

Controlling for sequentially (additive models):

■■■ 2005 CLA score and attributes prior to college entry
▨▨▨ College experiences
☐ Institutions attended

Figure 4.7. Predicted 2007 CLA score gaps between African-American and white students, adjusted for specific characteristics (based on table A4.5)

them to both read more than forty pages a week and write more than twenty pages over the course of a semester. These negative experiences do not entirely offset the positive ones, thus leading to the increase in the CLA gap between African-American and white students after including college experiences in the analysis.

Considering institutions attended reveals a different pattern. As reported in chapter 2, African-American students are less likely than their white peers to attend highly selective or selective institutions. Colleges attended by African-American and white students may also differ on other institutional characteristics. After controlling (i.e., statistically adjusting estimates) for institutions attended, the gap in learning between African-American and white students decreases by 15 percent. While this reduction may not appear substantial, it is remarkable given that our analyses already control for a host of individual characteristics and college experiences. African-American students are thus disadvantaged by attending colleges and universities that are less effective at facilitating students' development of critical thinking, complex reasoning, and writing skills. These findings highlight once again the importance of college experiences as well as institutions attended, not only for overall learning but also for inequality in learning between African-American and white students.

In the final analysis, after we adjust the CLA performance for a range of individual attributes, college experiences, and institutions attended, we could explain almost two-thirds of the gap in learning between African-American and white students. Although this is a notable feat, the gap between the two groups remains sizable and statistically significant. Moreover, although some recent studies have suggested "compensatory effects" of college experiences, indicating that students who enter college less advantaged gain more from positive experiences, we find no such evidence regarding growth in the CLA for African-American versus white students.[51] Persistent gaps in test performance between African-American and white students have been reported at other grade levels as well—no matter what controls are included in statistical analyses, the gaps persist. This pattern has led some authors to consider the role of more subtle cultural factors in producing the gaps in academic achievement between African-American and white students. [52]

A prominent early theory argued that due to the long history of discrimination and inequality, African-Americans have developed an oppositional culture, which defines behaviors and traits appropriate for the group in opposition to the dominant white culture. In the context of schooling, the argument goes, the oppositional culture of African-American adolescents has led them to eschew academic achievement. Strong peer pressures and accusations of "acting white" are argued to be keeping African-American students from doing well academically.[53] The empirical evidence for this theory is weak, and recent decades have presented multiple challenges to the oppositional culture argument.[54] However, this does not necessarily mean that culture is inconsequential for educational success. Instead of thinking about it as shaping preferences, we may want to think about culture as a "tool kit" of habits, skills, and styles.[55] Since African-American and white students grow up in different contexts, sociologist Douglas Downey has argued that "the skills, habits, and styles blacks are exposed to are, on average, less useful for academic success." From this definition of culture, the key to understanding academic performance does not lie with African-American attitudes about schooling but with the social isolation of African-American adolescents.[56]

An alternative explanation for the differences in academic achievement between African-American and white students that has received increasing support in recent decades is termed "stereotype threat." Emanating from the work of psychologists Claude Steele and Joshua Aronson, this argument proposes that African-American adolescents are well aware of the negative stereotypes regarding their groups' academic achievement. Whenever they are called on to perform academically, they face "stereotype threat" or the fear of confirming the negative stereotype. This fear leads to their lower performance.[57] Even subtle cues like being asked to identify one's race before a GRE-like verbal test can lead African-American students to perform less well.[58] Recent analyses of college students at selective institutions have supported this argument. The researchers found that stereotype threat is related to students' grade-point average, and that controlling for it helps to reduce the gap in academic performance between African-American and white students.[59] Although we cannot test these propositions given our data, more subtle mechanisms, resting on differences in "cultural tool kits" and/or the threats of confirming negative stereotypes, deserve further study to advance our understanding of the inequality in academic achievement.

Variation Across and Within Institutions

While students do not learn much on average, this chapter has illuminated how specific activities and experiences during college can either facilitate or thwart learning, creating variation among students and institutions. Twenty-nine percent of variance in 2007 CLA scores is found across institutions. Even if we focus specifically on growth (estimating 2007 CLA scores while controlling for the 2005 scores), 20 percent of the variance is found across institutions. Some of it is associated with the sorting of students into institutions (i.e., institutions enroll students with different characteristics, such as different levels of academic preparation). However, even if we control for a range of background characteristics, including race/ethnicity, socioeconomic background, academic preparation, and 2005 CLA scores, students in some institutions experience larger gains on average than others. The same finding has been reported in previous research with respect to other outcomes. For example, while student characteristics and school resources are important predictors of degree attainment, there are notable differences in graduation rates across institutions, even after accounting for many of these "input" characteristics.[60]

If we select top-performing institutions—institutions that show much larger gains on the CLA than others, net of individual characteristics—we find, not surprisingly, that their students report higher incidence of behaviors that are beneficial for learning (figure 4.8).[61] Students at these institutions report greater course requirements: almost two-thirds (62 percent) of their students reported taking courses that required both reading more than forty pages a week and writing more than twenty pages over the course of a semester. The average for other institutions is just over one-third (39 percent). In a finding perhaps related to higher coursework demands, students at high-performing institutions also spent more time studying, particularly alone—almost three more hours of solitary study

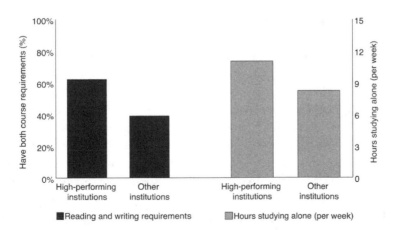

Figure 4.8. Reading/writing course requirements and hours spent studying alone at high-performing and other institutions

than students at other institutions. Three hours is a remarkable difference, considering that students overall on average spent less than nine hours studying alone. Since we have only 24 institutions in the sample, some of which have relatively small sample sizes, we are not able to delve deeply into institutional differences. However, even this brief discussion indicates that institutions differ in the extent to which they create contexts which facilitate positive behaviors and actions associated with learning.

Previous studies of institutional characteristics and practices substantiate these findings by showing that institutions vary notably in how they structure student experiences. George Kuh and his colleagues, for example, conducted in-depth studies of twenty four-year colleges and universities that had higher than predicted graduation rates and higher than predicted levels of student engagement (based on the National Survey of Student Engagement). Among other characteristics, these institutions had an "unshakeable focus on student learning." Their emphasis on undergraduate learning was manifested in a range of practices, from institutional openness to new and experimental instructional techniques to faculty investing more time in students and taking greater responsibility for them, as well as showing greater commitment to both providing and receiving feedback.[62] Moreover, although many existing college programs focus exclusively on retention, some have potential to facilitate learning. Learning communities—programs that enroll groups of students in a common set of courses and are frequently linked with residence life experiences—have shown positive association with a range of student outcomes including persistence, grades, and self-reported learning.[63] Researchers have yet to evaluate the effects of learning communities on standardized objective measures of learning—this is an important area of future research, as these programs are poised to facilitate persistence as well as learning.

While there is variation in student performance across colleges and universities, it is important to note that there is even more variation within institutions. This is the case for most educational outcomes, and it has been extensively documented with respect to student engagement in higher education.[64] High- as well as low-performing students are found at all institutions. If, for example, we consider students in the top 10 percent of the CLA growth distribution, we would find them at each of the institutions.[65] This is remarkable, given that these students are experiencing more than 1.5 standard deviation of growth between the beginning of their freshman and end of their sophomore year, which is more than eight times the average growth. Exploring variation within institutions highlights the often ignored and untapped potential for improvement. Even at the highest-performing schools there is room for growth, as not all students are performing equally well. And even colleges that are struggling have students who spend time studying and make notable progress in critical thinking, complex reasoning, and writing skills during their first two years. Given our sample-size limitations, we cannot provide a detailed account of what students at each institution look like and what institutions are doing to facilitate their learning. However, each institution can look within, as opposed to only looking across, to learn what works and what does not. High-performing students within institutions can serve as guides for thinking about and implementing meaningful change.

Focusing on Learning in Higher Education

Learning is a complex process—and thus, not surprisingly, myriad factors shape what and how much students learn in higher education. To make matters more challenging, many of these factors are related, such that students' backgrounds and academic preparation are related to the institutions they attend and their specific experiences within those institutions. We have aimed to untangle these different influences to the extent possible with our observational data, and to provide some insights into which factors may lead to greater growth in critical thinking, complex reasoning, and writing during the first two years in college.

Putting it all together, we present results from the final model (see table A4.5 in methodological appendix), which includes all relevant factors discussed throughout the chapter. The final model includes only college experiences that were deemed influential in preceding analyses. The overall framework representing this final analysis is illustrated in figure 4.9. What students bring to college matters; this is particularly the case with respect to their academic preparation. However, our primary focus in this chapter has been on what students do while they are in college, as those analyses help us illuminate the direction for improving higher-education policy and practice in the future. These final analyses confirm the results discussed in the preceding pages, reaffirming the importance of students' college experiences and institutions attended for their intellectual development.

What students do in higher education matters. But what faculty members do matters too. Faculty are most directly involved in shaping student experiences, although the support and incentives advocated by their deans, provosts, and presidents will influence whether and how they engage in activities that facilitate student learning. There are some clear examples of how faculty members may shape student actions and, by extension, their

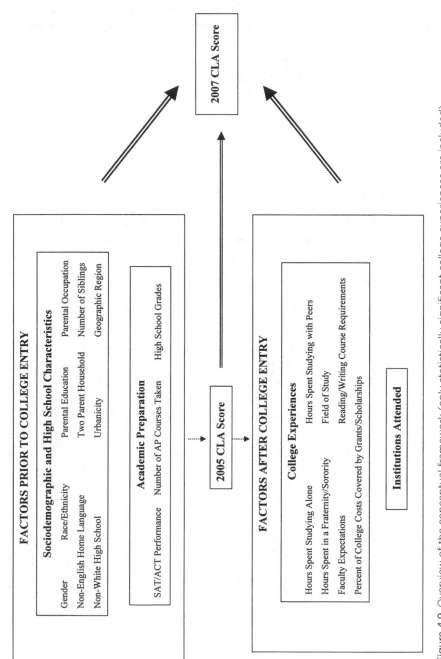

Figure 4.9. Overview of the conceptual framework (only statistically significant college experiences are included)

FACTORS PRIOR TO COLLEGE ENTRY

Sociodemographic and High School Characteristics

Gender   Race/Ethnicity   Parental Education   Parental Occupation

Non-English Home Language   Two Parent Household   Number of Siblings

Non-White High School   Urbanicity   Geographic Region

Academic Preparation

SAT/ACT Performance   Number of AP Courses Taken   High School Grades

2005 CLA Score

2007 CLA Score

FACTORS AFTER COLLEGE ENTRY

College Experiences

Hours Spent Studying Alone   Hours Spent Studying with Peers

Hours Spent in a Fraternity/Sorority   Field of Study

Faculty Expectations   Reading/Writing Course Requirements

Percent of College Costs Covered by Grants/Scholarships

Institutions Attended

learning. For example, college GPA is positively related to the 2007 CLA scores.[66] This indicates that faculty members indeed reward critical thinking, complex reasoning, and writing skills in the classroom. The relationship is not perfect but that is to be expected, as not all classes are likely to focus on the skills captured by the CLA. Nevertheless, this positive association indicates a potential for considering how those skills, which on surveys faculty report should be crucial components of undergraduate education, can be taught and rewarded in college classrooms across the nation.

Moreover, as we have seen, when faculty have high expectations and expect students to read and write reasonable amounts, students learn more. In addition, when students report that they have taken a class in which they had to read more than forty pages a week and write more than twenty pages over the course of a semester, they also report spending more time studying: more than two additional hours per week than students who do not have to meet such requirements.[67] Thus, requiring that students attend to their class work has the potential to shape their actions in ways that are conducive to their intellectual development.

While we have reported relationships between specific college experiences and learning, one may still wonder how much those factors really matter. One way to address this question is to evaluate the magnitude of the relationships, which we have aimed to do by presenting predicted CLA scores across different dimensions of college experiences. Another approach is to consider the proportion of variance in the CLA scores that is explained by a different set of factors. The final analysis—which includes all background measures, college experiences, and institutions attended—explains 42 percent of the variation in CLA scores. This is a substantial amount by social science standards, although it does imply that much more research is needed to understand the remaining variance. Within our analyses, college experiences and institutions attended explained an additional 6 percent of the variance, after controlling for academic preparation and other individual characteristics.[68] While that may appear to be a small contribution, academic preparation, which has received much attention in research and policy circles, explains only an additional 8 percent of the variance beyond students' background characteristics.[69] These estimates may seem low, but this is because of our analytic strategy: we are focusing on growth and are thus controlling for 2005 CLA scores, which, as would be expected, explain the largest portion of the variance in 2007 CLA performance. Thus, students' college experiences and institutions attended make almost as much of a difference as prior academic preparation. If the blame for low levels of critical thinking, complex reasoning, and writing skills of college students is to be placed on academic preparation, then almost an equal amount of responsibility rests with what happens after students enter higher education.

The analyses presented in this chapter illuminate the multiple actors contributing to the current state of limited learning on college campuses. Faculty members are perhaps the easiest to blame, as in some institutional settings they are often tempted to focus greater attention on research and other professional demands than on teaching; this reality presents a concrete set of practices that can be critiqued. And many higher-education institutions indeed deserve criticism for failing to focus adequately on the core mission of higher education: *educating* the next generation. Beyond faculty offices and tenure review procedures, however, there are students, who spend far more time socializing than studying.[70] Given the little time they spend studying, it is no surprise that they are not learning much on average. This is partly a consequence of lax demands and expectations, but it is wishful thinking to imagine that simply increasing faculty demands will produce greater learning. "Current cultural norms among U.S. undergraduates support a conception of schooling as an important, but part-time activity. Other parts of life, notably, social and leisure activities, are at least as important," sociologist Steven Brint recently observed.[71] Judging from students' use of time, we find that these social and leisure activities appear much more important than academic pursuits. The college experience is perceived by many students to be, at its core, a social experience.[72] The collegiate culture emphasizes sociability and encourages students to have fun—to do all the things they have not had a chance to do before, or may not have a chance to do after they enter "the real world" of the labor market. Faculty, administrators, policy makers, and parents are all implicated to a certain extent in accepting or at least partly acquiescing to contemporary collegiate culture.

5

A Mandate for Reform

"With regard to the quality of research, we tend to evaluate faculty the way the Michelin guide evaluates restaurants," Lee Shulman, former president of the Carnegie Foundation for the Advancement of Teaching, recently noted. "We ask, 'How high is the quality of this cuisine relative to the genre of food? How excellent is it?' With regard to teaching, the evaluation is done more in the style of the Board of Health. The question is, 'Is it safe to eat here?'"[1] Our research suggests that for many students currently enrolled in higher education, the answer is: not particularly. Growing numbers of students are sent to college at increasingly higher costs, but for a large proportion of them the gains in critical thinking, complex reasoning and written communication are either exceedingly small or empirically nonexistent. At least 45 percent of students in our sample did not demonstrate any statistically significant improvement in CLA performance during the first two years of college. While these students may have developed subject-specific skills that were not tested for by the CLA, in terms of general analytical competencies assessed, large numbers of U.S. college students can be accurately described as academically adrift. They might graduate, but they are failing to develop the higher-order cognitive skills that it is widely assumed college students should master. These findings are sobering and should be a cause for concern.

While higher education is expected to accomplish many tasks—and contemporary colleges and universities have indeed contributed to society in ways as diverse as producing pharmaceutical patents as well as prime-time athletic bowls—existing organizational cultures and practices too often do not prioritize undergraduate learning. Faculty and administrators, working to meet multiple and at times competing demands, too rarely focus on either improving instruction or demonstrating gains in student learning. More troubling still, the limited learning we have observed in terms of the absence of growth in CLA performance is largely consistent with the accounts of many students, who report that they spend increasing numbers of hours on nonacademic activities, including working, rather than on studying. They enroll in courses that do not require substantial reading or writing assignments; they interact with their professors outside of classrooms rarely, if ever; and they define and understand their college experiences as being focused more on social than on academic development. Moreover, we find that learning in higher education is characterized by persistent and/or growing inequality. There are significant differences in critical thinking, complex reasoning, and writing skills when comparing groups of students from different family backgrounds and racial/ethnic groups. More important, not only do students enter college with unequal demonstrated abilities, but their inequalities tend to persist—or, in the case of African-American students relative to white students, increase—while they are enrolled in higher education.

Despite the low average levels of learning and persistent inequality, we have also observed notable variation in student experiences and outcomes both across and within institutions. While the average level of performance indicates that students in general are often embedded in higher-education institutions where only very modest academic demands are placed on them, exceptional students, who have demonstrated impressive growth over time on CLA performance, exist in all the settings we examined. In addition, students attending certain high-performing institutions had more beneficial college experiences in terms of experiencing rigorous reading/writing requirements and spending greater numbers of hours studying. Students attending these institutions demonstrated significantly higher gains in critical thinking, complex reasoning and writing skills over time than students enrolled elsewhere.

The Implications of Limited Learning

Notwithstanding the variation and positive experiences in certain contexts, the prevalence of limited learning on today's college campuses is troubling indeed. While historian Helen Horowitz's work reminds us that the phenomenon of limited learning in higher education has a long and venerable tradition in this country—in the late eighteenth and early nineteenth century, for example, "college discipline conflicted with the genteel upbringing of the elite sons of Southern gentry and Northern merchants"—this outcome today occurs in a fundamentally different context.[2] Contemporary college graduates generally do not leave school with the assumption that they will ultimately inherit the plantations or businesses of their fathers. Occupational destinations in modern economies are increasingly dependent on an individual's academic achievements. The attainment of long-term occupational success in the economy requires not only academic credentials, but likely also academic skills. As report after national blue-ribbon report has reminded us, today's jobs require "knowledge, learning, information, and skilled-intelligence."[3] These are cognitive abilities that, unlike Herrnstein and Murray's immutable IQ construct, can be learned and developed at school.[4]

Something else has also changed. After World War II, the United States dramatically expanded its higher-education system and led the world for decades in the percentage of young people it graduated from college, often by a wide margin. Over the past two decades, while the U.S. higher education system has grown only marginally, the rest of the world has not been standing still. As Patrick Callan, president of the National Center for Higher Education and Public Policy, has observed: "In the 1990s, however, as the importance of a college-educated workforce in a global economy became clear, other nations began making the kinds of dramatic gains that had characterized American higher education earlier. In contrast, by the early 1990s, the progress the United States had made in increasing college participation had come to a virtual halt. For most of the 1990s, the United States ranked last among 14 nations in raising college participation rates, with almost no increase during the decade."[5]

For the first time in recent history, many countries today graduate higher percentages of their youth from college than does the United States. While the United States still ranks second of Organisation of Economic Cooperation and Development (OECD) countries in terms of adult workers' bachelor-level degree attainment, it has dropped to sixth when higher-education attainment of only the most recent cohort of young adults is considered.[6] "We may still have more than our share of the world's best universities. But a lot of other countries have followed our lead, *and they are now educating more of their citizens to more advanced levels than we are,*" the recent federal report *A Test of Leadership* observed. "Worse, they are passing us by at a time when education is more important to our collective prosperity than ever."[7]

The U.S. higher-education system has in recent years arguably been living off its reputation as being the best in the world. The findings in our study, however, should remind us that the system's international reputation—largely derived from graduate programs at a handful of elite public and private universities—serves as no guarantee that undergraduate students are being appropriately challenged or exposed to educational experiences that will lead to academic growth throughout the wide range of diverse U.S. colleges and universities. While the U.S. higher-education system still enjoys the competitive advantage of a sterling international reputation, in recent decades it has been increasingly surpassed in terms of quantity (i.e., the percentage of young adults it graduates), and its quality is coming under increasing scrutiny. The U.S. government's recent decision to participate in current international efforts led by the OECD to measure higher-education academic performance on a comparative basis cross-nationally, following the less-than-stellar comparative results observed in international comparisons of adult literacy, provides little reassurance that the system's reputation will not become increasingly challenged and debated.[8] In an increasingly globalized and competitive world system, the quality and quantity of outcomes of a country's education system are arguably related to a nation's future trajectory and international economic position.[9]

The changing economic and global context facing contemporary college graduates convinces us that the limited learning that exists on U.S. campuses—even if it has been a part of the higher-education landscape since the system's inception—qualifies today as a significant social problem and should be a subject of concern of policymakers, practitioners, parents, and citizens alike. While the phenomenon can accurately be described as a social problem, the situation that exists on today's college campuses in no way qualifies as a crisis, and we have consciously avoided the use of rhetoric here that would point to "a crisis in higher education."

Limited learning in the U.S. higher education system cannot be defined as a crisis because institutional and system-level organizational survival is not being threatened in any significant way. Parents—although somewhat disgruntled about increasing costs—want colleges to provide a safe environment where their children can mature, gain independence, and attain credentials that will help them be successful as adults. Students in general seek to enjoy the benefits of a full collegiate experience that is focused as much on social life as on academic pursuits, while earning high marks in their courses with relatively little investment of effort. Professors are eager to find time to concentrate on their scholarship and professional interests. Administrators have been asked to focus largely on external institutional rankings and the financial bottom line. Government funding agencies are primarily interested in the development of new scientific knowledge. In short, the system works. No actors in the system are primarily interested in undergraduate student academic growth, although many are interested in student retention and persistence. Limited learning on college campuses is not a crisis because the institutional actors implicated in the system are receiving the organizational outcomes that they seek, and therefore neither the institutions themselves nor the system as a whole is in any way challenged or threatened.

While in the long term this country's global competitiveness is likely weakened by a white-collar workforce that is not uniformly trained at a rigorous level, colleges where limited academic learning occurs in the short term can still fulfill their primary social functions: students are allocated to occupational positions based on their credentials, not their skills; students are provided settings where they can experiment with new forms of social behavior and develop independent identities; and, as we have shown elsewhere, students' subsequent marital choices can in part be structured by their college pedigrees.[10] This evaluation can be contrasted with the situation that exists in U.S. elementary and secondary schools, where a "crisis in moral authority" has prevented many public schools from socializing youth effectively and has "undermined public school legitimacy, eroded popular support necessary for maintenance and expansion of these institutions, stimulated political challenges and the growth of competitive organizations, and thus [has] come to threaten public school organizational survival in many state and local settings."[11] Socialization of elementary and secondary school students is a core institutional function, but academic learning at colleges unfortunately has not been recognized as such.

Transforming Higher Education

Given that the problem of limited learning in higher education has such a diverse set of causes, potential efforts towards educational reform must be multifaceted, and must be directed at various levels for significant change to occur. Specifically, we propose here recommendations for improved educational practices at the institutional level as well as policy changes that are focused at the system level. Before discussing these potential reforms, we briefly discuss the need for improved elementary- and secondary-school student preparation. While the latter issue is largely beyond the scope of this book, we would be remiss not to identify and bring attention to the topic here.

Student preparation

Our study provides evidence supporting the proposition that students who come into college with higher levels of academic preparation (in terms of either prior advanced placement coursework or SAT/ACT performance) are better positioned to learn more while in college. These findings resonate with prior research that has emphasized the importance of rigorous academic work in high school. Clifford Adelman, for example, has demonstrated that "the intensity and quality of one's secondary school curriculum was the strongest influence not merely on college entrance, but more importantly, on bachelor's degree completion for students who attended a four-year college."[12] Many students come into college with such inadequate levels of preparation that they must spend much of their early coursework in remedial education classes where gains in higher-order critical thinking and complex reasoning are unlikely to occur. One-third of recent four-year college students took at least one remedial course in college.[13]

In terms of needed reforms in elementary and secondary schools, however, we believe that improving academic preparation is only half the story. Many students emerging from these schools have also not developed norms, values, and behaviors conducive to assuming productive lives as responsible adults, let alone the ability and interest to focus on academic learning at college.[14] While students today express very high educational expectations and professional ambitions, as Barbara Schneider and David Stevenson have well documented, they have failed to develop realistic understandings of the steps necessary to achieve their goals.[15] These students have not formulated what the social psychologist William Damon calls "paths to purpose"—that is, moral grounding that anchors their ambitions in the tasks, behaviors, and practices required to achieve the ends they view as meaningful. Youth today have been unable to develop a sense of purpose in their lives not only because of general changes in parenting and the larger culture, Damon argues, but because schools have turned away from accepting responsibility for youth socialization and moral education. Elementary and secondary educational reform has focused almost exclusively on improving students' standardized test scores. "Often squeezed entirely out of the school day are questions of meaning and purpose that should underlie every academic exercise," Damon notes. "Our obsessive reliance on standardized test scores deters both teachers and students from concentrating on the real mission of schooling: developing a love of learning for learning's sake—a love that will then lead to self-maintained learning throughout the lifespan."[16]

Higher education leadership

"Ultimately, it's about the culture . . ." was a conclusion drawn by researchers studying twenty high-performing four-year institutions.[17] Institutions need to develop a culture of learning if undergraduate education is to be improved. This is not an easy or an overnight process, but one that requires strong leadership—including presidents, deans, provosts, and others demonstrating a commitment to these goals. "Student success becomes an institutional priority when leaders make it so."[18] Setting student success, and learning in particular, as a priority provides guidance and focus for future action; staying the course over the long haul is crucial, as many aspects of an institution may need changing, implementing the change takes time, and seeing the results of specific policies and practices takes even longer. Leaders at successful institutions have a strong sense of purpose; they engage other members of the community in achieving the vision, and they make decisions about hiring and programs that support the achievement of these goals. Effective administrators provide the vision; motivate broad engagement and openness to change, continuous evaluation, and growth; and "get and keep the right people"—those committed to undergraduate learning.[19]

We believe that one way for higher-education leaders to communicate a greater sense of institutional purpose is for them to articulate to their respective communities that colleges and universities need to take greater responsibility for shaping the developmental trajectories of students, and to prioritize these organizational goals in decision-making. It is not enough for higher-education institutions simply to confer educational degrees on students, if the credentials do not reflect substantive academic accomplishments and if the students have not developed an appreciation of the meaning and responsibilities associated with their acquisition. Many higher-education administrators and faculty today have largely turned away from earlier conceptions of their roles that recognized that providing support for student academic and social development was a moral imperative worth sacrificing for personally, professionally, and institutionally.

Consider, for example, the issue of college dormitories. College dormitories were originally developed in the first quarter of the twentieth century, according to historian Julie Reuben, because "university administrators recognized that it was almost impossible to mold the social lives of students when they lived outside the college."[20] Lyman Wilbur, Stanford University's president at the time, wrote that "when students are housed together there is developed a strong cooperative sense of loyalty and enthusiasm called 'college spirit' which has a profound effect upon the development of the character of the students and upon the welfare of the institution." At Harvard University a similar sentiment was expressed. "The problem of the college," Harvard's president A. Lawrence Lowell asserted, "is a moral one, deepening the desire to develop one's mind, body, and character; and this is much promoted by living in surroundings and an atmosphere congenial to the object." For Lowell and other university leaders at the time, the dormitory was a "social device for a moral purpose."[21]

Today, rather than instruments designed for shaping students' individual social and academic development at college, residence halls are often viewed as "revenue and cost centers" that need to be managed primarily for financial ends. Many colleges and universities today are building private-suite residence halls to cater to student demands for increased privacy and comfort. At the Midwestern public university where sociologist Mary Grigsby studied, four new dorms that together can house five thousand students have been built featuring "two-bedroom suites with a shared bathroom and single rooms with private baths." Grigsby notes that "competition for students by universities and perceptions on the part of decision makers that parent and student consumers want upscale facilities, along with beautiful grounds, up-to date recreation centers, and glamorous sports stadiums, have led Midwest to invest heavily in such construction." Grigsby's study of undergraduate culture, however, reveals that while these new forms of private residences are popular among student and parent consumers, they have significantly altered the collegiate atmosphere. In traditional shared-room dormitories with communal bathrooms, Grigsby found open doors and very high levels of interpersonal interaction; in the new private-suite residences doors were closed, little interpersonal interaction occurred, and the atmosphere was similar to that of modern apartment buildings. In terms of the role of adult authority in these two settings, Grigsby notes the comments of a resident assistant who had served in both traditional shared-room and new private-suite halls: "Where students in the other dorms (with shared rooms and communal baths) resented my enforcing rules because they said I was 'just one of them,' in this [private-suite] dorm they complain because I'm just 'the hired help' and have no right to tell them what to do, since they are paying for their privacy and have a right to do what they want in their rooms."[22] In their efforts to cater to student consumers, colleges and universities have arguably moved even further away from their responsibility to structure social behavior and provide a setting conducive to rigorous academic instruction and moral development. While these new dormitories potentially provide increased opportunities for students to study alone, the ability to develop a shared sense of mission and collegiate identity is lost—as, too, is the possibility to tie these larger communal sentiments to the development of individual purpose and meaning in the lives of undergraduate students.

Improving curriculum and instruction

While it would be naïve to base policy reform on appeals for higher education actors to embrace a call for institutional renewal on moral terms, all higher-education institutions could focus increased attention on the academic component of undergraduate learning without fundamental challenges to the existing system. Our findings provide clear empirical evidence that academically rigorous instruction is associated with improved performance on tasks requiring critical thinking, complex reasoning, and written communication. Spending time studying, having faculty who hold high expectations, and offering courses that require reasonable amounts of reading and writing are associated with students' learning during the first two years of college. These practices focus attention on the fact that students benefit when they are in instructional settings where faculty demand and students engage in rigorous academic endeavors. Prior sociological literature has at times applied the term "academic press" to elementary and secondary schools whose organizational climates encourage student academic engagement and effort.[23]

Given the large number of students who were not exposed to courses that required more than forty pages of reading per week and more than twenty pages of writing over the course of the semester, we believe that it is incumbent on higher-education institutions to take seriously their responsibility to monitor and enhance the academic requirements of courses. While at most colleges and universities course syllabi are collected from instructors and administratively filed (typically at the department level), there is often little evidence that faculty have come together to ensure that coursework is appropriately demanding and requires significant reading, writing, and critical thinking. Faculty share a collective responsibility to address this issue.

In addition to reading and writing requirements associated with coursework, we have found that students who report that faculty have high expectations of their performance demonstrate improved rates of undergraduate learning. Just as they need to ensure rigorous assignments associated with coursework, colleges also need to encourage faculty to communicate high expectations to all their students. At least since the publication of *Pygmalion in the Classroom* in 1968, elementary and secondary school teachers have understood the importance of high expectations for all students, and have been institutionally encouraged to demonstrate them.[24] Unlike elementary and secondary school teachers, however, college professors have typically not received formal training in instruction that has emphasized the pedagogical functions of educational expectations. Our findings suggest that high expectations for students and increased academic requirements in syllabi, if coupled with rigorous grading standards that encourage students to spend more time studying, might potentially yield significant payoffs in terms of undergraduate learning outcomes.

Academic press is one element of effective instructional practices that has been advocated by higher education reformers in recent decades. The importance of active learning and related academic experiences has been repeatedly emphasized in scholarship on effective practices in higher education. In their seminal work titled *Principles of Good Practice for Undergraduate Education*, for example, Chickering and Gamson outlined seven categories of effective educational practices, including those that encourage the following activities: student-faculty contact, cooperation among students, active learning, prompt feedback, time on task, high expectations, and respect for diverse talents and ways of learning. These principles are reflected in the five benchmarks of academic engagement of the National Survey of Student Engagement (NSSE).[25] Based on Chickering and Gamson's work as well as other research on effective practices in higher education, Kuh and his colleagues have identified five clusters of desirable educational practices: academic challenge, active/collaborative learning, student-faculty interaction, enriching educational experiences, and supportive campus environments.[26]

Of the five categories of effective practice, the academic challenge benchmark is most clearly associated with the sociological concept of "academic press" and corresponds with key factors identified as facilitating student learning in our study. In the NSSE framework, academic challenge includes questions regarding time spent preparing for class, course demands (including reading, writing, using higher-order thinking skills, and working harder than students thought they could to meet the standards), and institutional emphasis on studying and academic work. The results from NSSE indicate that academic challenge has a strong relationship with student persistence and grades.[27] Results from the ongoing Wabash National Study, which uses slightly different measures of engagement, indicate that academic challenge and effective teaching—including factors such as prompt feedback and faculty interest in teaching and student development—are related to most of the twenty-nine indicators of student development in college, from moral reasoning and psychological well-being to academic motivation and critical thinking.[28] While what faculty members do matters, how much time and effort students invest in their classes is paramount: Studying is crucial for strong academic performance as "nothing substitutes for time on task."[29] It is worth emphasizing that faculty demands and students' time on task are related: when the students in our study reported that they had taken a class where they had to read more than forty pages a week and a class where they had to write more than twenty pages during the semester, they also reported spending more time studying.

At the core, changing higher education to focus on learning will require transforming students' curricular experiences—not only the time they spend sitting in their chairs during a given class period, but everything associated with coursework, from faculty expectations and approaches to teaching to course requirements and feedback. Scholarship on teaching and learning has burgeoned over the past several decades and has emphasized the importance of shifting attention from faculty teaching to student learning.[30] Once student learning is the focus of the enterprise, faculty can attend to the strategies that improve it. Research by members of Harvard Project Zero, for example, provides ample clues about strategies that facilitate student learning, including clearly stating course objectives, clearly presenting material, linking course content to course objectives, providing students with examples of what is expected, creating ample opportunities for students to apply what they have learned and perform their knowledge publicly, and assessing learning frequently and adjusting teaching accordingly. Education is not a process of simply accumulating "facts, concepts and skills," but one that facilitates students' "ever-increasing grasp of the world."[31]

Scholarship on effective college teaching and learning in recent decades has emphasized student engagement and has focused on active and collaborative curricular activities. Although there are different definitions and emphases, at the core of active/collaborative learning is the idea that students should not passively absorb the information but instead should engage in the learning process, often through applying what they have learned and working with others. The NSSE benchmark for active/collaborative learning, for example, includes factors such as asking questions in class, making class presentations, working with classmates during and/or outside of class, tutoring or teaching students, participating in community-based projects, and discussing ideas from class/readings with others. Based on these measures, college students appear to be quite engaged in their learning: virtually all contribute to class discussion, and the vast majority have made class presentations and worked with peers inside and outside of the classroom.[32]

Although preference for active engagement in the learning process over passive acquisition of information can hardly be disputed, there is a question of what "active/collaborative learning" really entails in the day-to-day activities of a classroom. Has adopting active/collaborative learning meant mostly that we have made classrooms more lively and interesting, but not more demanding and challenging? Sociologist Steven Brint has recently raised concerns about the overarching emphasis on student engagement in higher education, which he describes as "new progressivism." According to Brint, the new progressivism "advocated active learning experiences, commitment to diversity and civic engagement, and challenging academic standards. However, [this] advocacy of challenging academic standards proved to be no match for the consumerism and utilitarianism of college student life. The trajectory of the new progressivism consequently mirrored the pattern of K–12 progressive education in the early 20th century, when followers of John Dewey, such as William Heard Kilpatrick, de-emphasized Dewey's insistence on rigor and frequent assessment and highlighted student-centered, active learning, and community engagement themes."[33]

Indeed, while approximately 90 percent of college seniors say they have worked on projects and assignments with classmates inside and outside of the classroom, 50 percent have not written a twenty-page paper, only one-third have taken coursework that "very much" emphasized synthesizing and organizing ideas, only approximately 40 percent have taken coursework that "very much" focused on applying or analyzing theories or concepts, and the vast majority spent less than fifteen hours a week studying.[34] Given these trends, perhaps it is not surprising that NSSE measures of engagement do not track strongly or consistently with objective measures of learning.[35] Our own findings also caution specifically against an overemphasis on studying with peers.

Engaging activities and peer collaboration do not have to be antithetical to learning, but they are likely conducive only in specifically structured contexts that focus students' attention appropriately on learning. In a recent national survey, only approximately 50 percent of students reported that they were "very successful" at developing effective study skills in college.[36] This raises the question of whether students know how to study, particularly in groups or collaboratively. Active/collaborative learning approaches are expected to increase student engagement and time on task. As Kuh and his colleagues claimed: "Active and collaborative learning is an effective educational practice because students learn more when they are intensely involved in their education and are asked to think about and apply what they are learning in different settings."[37] What we need to delve into more deeply is whether students are indeed using active and collaborative learning activities in these expected ways, and in particular whether these activities lead to notable gains on objective measures of learning. Studies rarely gauge the content, depth, or actual learning that takes place in collaborative experiences, thus leaving open the question of whether in practice those experiences are as beneficial for mastering complex skills such as critical thinking, complex reasoning, and writing as they should be, based on theories of learning and cognitive development or on students' self-reports.

It is not only students who may not put active and collaborative learning activities to best use. Faculty are not very skilled at doing so either. During graduate training, future faculty members receive little if any formal instruction on teaching. Doctoral training focuses primarily, and at times exclusively, on research. Although recent decades have seen a proliferation of interest in improving the preparation of graduate students, a recent survey of doctoral students indicated that only 50 percent either had an opportunity to take a teaching assistant's training course lasting at least one term, or reported that they had an opportunity to learn about teaching in their respective disciplines through workshops and seminars.[38] Not surprisingly, one of the main concerns of students in doctoral programs is a lack of systematic opportunities to help them learn how to teach.[39]

Graduate students are not only entering classrooms without much preparation, but more problematically, they are learning in their graduate programs to deprioritize and perhaps even devalue teaching. Frederick, a graduate student in history interviewed in a recent study of graduate school experience by Jody Nyquist and her colleagues, made the following remark about the comments and choices of faculty members in his department: "I have learned that the people who call the shots do not value teaching. And I've learned that I can't spend as much time on my teaching as I have." Alice, a graduate student in math, conveyed even stronger sentiments: "What kind of messages have I received about being a teacher? That it's really settling for a lesser thing. That if you are going to be a real person, you're going to do research . . . ."[40] This aspect of graduate training, which neither prepares students to teach nor always instills in them a respect for the importance of teaching, is problematic not only on principled grounds but also from a functional standpoint: "Many, if not most [PhDs], will not be tenure-track faculty members," and only a few will have jobs at research universities.[41]

A number of organizations and major foundations have spent recent decades conducting studies, sponsoring initiatives, and organizing conferences and roundtables to address the current state of affairs and the future of the doctorate. Some of the programs, such as the Preparing Future Faculty (PFF) program, appear effective at increasing the interest and preparation of graduate students for teaching.[42] Those important endeavors are chipping away at the ivory tower. However, transformational change will remain elusive as long as the principal tenets of the academy remain in place: as long as teaching remains a solitary activity as opposed to one that is shared and valued in a scholarly community; as long as faculty members spend little time reflecting on teaching or engaging in the scholarship of teaching, and have little incentive to do so; and as long as a doctorate is fundamentally defined as a research degree, as opposed also to at least to some extent as a teaching degree.[43]

The institutional reforms we have articulated above, which focus on enhanced academic rigor in undergraduate instruction, appear as rather straightforward and perhaps easy to implement. While this is partially true, such an assessment ignores the extent to which current instructional practices have developed over time as a result of the complex incentive structures that exist in these educational settings. Faculty throughout the higher-education system have learned that research productivity is rewarded not just with increased salary, but often with reduced course loads—and they have come to believe that to the extent that undergraduate instruction matters at all in these institutions, it is assessed primarily in terms of student satisfaction on course evaluations. Faculty working in such settings encounter a classic collective action problem. If they raise course demands on their students but their peers do not, they will potentially be disadvantaged by course evaluations in which students express dissatisfaction. If they devote more time to instruction but their colleagues do not, their career development will suffer (absent changing institutional and professional reward structures). While enforcement of common institutional standards for course requirements and grading schemas can address some of these issues, other related problems associated with altering professional incentive structures that are not currently well aligned with undergraduate instruction, will likely require system-level reforms to address.

Facilitating learning, not just persistence

The results from our work show that learning is related first and foremost to academic activities, and particularly to individual studying. Social activities, including studying with peers, have either no consequences or negative consequences for learning. While this may not be surprising, it points to the importance of reevaluating our common understandings of collegiate outcomes and thinking about important distinctions between persistence and learning. Prior research has highlighted the importance of both social and academic integration for student outcomes in college. This was particularly the case in higher-education researcher Vincent Tinto's early scholarship on persistence, where academic factors in particular were emphasized. Tinto wrote: "But unlike most communities, institutions of higher education are first and foremost *educational communities* whose activities center about their *intellectual life*."[44] While academics, and specifically activities within the classroom, are prominent in Tinto's theory, those factors seem to have been overwhelmed by the extensive current focus on students' social experiences.

Recent research has increasingly emphasized the importance of social interactions for college success. This could in part reflect researchers yielding to the realities of students' lives: students spend considerably more time socializing than they do studying. The emphasis on social integration may also partly reflect the focus of earlier research on retention. As higher-education researcher Alexander Astin has noted: "Retention is facilitated by both student-student and student-faculty interaction, hours per week spent socializing with friends, partying, talking with faculty outside of class, and being a guest in a professor's home."[45] While these social experiences may yield higher graduation rates, it is not clear that they would also facilitate students' cognitive development. In our analyses, interactions neither with peers nor with faculty outside the classroom had positive consequences for learning.

The potential tension between learning and persistence was noted in a recent study that reported "the existence of two parallel processes at work among students attending selective colleges and universities in the United States: a mostly *social process of persistence* by which students derive satisfaction and become attached to the institution, and a mostly *academic process of achievement* whereby students earn good grades and steadily accumulate course credits."[46] This implies that we cannot simply take the prevailing focus on social integration from the literature on retention and assume that these social experiences will have equally beneficial effects on learning. Learning is a distinct outcome, which in some instances may be affected by institutional interventions in the opposite direction from persistence.

Choosing between learning and persistence is not inevitable; the question is how we conceive of their relationship. Tinto argued that "quite simply, the more students invest in learning activities, the more they learn. . . . Involvement, especially academic involvement, seems to generate heightened student effort. That effort, in turn, leads to enhanced learning. As to the latter, we also know that student learning is linked to persistence."[47] In this line of reasoning, the focus of the college experience is on learning, which in turn may facilitate persistence. In recent decades, many have turned this argument upside down. Policy makers and practitioners alike have focused on keeping students in college, assuming that if they stay they will learn. But the causal arrows do not seem to work in that direction. The simple act of staying enrolled does not ensure that students are learning much. If, on the other hand, students are learning and engaged, they will likely stay enrolled and graduate.

Institutional transparency and accountability

While faculty and leaders of higher-education institutions are in a unique position to shape the future of the enterprise, they operate in broader social, fiscal, regulatory, and political contexts. The responsibility for change thus rests not only with those on college campuses but beyond. At the system level, it is worth reflecting on the costs and benefits associated with the consumer-driven character of U.S. higher education. On the one hand, the empowerment of students and families to make choices in the marketplace through government-supported student aid and loan programs has produced significant gains for the system as a whole. As we have empirically demonstrated with our colleagues elsewhere in comparative work, an increased reliance on private higher-education financing has led to an expansion and diversification of higher education. More students attend college than would otherwise have been the case. In addition, although diversification of higher-education systems is associated with increased inequality in educational access, the expansion of higher education that accompanies diversification overall has counterbalanced these increases, and the system as a whole has provided improved access to disadvantaged youth without any overall growth in inequality.[48] Neoliberal policy makers who have advocated for increased privatization and market-based educational reforms have produced a system that has expanded opportunity for all.

What conservative policy makers have missed, however, is that market-based educational reforms that elevate the role of students as "consumers" do not necessarily yield improved outcomes in terms of student learning. While part of this disconnect between market-based reforms and student learning outcomes is likely the result of inadequate information on school performance being provided to students and parents—a problem that could be remedied by greater institutional transparency in reporting student academic outcomes—a greater and more enduring problem emerges in consumer preferences themselves. There is no reason to expect that students and parents as consumers will prioritize undergraduate learning as an outcome. Rather, it is likely that other features of institutions will largely be focused on, including the quality of student residential and social life, as well as the ability with relatively modest investments of effort to earn a credential that can be subsequently exchanged for labor market— and potentially marriage market—success. The educational philosopher John Dewey once asserted that schools should be designed so they manifested "what the best and wisest parent wants for his own child."[49] While we find it likely that the "best and wisest parent" would indeed focus on student learning, particularly if better information was made available on school performance in this area, we are profoundly skeptical that students in general, empowered as consumers or clients, will necessarily place much of an emphasis on this particular collegiate outcome.

One proposed remedy for higher-education inattention to student learning is the implementation of externally mandated accountability systems on public colleges and universities similar to the ones required and promoted in elementary and secondary school systems through policies such as No Child Left Behind (NCLB). Private colleges could be compelled by their reliance on federal subsidies, such as student aid grants, to participate in these systems at a level that at a minimum would require that they made data on student outcomes publicly available. One of the clearest and most significant calls for such a set of changes came recently in the 2006 Spellings Commission national report *A Test of Leadership: Charting the Future of U.S. Higher Education*, which asserted that "we want to bring much-needed transparency and accountability to our colleges and universities."[50] In justifying a call for an accountability system in higher education, the report noted that "better data about real performance and lifelong working and learning ability is absolutely essential if we are to meet national needs and improve institutional performance."[51] Specifically, systems were called for that would make data on student outcomes more transparent and available, since "despite increased attention to student learning results by colleges and universities and accreditation agencies, parents and students have no solid evidence, comparable across institutions, of how much students learn in colleges or whether they learn more at one college than another. Similarly, policymakers need more comprehensive data to help them decide whether the national investment in higher education is paying off and how taxpayer dollars could be used more effectively."[52] The Spellings Commission report identified in particular the CLA indicator we have relied on for this project as a potential state-of-the-art instrument to measure undergraduate learning. The report specifically noted that "among the most comprehensive national efforts to measure how much students actually learn at different campuses, the Collegiate Learning Assessment (CLA) promotes a culture of evidence-based assessment in higher education."[53]

The demand for greater accountability of student learning outcomes in higher education has been met with some ambivalence from actors within the system. For example, the former president of Harvard University, Derek Bok, who has been one of the most long-standing and articulate advocates of colleges focusing increased attention on undergraduate instruction, has observed:

> Though well intended, these efforts to impose accountability have not proved notably effective. For one thing, the standards have typically been devised without input from faculty representatives, thus greatly reducing their chances of having any effect on what goes on in college classrooms. For another, the measures used are generally too crude to be helpful. Some of them track outcomes that are largely beyond the college's control, such as how many graduates remain in the state or how many are employed (and at what average salary) a year after graduation. Other indicators look at how well students perform on standardized tests in their senior year, but the tests are often crude and the results usually tell us more about how intelligent students were when they entered college than about what they learned during their four years there.
>
> Officials may correct some of these defects. Past experience, however, suggests an even greater risk that states will put undue emphasis on

standardized test scores that do not accurately measure what a good liberal education should be trying to accomplish and cause college authorities to concentrate on excelling in the test at the expense of other, more important educational goals.[54]

To avoid the perceived pitfalls and institutional risks associated with externally imposed accountability systems, a growing number of institutions and other higher-education agencies are working internally to assess and improve performance in undergraduate education. A newly released report by the Association of American Colleges and Universities and the Council for Higher Education Accreditation, for example, urges all institutions to develop "ambitious, specific, and clearly stated goals for student learning" and to "gather evidence about how well students in various programs are achieving learning goals."[55] Other national organizations of colleges and universities have launched similar initiatives, and prominent voices in higher education have increasingly called for results of such efforts to be made publicly available.

These internal efforts towards self-assessment of student learning are widely supported and relatively uncontroversial steps towards embracing what the Spellings Commission has termed "a robust culture of accountability and transparency throughout higher education."[56] Internal self-assessment efforts ideally would be built on a diverse set of measures tracking teaching and learning within an institution. While such measures could include the CLA, one would expect institutions also to adopt alternative performance indicators; the Association of American Colleges and Universities, for example, has noted that "capstone courses and portfolios provide promising anchors for a meaningful approach to educational accountability."[57] Colleges and universities should routinely collect diverse sources of evaluation and assessment data to improve instruction and student learning on an ongoing basis. Given that we found great variation in student performance within colleges and universities in our study, all schools would benefit from developing internal organizational cultures that reflect on the strengths and weaknesses of curricular programs within their own institutions.

At the same time, however, internal organizational self-assessment efforts are premised on what Frederick Hess, director of education policy at the American Enterprise Institute, has termed "suggestive" as opposed to "coercive" accountability mechanisms. The former approach presumes "that the key to school improvement is to provide educators with more resources, expertise, training, support and 'capacity.'" Accountability systems of this character seek "to improve schooling by developing standards, applying informal social pressures, using testing as a diagnostic device, increasing coordination across schools and classrooms, and making more efficient use of school resources through standardization." The problem with such an approach, says Hess, is that "left to their own devices, most employees in any line of work will resist changes that require them to take on more responsibility, disrupt their routines, or threaten their jobs or wages." He argues that to significantly improve student outcomes, what is typically required is coercive accountability that not only makes individuals work harder but forces "managers and leaders to rethink systems and practices."[58]

While the coercive pressure that Hess believes necessary for significant improvement in school performance may appear as an attractive policy option to legislators and policy makers frustrated with the current state of undergraduate education, we believe that it is not likely to occur or be successfully implemented in the near term for two reasons. First, the higher-education system will likely be much more effective than elementary and secondary schools at resisting externally imposed accountability systems. The system as a whole is effectively organized in terms of national associations and influential lobbyists. In addition, university and college educators have significantly greater status and power in society than their peers who teach at lower grade levels. As knowledge producers, they are trained to use their pens effectively and would no doubt be quite persuasive in op-ed articles, policy reports, and book monographs about the risks and undesirability of any externally imposed accountability schema. In addition, although four-year colleges and universities are dependent on public largesse in the form of tax credits, student aid, and indirect charges associated with research grants, a much greater portion of them are in the private sector than is true for elementary and secondary education, and thus the system as a whole is in a stronger position to resist externally imposed regulatory pressure.

Coercive accountability in higher education will also not likely be effective—nor warranted or desirable in the short term—because the measurement and understanding of learning processes in higher education are considerably underdeveloped. For example, the research presented in this book on individual, social, and institutional factors associated with learning in higher education, while innovative and significant in developing our understanding of undergraduate learning, was based solely on nonexperimental data—the type that has been widely available and has facilitated research on elementary and secondary learning outcomes for the past several decades. Given that students are sorted and self-selected into various high school and college experiences, academic programs, and higher-education institutions, however, our findings here can do little more than identify factors associated with improvement in critical thinking, complex reasoning, and written communication. Future longitudinal research, including experimental and quasi-experimental approaches, is needed to determine the character and robustness of the associations identified in our research. In addition, while the CLA instrument as a measure of learning tracks remarkably well with sociological factors at the aggregate group or institutional level, there are limitations to its precision at the individual level that should caution policy makers from imposing high-stakes accountability schemes based on it or similar assessment indicators. We find that although from a sociological perspective the CLA appears quite promising and worthy of further research and development, we are simply not at a stage of scientific knowledge where college students' learning outcomes can be measured with sufficient precision to justify embracing a coercive accountability system without significant reservations.

Finally, while we do not believe that federal and state governments should or could yet effectively implement an accountability system for learning in higher education; they have other ways to address the current problems with undergraduate education that are worth considering. Today, federal policies largely have exacerbated the situation. Financial aid has so empowered students as consumers that higher-education institutions now compete for applicants by focusing on student services and organizational goals aligned more with *U.S. News and World Report* college rankings than with undergraduate learning. While the federal government has devoted resources to the Department of Education's Fund for the Improvement of Postsecondary Education, its level of support is insignificant when considered relative to the competing funds that encourage faculty and institutions to focus on scientific research. For example, in 2009 the federal budget for research and development was $151.1 billion, including $40.9 billion for the National Institutes of Health and $7.5 billion for the National Science Foundation. These outlays can be compared to $134 million for the Department of Education's Postsecondary Education Improvement Fund.[59] While public investment in research supporting knowledge production is a worthy end, federal and state governments would do well to balance these institutional incentives with greater funding commitments tied to the improvement of undergraduate learning.

Existing government commitments to individual student aid and grant programs could also be tied to—or partially redirected to support—insti-

tutional grants that require colleges and universities to adopt school improvement efforts that track and demonstrate student progress in undergraduate learning. Our research has demonstrated that existing student
grant programs are associated with increased undergraduate learning,
while reliance on loans to finance college was not associated either positively or negatively with learning. While individual forms of grant support potentially facilitate undergraduate learning, institutional school
improvement grants—similar to elementary and secondary school reform
programs—could encourage innovation by empowering local institutional
actors to design and develop policies and practices to enhance undergraduate education outcomes and measurably improve student learning. These
grants would provide support for organizational entrepreneurs within the
system to develop innovative educational policies and practices. Although
some higher-education institutions might resist these changes, their participation in the programs would be voluntary, and thus their resistance
would be muted or passive. In addition, while it may be comfortable for
many colleges and universities to continue under the present arrangements, it would be unrealistic for them to expect that federal and state support for undergraduate tuition would continue indefinitely without more
substantive conditions and requirements eventually being attached.

Reaching for the Moon

While limited learning in higher education is indeed cause for concern, it
will probably not be easily or quickly remedied without some form of ex-
ogenous shock to the system. Social scientists have no particular expertise
in predicting the particular form and timing of such an occurrence. We
are familiar enough with U.S. history, however, to know that these shocks
do periodically transpire. The Sputnik launch in 1957, for example, led
within a year to legislation that significantly increased federal support for
education and provided increased attention to science and mathematics instruction in particular. A few years later, President John F. Kennedy would
pick a university setting to proclaim that the United States would send an
astronaut to the moon within a decade. Many said such a goal could never
be attained.

Standing in the way of significant reform efforts are, of course, a set
of entrenched organizational interests and deeply ingrained institutional
practices. While the lack of undergraduate academic learning has gener-
ated increased hand-wringing in various quarters, efforts to address the
problem have been feeble and ineffective to date. A primary reason is that

undergraduate learning is peripheral to the concerns of the vast majority of those involved with the higher-education system. Limited learning is in no way perceived as a formidable crisis that threatens the survival of organizational actors, institutions, or the system as a whole. We believe that students, parents, faculty, and administrators are not overly concerned with the lack of academic learning currently occurring in colleges and universities, as long as other organizational outcomes more important to them are being achieved.

The dissatisfaction of corporate leaders in the private sector with the quality of U.S. undergraduate education has, however, become palpable as they claim that "the current state of affairs is unacceptable" and that "many of the skills and abilities they seek can—and should—be taught on campus."[60] More than 90 percent of employers rate written communication, critical thinking, and problem solving as "very important" for the job success of new labor market entrants. At the same time, they note that only a small proportion of four-year college graduates excel in these skills: 16 percent excel in written communication and 28 percent in critical thinking/problem solving.[61] In another recent survey, commissioned by the Association of American Colleges and Universities, employers rated only 26 percent of college graduates as being very well prepared in writing, and 22 percent as being very well prepared to think critically.[62]

While employers might lament the capacities that current college graduates bring to the workplace, industry has already largely adapted by turning to graduate schools and foreign sources of labor to fill positions that require sophisticated technical expertise, and it has often relegated U.S. college graduates to routine nonmanual occupations within firms. And while those who are committed to promoting a democratic citizenry might bemoan the consequences of limited learning on the public's ability to reflect critically on contemporary political issues, critical thinking and complex reasoning capacities are of little use if future citizens are largely disengaged and tuned out from societal events altogether. The extent of disengagement in young adults today is highlighted by recent findings that suggest that of individuals aged eighteen to twenty-four—many of whom are enrolled in higher-education institutions—only 24 percent report that they even read a print or on-line version of a newspaper, while 34 percent admit that on a typical day they receive no news from any source.[63]

The increases in cognitive disengagement from societal events and in the institutional marginalization of undergraduate learning should remind us that solutions to the problem of limited learning will require not only technical fixes but also a recommitment to recognizing that providing future college students with rigorous and high-quality educational experiences is a moral imperative. Federal incentives to alter individual and institutional incentives will not likely prove sufficient to change educational practices without more fundamental change to college and university organizational cultures. Historians remind us that higher-education institutions initially were created largely to achieve moral ends. A renewed commitment to improving undergraduate education is unlikely to occur without changes to the organizational cultures of colleges and universities that reestablish the institutional primacy of these functions—instilling in the next generation of young adults a lifelong love of learning, an ability to think critically and communicate effectively, and a willingness to embrace and assume adult responsibilities. Although our higher-education institutions currently are academically adrift, they can commit to a change of course that will reconnect them with their earlier design and functions. We should choose paths of purpose such as these, as Kennedy reminded us when he exhorted us to reach for the moon, "not because they are easy, but because they are hard, because that goal will serve to organize and measure the best of our energies and skills, because that challenge is one that we are willing to accept, one we are unwilling to postpone, and one which we intend to win."[64]

Methodological Appendix

Data, Methods and Statistical Analyses

The data analyses presented in this book are based on the Determinants of College Learning (DCL) dataset, which was developed in partnership with the Council for Aid to Education (CAE). The CAE initiated the Collegiate Learning Assessment (CLA) Longitudinal Project in the fall of 2005, administering a short survey and the CLA instrument to a sample of freshmen at four-year institutions. The same students were contacted for the sophomore-year follow-up in the spring of 2007. The Social Science Research Council (SSRC) joined the project at this time, broadening the original CAE questionnaire to include a range of survey questions regarding students' family backgrounds, high school characteristics, and college experiences. The SSRC collected course transcript data from participating institutions and obtained survey and test assessment data from the CAE for students who signed the SSRC consent form permitting the release of this information. This sample included 2,362 students across twenty-four four-year institutions. The analytic sample used in this report includes 2,322 students who had valid demographic information (race/ethnicity and gender) and test scores for both survey years.

Institutions participating in this project include schools of varying sizes, selectivity, and missions. The sample includes private residential

Melissa Velez coauthored this appendix.

liberal arts colleges and large research institutions as well as a number of His-torically Black Colleges and Universities (HSBUs) and Hispanic Serving Institu-tions (HSIs). Colleges and universities were located in all four census regions of the country. Participating institutions implemented their own sampling and retention strategies. Although the CAE provided overall advice and guidance on random sampling, each institution worked independently to recruit and retain students in the sample. The overall retention rate from freshman to sophomore year across the twenty-four institutions included in the DCL dataset was slightly under 50 percent, although this varied notably across institutions and groups of students. If bias is introduced into our analyses by processes of selective attrition, however, it is likely in a direction that leads us to overestimate the overall rate of academic growth that is occurring in these institutions—that is, the dearth of learning we have identified would likely be even more pronounced if we had been able to track down and continue assessing the students who dropped out of the study and/or the institutions they originally attended.

Joining the ongoing CAE endeavor has facilitated a quick start-up of the project and substantially reduced research costs. However, this approach has also produced a unique sample of institutions and students. To illuminate the characteristics of the DCL sample, we have conducted several comparisons with national datasets. First, we compared students in the DCL sample to students en-tering postsecondary institutions in the 2003–04 academic year using the Begin-ning Postsecondary Students (BPS) Longitudinal Study. We restricted the BPS sample to students of traditional age (nineteen or younger as of December 31, 2003) who entered four-year institutions. These restrictions are necessary since our sample includes only four-year institutions and the students were on average 19.5 years old in their sophomore year. Comparison with the BPS provides infor-mation about student demographics as well as some of their college experiences. As table A1.1 shows, the experiences of students in the DCL sample are quite similar to those of nationally representative samples with respect to studying with peers and meeting with faculty, although DCL students report less commit-ment to the labor market in terms of hours worked (see note 40 in chapter 4 for further discussion). The students' social and academic backgrounds across the two samples are fairly similar as well. These comparisons offer some assurance that students in the DCL sample capture reasonably well the characteristics and experiences of students attending four-year institutions nationwide.

Next, we compared the school-level characteristics of DCL institutions to all four-year institutions in the Integrated Postsecondary Education Data System (IPEDS; table A1.2). The institutional demographic and selectivity character-istics for DCL schools and all four-year institutions are virtually identical, in-dicating that our institutions closely resemble four-year institutions nationally, at least with respect to the characteristics examined. Moreover, if we estimated institutional characteristics for the DCL schools based on the students in our sample, they would relatively closely match official institutional reports from IPEDS for race/ethnicity and the 75th percentile of the SAT/ACT distribution. The DCL sample, however, includes a higher proportion of women and the 25th percentile of the SAT/ACT distribution is slightly higher, implying that the DCL sample includes better academically prepared students in the bottom quartile.

Moreover, we compared the characteristics of high schools from which DCL students graduated to those of all U.S. high schools as identified by data combined from two sources: the Common Core of Data and the Private School Universe Survey (table A1.3). Demographic and other school characteristics represented in the DCL sample are quite similar to national statistics. The DCL sample includes a lower proportion of racially segregated high schools, and high schools with high proportions of students receiving free or reduced-price lunch. This pattern is exactly what would be expected given the inequality in entry into higher education, and particularly into four-year institutions. Thus, although the DCL sample was not obtained through national probability sampling procedures, the students and institutions in the sample display a relatively close resemblance to students attending postsecondary institutions throughout the United States.

Table A1.4 provides description of variable coding for all measures used in the analysis. We used the performance task of the CLA to assess student learning. The CLA measures student learning by asking students to write open-ended arguments in response to "real-world" scenarios. Using these questions, it aims to measure general skills-based competencies such as critical thinking, complex reasoning (such as analytical reasoning and problem solving), and written communication rather than academic aptitude, general intelligence, or subject- and content-specific skills. Measures used to assess student learning consist of three sets of open-ended prompts which have been carefully constructed in consultation with experts on student assessment, and elaborately pre-tested and piloted in prior work. The three components include the performance task, "make an argument," and "break an argument." We focused on the performance task since that component of the CLA was administered most uniformly across institutions, had the largest completion rates, and is the state-of-the-art component of the assessment instrument (for further discussion of the CLA, see chapter 1).

Given that the CLA performance task measures student performance on one ninety-minute complex cognitive task, significant measurement error is introduced at the individual level that otherwise would be reduced with multiple choice indicators that require student responses on hundreds of shorter items. The precision of the individual-level measurement of CLA performance thus is not ideal. While the CLA performance of students would thus not be appropriate as a basis for high-stakes individual consequences (assuming that one even sought such a coercive and punitive accountability system), when analysis is done at the aggregate level, the lack of precision in measurement simply leads to larger standard errors, and makes it more difficult to identify statistically significant findings than would otherwise be the case. Moreover, the CLA measure is desirable and appropriate as a research instrument, as it can gauge student competencies on simulated scenarios of real-world tasks that respondents potentially will later encounter as college graduates. The measure is also sufficiently broad-based in the competencies assessed that it avoids the pitfalls of being excessively reductionistic and intellectually narrow in the outcomes measured.

Statistical Analyses

In chapter 2 we examined the overall patterns of learning in higher education as assessed by change over time in the CLA measure of critical thinking, analytical reasoning, and expository skills for different groups of students. We focused on what are typically considered measures of student social background to understand the extent to which broader patterns of stratification are manifested in learning outcomes in higher education. We began by considering students' self-reported race/ethnicity, divided into the following categories: white, African-American, Hispanic, Asian, and other racial/ethnic groups. Next, we considered family background, including both parental occupation and education. Since parental occupation did not show a statistically significant relationship to growth in learning net of parental education, we focused discussion on the latter. This variable captures the highest level of education completed by either parent, as reported by students, and is divided into the following categories: high school or less, some college, bachelor's degree, and graduate or professional degree.

In addition to these often-discussed measures of social background, we examined two other characteristics: whether a student attended a high school with predominantly non-white students (70 percent or more), and whether a student's home language was English (based on the question: Was English the primary language spoken in your home when you were growing up?). For each measure we first examined descriptive statistics, considering the distribution of 2005 CLA scores, 2007 CLA scores, and the difference between the two scores for each group of students. To express differences across groups in standard deviation terms, we divided the mean difference between groups by the standard deviation for the full sample.

Following the discussion of descriptive results, we examined the relationship between students' social background and CLA scores in a multivariate framework. We conducted a series of regression models which predicted the 2007 CLA score while controlling for the 2005 CLA score. Presented results thus, in effect, estimate the relationship between specific variables of interest and improvement in CLA performance between freshman and sophomore years. All analyses are adjusted for clustering at the institutional level. We used mean substitution for missing data on covariates in the models, replacing missing values and including dummy variables (coded 1) when the substitution was made. Mean substituted data is used in regression analyses, but not for descriptive results.

We present several regression models that successively add more controls. The first model begins simply by controlling for the 2005 CLA score. This model thus reports differences across groups in their 2007 CLA scores, adjusted for their performance at the point of entry into higher education. However, students may perform differently on the CLA for a number of reasons, such as their social background or their academic preparation. The subsequent models thus control for a range of students' sociodemographic attributes (race/ethnicity, gender, parental education and occupation, English as home language, number of siblings, and two-parent household), high school characteristics (region, urbanicity, and racial composition—i.e., high school 70 percent or more non-white), and academic preparation (number of advanced placement courses taken, high school GPA, and SAT/ACT performance).

Table A2.1 reports mean differences in 2005 and 2007 CLA scores and change in CLA scores between 2005 and 2007 for different groups of students. We compare students who come from different social backgrounds based on their race/ethnicity, parental education, gender, home language, and high school's racial composition (i.e., whether the high school is 70 percent or more non-white). We also compare CLA scores of students with different high school academic experiences, including number of advanced placement courses taken, high school GPA, and SAT/ACT performance. Each variable of interest is divided into categories for ease of presentation. High school GPA and SAT/ACT scores are divided into quintiles, with results presented for the bottom, middle three, and top quintiles. The top quintile includes students who scored the equivalent of a combined verbal and math SAT score of 1,320 or higher; the bottom quintile is the equivalent of a combined SAT score lower than 990 points. For each variable we have chosen a reference category to which all other categories are compared.

Since students' social background and academic experiences are related, table A2.2 reports the proportion of students who took different numbers of AP courses, had a GPA in a particular quintile, or scored in a particular quintile of the SAT/ACT distribution for students from different social backgrounds. Following these descriptive results, table A2.3 reports mean differences in test scores across different groups of students after adjusting estimates for 2005 CLA scores, students' sociodemographic and high school characteristics, and finally students' academic preparation. The sequential models allow us to evaluate the extent to which gaps in CLA performance across groups emerge from different sources. Finally, we consider how students' social and academic backgrounds are related to their higher-education destinations. Table A2.4 reports the propor-

tions of students who attended highly selective, selective, and less selective institutions. Again, we consider the distribution of students from different sociodemographic groups across these institutional contexts. College selectivity is based
on institutional reports of the combined SAT scores at the 25th percentile of the
incoming freshman class. Highly selective colleges were defined as schools with
students at the 25th percentile having combined verbal and math SAT scores
higher than 1,150 (four schools with 25.2 percent of the overall sample fell into
this category); less selective colleges were defined as schools with students at the
25th percentile having combined scores lower than 950 (six schools with 24.2
percent of the overall sample fell into this category).

In chapter 3 we examined how students' college experiences varied by individual background, as well as with respect to the higher-education institutions
they attended. We explored group differences by race/ethnicity, parental education, gender, English as home language, and high school racial composition
(measured by whether the school was 70 percent or more non-white). In addition, we looked for group differences based on students' SAT/ACT scores and the
selectivity of the four-year college attended (measured by the SAT scores at the
25th percentile of incoming students).

After discussing mean differences across groups, we identify the proportion
of the variance that occurs across schools for each measure of students' college
experiences. We provide this identification of proportion variance across schools
for an intercept model, which includes no statistical adjustments other than a
random error term for college attended. We also report estimates of proportion
variance across schools after controlling for individual-level social and academic
background (i.e., race/ethnicity, gender, parental education and occupation, English as home language, number of siblings, two-parent household, high school
racial composition, region, urbanicity, number of advanced placement courses
taken, high school GPA, and SAT/ACT performance). The proportion of variance across schools is also estimated after controlling for the selectivity of the
college attended at the institutional level, in addition to social and academic
background at the individual level. By comparing changes to the proportion variance under these different specifications, one can estimate how much variance
across schools is accounted for by the inclusion of individual-level factors as well
as by our institutional-level measure of college selectivity.[1] While our reports of
proportion variance across schools rely on modeling with random institutional
effects, we also provide estimates of R-squared explained variance in models that
first solely include our measures of individual-level social and academic background, and then add institutional-level fixed effects. The change in R-squared
between these models provides an alternative approach to estimating the extent
to which institutional-level differences are associated with the measures examined. We run similar models for both continuous and dichotomous variables

in chapter 3, as we seek to facilitate comparisons across variables and are not interested, in this particular analysis, in the statistical significance of specific coefficients or the overall statistical fit of the model that might be improved with logistic or ordered/adjacent logit regression models.

In table A3.1 we examine student reports of faculty being approachable, having high standards, and holding high expectations, as well as the frequency and prevalence of faculty-student interactions outside of the classroom during the prior semester. Students' ratings of the faculty are standardized to a scale with a mean of zero and a standard deviation of one to facilitate comparisons across measures. In table A3.2 we explore students' reports of whether peers have high expectations, help others to succeed, and work hard to succeed. In addition, we measure the percentage of time studying that occurs with peers. Students' assessments of their peers are also standardized to a scale with a mean of zero and a standard deviation of one. Table A3.3 identifies curricular experiences measured by the number of hours students spent studying and whether students took courses in the previous semester that required more than twenty pages of writing per semester or more than forty pages of reading per week. Table A3.4 presents transcript-based measures of the percentage of coursework taken in the following subject areas: business, education and social work, communications, health, science and mathematics, and humanities and social sciences. In addition, the transcript-based college GPA is identified. In table A3.5 we examine course concentrators in these different subject areas (defined as students whose transcripts report that they have taken one standard deviation more coursework in a particular area than an average student) and explore how their curricular experiences vary. We measure curricular experiences in this table as the number of times students met with faculty, the number of hours they spent studying per week, and whether they took courses during the previous semester that required more than twenty pages of writing per semester or more than forty pages of reading per week. Table A3.6 identifies social aspects of college life and reports measures of whether or not students lived in a college dormitory, as well as the number of hours students spent in fraternities and sororities, involved with student clubs and volunteering. Table A3.7 presents information on college financing and student employment. Measured in this table are whether students work for pay, the number of hours spent working for pay (for students who reported working), and the percentage of college costs covered by loans, grants, and scholarships.

The analyses in chapter 4 explore the relationship between students' college experiences and their CLA performance. All the analyses are presented as sequential regression models, wherein the first model controls only for the 2005 CLA scores; the second controls for students' sociodemographic backgrounds (race/ethnicity, gender, parental education and occupation, English as home language, number of siblings, and two-parent household), high school characteristics (region, urbanicity, and racial composition—i.e., high school 70 percent or more non-white), and academic preparation (number of advanced placement courses taken, high school GPA, and SAT/ACT performance); and the final model includes institutional fixed effects. Fixed effects models include a dummy variable for each of the institutions except for one, which serves as a reference (the institution with no growth in CLA scores between 2005 and 2007 was chosen). As a robustness check of our results, we also ran random effect models. The results from random effects models were virtually identical to those from fixed effects models; the coefficients were of similar magnitude and significance tests led to the same substantive conclusions. All the analyses are adjusted for clustering at the institutional level. We used mean substitution for missing data, replacing missing values and including dummy variables (coded 1) when the substitution was made.

To present a more intuitive interpretation of results, we often calculate predicted 2007 CLA scores based on different regression specifications. In these predictions, all continuous variables (2005 CLA scores, high school GPA, and SAT/ACT performance) are set at their means. This implies that on those measures we are predicting 2007 CLA scores for an average student with a mean 2005 CLA score, as well as a mean high school GPA and a mean SAT/ACT performance. For categorical variables, our predictions are based on the reference category. Our focus is not on the specific values of the estimates, but on the trends across students' college experiences. Thus, the actual value of the predicted 2007 CLA score is of less interest than whether the scores increase or decrease with specific college experiences.

Table A4.1 presents predicted 2007 CLA scores for students who reported different academic and social climates. For academic climates, we consider students' ratings of whether faculty members are approachable and have high standards and high expectations, whether students ever met with faculty, and whether they reported having reading and writing requirements during the prior semester (i.e., reading more than forty pages per week or writing more than twenty pages over the course of the semester). Social climates include students' ratings of whether their peers had high expectations, worked hard to succeed, and helped others succeed. We first predict 2007 CLA scores for students with these different college experiences while controlling only for the 2005 CLA scores, and then we adjust estimates for students' social backgrounds, academic preparation, and institutions attended (through fixed effects).

Following the same procedures, table A4.2 examines the relationship between students' time use and CLA scores. Here, we first examine the number of hours students spent studying and the number of hours they spent in extracurricular activities. Next, we present a more nuanced account of students' time, examining the number of hours they spent studying with peers and alone, the number of hours they spent working on and off campus, and the number of hours they spent in student clubs, fraternities/sororities, or volunteering. We explore variation in CLA performance across different fields of study, based on students' reported major at the end of their sophomore year (table A4.3). We also explore how students' financial experiences are related to their CLA performance by considering the percentage of their college costs covered by grants, scholarships, and loans in table A4.4. The final table, A4.5, presents a series of regression models which sequentially add different controls: 2005 CLA scores, sociodemographic and high school characteristics (model 1), academic preparation in high school (model 2), college experiences (model 3), and institutions attended (i.e., fixed effects, model 4). In addition to considering the relationships between different factors and CLA scores, we also report the proportion of the variance that is accounted for by different factors by comparing R-squared values across models.

Robustness Checks: Scaling, Ceiling and Motivation Effects

The CLA instrument was scaled slightly differently in 2005 and 2007. In 2005 the scores were capped at 1,600, while in 2007 they were allowed to range up to 1,800. Sixty-five students scored above 1,600 in 2007. We conducted several checks to evaluate the implications of this change in scoring for our results. First, we capped the 2007 scores at 1,600. This procedure slightly decreases the mean of the 2007 scores (from 1166 to 1163), and consequently lowers the growth estimate (0.16 standard deviation, compared to the 0.18 standard deviation based on the original scores). Similarly, some of the differences between groups (e.g., parental education and race/ethnicity) are one to two points lower with the capped 2007 measure, at least in the baseline models. The differences are often smaller, and in some cases nonexistent, after a full set of controls is included in the models. Similarly, regression coefficients for college activities at times differ by approximately one point from those reported. Overall, the differences between the 2007 capped measure and the one used in the reported models are of negligible magnitude and do not alter the substantive findings.

Our second approach for checking the consequences of test-score scaling differences was to keep 2007 scores as they were, but include a dummy variable in regression models for students who scored 1,600 in 2005 (many of whom likely scored higher but were scaled to 1,600). Thirty-nine students had a score of 1,600 in 2005. In most models, the dummy variable representing these students is just barely statistically significant (e.g., in the final models reported in table A4.5, the p-value ranges from 0.027 to 0.046). More importantly, including this dummy variable in the models does not notably alter the magnitude or statistical significance of the other variables of interest, specifically parental education, race/ethnicity, and academic and social experiences during college. Substantively identical conclusions are thus reached regardless of the estimation procedure used.

We also checked our results to ensure that they were not an artifact of ceiling effects of the CLA instrument. We first divided the sample into quartiles by high school GPA and SAT/ACT scores. Students in the top quartiles on both measures made equal or larger gains than students in lower quartiles. Next, we conducted a more fine-grained analysis by dividing students into deciles based on their SAT/ACT scores. There was much variation in growth across deciles, but no clear indication that higher deciles gained less (indeed, students in the highest SAT/ACT decile showed the largest gains in the performance task score between their freshman and sophomore years). While there were no ceiling or floor effects on the CLA instrument with respect to prior high school performance and SAT/ACT scores, we did observe some evidence of regression toward the mean when 2007 CLA scores were compared to 2005 CLA scores. This tendency was relatively modest and is likely a product of the compromises to the precision of the individual-level measurement that occur when relying on an open-ended, in-depth essay prompt.

Moreover, it is possible that reported test scores do not only reflect students' critical thinking, analytical reasoning, and written communication skills, but also the degree of motivation and effort they invested in the test. This is a particularly important issue to consider, given our focus on differences between students from various social and academic backgrounds; those differences may emerge not because certain groups have lower skills, but because of their lower levels of investment in the assessment activity. After the completion of the CLA instrument in 2005, CAE asked students a range of questions regarding their experience of the test. Among these were questions about effort (e.g., whether students engaged in good effort throughout the test and gave it their full attention) and importance (e.g., the extent to which doing well on the test was important to students). Based on these questions, we used factor analysis to identify items that measured similar underlying constructs. Based on the results of the factor analysis we created two scales, one measuring the degree of effort invested in the test and the other capturing the importance of performing well. Since the measurement of these scales occurred in 2005, we can explore the extent to which they can act as proxies for underlying individual traits around test-taking motivation and can be associated with differential test score performance.

As would be expected, adding these scales to the full model indicates that students scored higher when they exerted more effort and cared more about performing well. What is crucial for our analysis, however, is that there were only relatively small differences in reported effort and importance of the test between different groups of students, whether the groups were defined by sociodemographic background and academic preparation or by the students' college experiences. Consequently, including these scales in the full model did not alter any of the substantive results discussed. Thus, while effort and the importance of performing well matter for individuals, they are similarly distributed across students and do not help to explain differential performance of students across social backgrounds or across groups engaging in specific types of college activities.

Table A1.1. Student characteristics and experiences in the DCL and BPS samples

	DCL sample Mean	BPS sample[1] Mean
Background characteristics		
Race/ethnicity		
White	0.64	0.70
African-American	0.15	0.09
Hispanic	0.05	0.10
Asian	0.10	0.05
Other	0.05	0.06
English not primary language	0.13	0.10
Parental education		
High school or less	0.14	0.23
Some college	0.21	0.18
Bachelor's degree	0.29	0.29
Graduate/professional degree	0.36	0.30
High school GPA		
D or lower	0.00	0.00
C−/C	0.00	0.01
C/B−	0.03	0.05
B−/B	0.10	0.10
B/A−	0.38	0.35
A−/A	0.48	0.49
College experiences		
Employment		
Not working	0.35	0.29
Average number of hours working (if employed)	12.48	20.50
Studying with peers[2]		
Never	0.23	0.24
Sometimes	0.61	0.58
Often	0.16	0.18
Meeting with faculty outside of class[2]		
Never	0.09	0.09
Sometimes	0.60	0.55
Often	0.32	0.36

[1] Beginning Postsecondary Students (BPS) Longitudinal Study, 2003–04 cohort. The sample is restricted to students who entered four-year institutions and were 19 years of age or younger as of 12/31/2003. College experiences are based on the 2006 survey and thus typically reference students' junior year.
[2] These categories represent BPS coding. DCL questions were mapped as closely as possible to these categories (for hours studying with peers: 0 = never, 1–5 hours = sometimes, above 5 hours = often; for times met with faculty: 0 = never, 1–4 times = sometimes, more than 4 times = often). For more details on the DCL questions, see table A1.4.

Table A1.2. Institutional characteristics of colleges and universities in the DCL sample compared to IPEDS reports

| | Our sample: DCL schools | IPEDS: DCL schools only[1] | IPEDS: All four-year institutions[1] |
	Mean	Mean	Mean
Institutional demographics			
% Male	0.37	0.46	0.45
% White	0.59	0.61	0.59
% African-American	0.19	0.14	0.13
% Hispanic	0.05	0.08	0.13
% Asian	0.11	0.10	0.06
% Other[2]	0.05	0.07	0.09
Institutional selectivity			
SAT, 25th percentile	1052.83	995.15	993.14
SAT, 75th percentile	1212.83	1219.02	1219.23
ACT 25th percentile	22.05	20.86	20.33
ACT 75th percentile	26.29	25.77	25.31

[1] Integrated Postsecondary Education Data System (IPEDS) data includes first-time, degree-seeking undergraduates and is weighted by enrollment.

[2] For the IPEDS sample, this category inncludes American Indians, students of unknown background, and non-resident aliens. For the DCL sample, this category includes American Indians and any students who self-identified as "other" race/ethnicity.

Table A1.3. Institutional characteristics of high schools in the DCL and national samples

	DCL sample Mean	National sample Mean
High school institutional characteristics		
Student Composition		
% White	0.69	0.63
% African-American	0.14	0.15
% Hispanic	0.09	0.16
% Asian	0.06	0.05
% American Indian	0.01	0.01
% total minority	0.30	0.37
Segregated school (70% or more non-white)	0.13	0.21
% free/reduced-price lunch[1]	0.23	0.32
School sector		
Public school	0.86	0.88
Charter school[1]	0.01	0.03
Magnet school[1]	0.09	0.07
Private school	0.14	0.12
School location		
Urban	0.31	0.31
Rural	0.20	0.23
Suburban	0.49	0.47
Northeast	0.18	0.18
Midwest	0.36	0.22
South	0.26	0.36
West	0.19	0.24
Student-teacher ratio	17.30	18.55
School size	1363.00	1382.77

[1] Only available for public high schools.
Note: Data on high school characteristics were obtained from the Common Core of Data (CCD) and Private School Universe Survey (PSS). Descriptives for the national sample are weighted by school size.

Table A1.4. Description of the variables used in analyses

Variable name	Variable coding

College: Academic and social experiences

College climate

Faculty are approachable — Students' responses to the statement: "Faculty members at my institution are approachable, helpful, and understanding." Answers recorded on a 1 (strongly disagree) to 7 (strongly agree) scale and then standardized to a mean of 0 and standard deviation (sd) of 1. Measure also divided into dummy variables indicating high (1 sd above the mean), medium (between 1 sd above and 1 sd below the mean), and low (1 sd below the mean; reference).

Faculty have high standards — Students' responses to the statement: "Faculty members at my institution hold students to high standards." Answers recorded on a 1 (strongly disagree) to 7 (strongly agree) scale and then standardized to a mean of 0 and standard deviation (sd) of 1. Measure also divided into dummy variables indicating high (1 sd above the mean), medium (between 1 sd above and 1 sd below the mean), and low (1 sd below the mean; reference).

Faculty have high expectations — Students' responses to the statement: "Faculty members at my institution have high expectations for students like me." Answers recorded on a 1 (strongly disagree) to 7 (strongly agree) scale and then standardized to a mean of 0 and standard deviation (sd) of 1. Measure also divided into dummy variables indicating high (1 sd above the mean), medium (between 1 sd above and 1 sd below the mean), and low (1 sd below the mean; reference).

Meeting with faculty — Students' reports of how many times they met with a faculty member outside of class in the previous semester. Response categories were 0, 1–2, 3–4, 5–6, and 7+ times. Continuous variable created from the categories, equaling the average of each category (e.g., 1–2 times equals 1.5). Responses also coded as dummy variables indicating never (reference) or at least once for certain descriptive analyses.

Reading course requirement — Dummy variable indicating whether students took a course where they reported reading more than 40 pages a week the previous semester.

Variable name	Variable coding
Writing course requirement	Dummy variable indicating whether students took a course where they reported writing more than 20 pages during the previous semester.
Reading and writing course requirements	Dummy variable indicating whether students took both a course where they reported reading more than 40 pages a week and a course where they reported writing more than 20 pages the previous semester.
Students have high expectations	Students' responses to the statement: "Students at my institution have high academic aspirations." Answers recorded on a 1 (strongly disagree) to 7 (strongly agree) scale and then standardized to a mean of 0 and standard deviation (sd) of 1. Measure also divided into dummy variables indicating high (1 sd above the mean), medium (between 1 sd above and 1 sd below the mean), and low (1 sd below the mean; reference).
Students help others succeed	Students' responses to the statement: "Students at my institution help each other succeed." Answers recorded on a 1 (strongly disagree) to 7 (strongly agree) scale and then standardized to a mean of 0 and standard deviation (sd) of 1. Measure also divided into dummy variables indicating high (1 sd above the mean), medium (between 1 sd above and 1 sd below the mean), and low (1 sd below the mean; reference).
Students work hard to succeed	Students' responses to the statement: "Students at my institution work hard to succeed academically." Answers recorded on a 1 (strongly disagree) to 7 (strongly agree) scale and then standardized to a mean of 0 and standard deviation (sd) of 1. Measure also divided into dummy variables indicating high (1 sd above the mean), medium (between 1 sd above and 1 sd below the mean), and low (1 sd below the mean; reference).
Time use	
Hours studying alone	Students' reports of the number of hours spent studying alone in a typical week. Response categories were 0, 1–5, 6–10, 11–15, 16–20, and 20+. Continuous variable created from these categories, equaling the average of each category (e.g., 1–5 category equals 3).
Hours studying with peers	Students' reports of the number of hours spent studying with peers in a typical week. Response categories were 0, 1–5, 6–10, 11–15, 16–20, and 20+. Continuous variable created from these categories, equaling the average of each category (e.g., 1–5 category equals 3).

Variable name	Variable coding
Hours studying	Sum of students' reports of the number of hours spent studying alone and studying with peers.
Percentage of time studying with peers	Number of hours spent studying with peers divided by total hours spent studying in a typical week.
Hours working on campus	Students' reports of the number of hours spent working on campus in a typical week. Response categories were 0, 1–5, 6–10, 11–15, 16–20, and 20+. Continuous variable created from these categories, equaling the average of each category (e.g., 1–5 category equals 3).
Hours working off campus	Students' reports of the number of hours spent working off campus in a typical week. Response categories were 0, 1–5, 6–10, 11–15, 16–20, and 20+. Continuous variable created from these categories, equaling the average of each category (e.g., 1–5 category equals 3).
Hours working for pay	Sum of students' reports of the number of hours spent working on and off campus.
Not working for pay	Dummy variable indicating that students were working zero hours on or off campus.
Hours volunteering	Students' reports of the number of hours spent volunteering in a typical week. Response categories were 0, 1–5, 6–10, 11–15, 16–20, and 20+. Continuous variable created from these categories, equaling the average of each category (e.g., 1–5 category equals 3).
Hours in student clubs	Students' reports of the number of hours spent in student clubs in a typical week. Response categories were 0, 1–5, 6–10, 11–15, 16–20, and 20+. Continuous variable created from these categories, equaling the average of each category (e.g., 1–5 category equals 3).
Hours in fraternities/sororities	Students' reports of the number of hours spent in fraternities/sororities in a typical week. Response categories were 0, 1–5, 6–10, 11–15, 16–20, and 20+. Continuous variable created from these categories, equaling the average of each category (e.g., 1–5 category equals 3).
Hours in extracurricular activities	Sum of students' reports of the number of hours spent working on campus, working off campus, volunteering, in student clubs, and in fraternities/sororities.

Variable name	Variable coding
College major	Dummy variables indicating students' self-reported majors or expected majors, aggregated into the following broad categories: business (reference), education/social work, engineering/computer science, communications, health, social science/humanities, science/mathematics, and other.
Course concentrations	Course concentration was defined as taking greater than one standard deviation above the mean of the percentage of courses in a given subject area (business, education/social work, engineering/computer science, communications, health, social science/humanities, and science/mathematics). Students taking fewer than that percentage represented the reference category for each concentration. Course-taking patterns were evaluated using transcript data collected from participating institutions.
College location/context	
College selectivity	Institutional measure of the average combined math and verbal SAT scores at the 25th percentile for the incoming freshman class at each institution. Data on SAT scores were obtained from the Integrated Postsecondary Education Data System (IPEDS) database. For certain analyses, dummy variables indicating highly selective, selective, and less selective (reference) institutions were used. Highly selective colleges were defined as schools with students scoring higher than 1,150 on their combined SAT at the 25th percentile; less selective colleges were defined as schools with students scoring lower than 950 on their combined SAT at the 25th percentile. Selective schools fell between these cutoffs.
Dorm residence	Dummy variable indicating that students reported living in "university housing (on or off campus)."
College financing	
Percentage of college costs covered by grants/scholarships	Students' reports of the percentage of college costs covered by grants and scholarships in the current semester. Response categories were 0–9, 10–39, 40–59, 60–89, and 90–100%. A continuous measure was then created by taking the average of the response category (e.g., 0–9 equals 4.5%).

Variable name	Variable coding
Percentage of college costs covered by loans	Students' reports of the percentage of college costs covered by loans in the current semester. Response categories were 0–9, 10–39, 40–59, 60–89, and 90–100%. A continuous measure was then created by taking the average of the response category (e.g., 0–9 equals 4.5%).

Academic preparation

SAT/ACT	Students' average combined math and verbal SAT scores (or ACT scores converted to an SAT scale, if SAT scores were not available) as reported by participating colleges. In addition to the continuous variable, for certain analyses, dummy variables were created indicating students in the top quintile, middle 3 quintiles, and bottom quintile (reference) of the test score distribution.
High school GPA	Students' high school GPA on a 4.0 scale reported by participating institutions. High school GPAs reported to colleges on a 0–100 scale converted to a 4.0 scale. If the college-reported high school GPA was missing, students' self-reported high school grades were used. In addition to the continuous variables, dummy variables were created to indicate students in the top quintile, middle 3 quintiles, and bottom quintile (reference) of the high school GPA distribution.
Advanced placement courses	Dummy variables indicating the number of advanced placement classes students reported taking in high school: 0 (reference), 1, 2, 3, 4, or more than 4.

Sociodemographic characteristics

Parental education	Dummy variables indicating the highest degree attained by either parent and categorized into high school or less (reference), some college (includes associate and technical degrees), bachelor's degree, and graduate/professional degree.
Parental occupation	Dummy variables indicating parental occupation in skilled manual (reference), professional/managerial, routine nonmanual, petty bourgeoisie, and unskilled categories. Parental occupation data was collected from student open-ended reports and coded using the Erikson-Goldthorpe-Portocarero (EGP) occupational coding schema. Final variable equaled father's occupation if available, mother's occupation otherwise.

Variable name	Variable coding
Race/ethnicity	Dummy variables indicating students' self-reported race/ethnicity, categorized as white (reference), African-American, Asian, Hispanic, or other racial/ ethnic group.
Male	Dummy variable indicating that student's gender is male.
Non-English home language	Dummy variable indicating students who reported that English was not the primary language spoken in their home growing up.
Two-parent household	Dummy variable indicating that students reported living in a two-parent household (i.e., with their mother and father, mother and male guardian, or father and female guardian) at age 16.
Number of siblings	Continuous variable of the number of self-reported siblings (capped at 4).
High school characteristics	
70% or more non-white	Dummy variable indicating that students' high schools enrolled 70% or more non-white students (i.e., American Indians/Alaskan Natives, Asians/Pacific Islanders, Hispanics, and/or African-Americans).
Urbanicity	Dummy variables indicating the urbanicity of students' high schools divided into suburban (reference), urban, and rural settings based on the National Center for Education Statistics (NCES) classifications. Urban settings include large and midsize cities. Suburban settings include urban fringes of a large or midsize city, large towns, and small towns. Rural settings include areas defined as rural by the U.S. Census Bureau.
Geographic region	Dummy variables indicating that students' high schools were in the Northeast (reference), Midwest, South, or West based on the U. S. Census Bureau's region codes.

Table A2.1. 2005 and 2007 CLA performance

	2005 CLA score		2007 CLA score		2007–05 change in CLA score	
	Mean (SD)	Score gap from comparison category	Mean (SD)	Score gap from comparison category	Mean (SD)	Score gap from comparison category
Sociodemographic and high school characteristics						
Parents' education: high school or less†	1063.34 (177.75)		1102.01 (186.40)		38.67 (201.72)	
Parents' education: some college	1083.18 (177.18)	19.84	1116.50 (200.09)	14.49	33.32 (199.80)	−5.35
Parents' education: bachelor's degree	1139.61 (179.46)	76.27**	1171.11 (207.87)	69.10**	31.50 (210.76)	−7.17
Parents' education: graduate/professional degree	1183.36 (188.94)	120.02**	1218.42 (215.91)	116.41**	35.06 (218.58)	−3.61
African-American	994.59 (167.15)	−175.80**	1001.35 (164.40)	−210.12**	6.76 (187.12)	−34.32*
Asian	1118.67 (174.82)	−51.72**	1145.68 (188.30)	−65.79**	27.01 (197.57)	−14.07
Hispanic	1102.67 (172.90)	−67.72**	1151.77 (186.69)	−59.70*	49.10 (213.75)	8.02
Other racial/ethnic group	1108.05 (194.72)	−62.34*	1137.23 (197.25)	−74.24**	29.18 (213.02)	−11.90

White†	1170.39 (178.96)		1211.47 (207.13)		41.08 (215.75)	
Male	1139.39 (192.10)	−11.91	1173.18 (208.34)	−11.05	33.79 (212.21)	−0.86
Female†	1127.48 (185.03)		1162.13 (212.63)		34.65 (208.46)	
Non-English home language	1101.22 (181.90)	−35.14	1124.30 (176.65)	−48.00*	23.08 (202.55)	−12.86
English home language†	1136.36 (188.21)		1172.30 (214.92)		35.94 (210.85)	
High school 70% or more non-white	1047.07 (166.88)	−98.75**	1068.58 (187.50)	−114.93**	21.51 (193.05)	−16.18
High school less than 70% non-white†	1145.82 (186.93)		1183.51 (209.50)		37.69 (212.34)	
Academic preparation						
Took 0 AP courses†	1053.26 (179.71)		1100.27 (195.37)		47.01 (198.50)	
Took 1 AP course	1109.20 (175.36)	55.94**	1139.06 (187.59)	38.79*	29.86 (205.10)	−17.15
Took 2 AP courses	1120.31 (178.01)	67.05**	1147.07 (202.70)	46.80*	26.76 (208.21)	−20.25
Took 3 AP courses	1160.30 (166.36)	107.04**	1171.69 (202.90)	71.42**	11.39 (195.82)	−35.62*

	2005 CLA score		2007 CLA score		2007–05 change in CLA score	
	Mean (SD)	Score gap from comparison category	Mean (SD)	Score gap from comparison category	Mean (SD)	Score gap from comparison category
Took 4 AP courses	1194.37 (173.51)	141.11**	1220.90 (208.22)	120.63**	26.53 (223.33)	−20.48
Took more than 4 AP courses	1228.20 (182.84)	174.94**	1275.21 (220.15)	174.94**	47.01 (231.77)	0.00
Top quintile HS GPA	1198.70 (175.31)	169.15**	1236.79 (200.88)	176.07**	38.09 (206.43)	6.92
Middle (3) quintiles HS GPA	1144.10 (179.01)	114.55**	1178.51 (208.54)	117.79**	34.41 (214.84)	3.24
Bottom quintile HS GPA†	1029.55 (184.69)		1060.72 (187.80)		31.17 (197.35)	
Top quintile SAT/ACT performance	1277.72 (168.46)	285.49**	1330.34 (207.52)	322.25**	52.62 (238.70)	36.76
Middle (3) quintiles SAT/ACT performance	1126.12 (163.74)	133.89**	1159.28 (183.56)	151.19**	33.16 (206.79)	17.30
Bottom quintile SAT/ACT performance†	992.23 (159.42)		1008.09 (159.23)		15.86 (182.95)	
All students	1131.94 (187.76)		1166.26 (211.06)		34.32 (209.82)	

*p < .05, **p < .01 (differences from comparison category). Significance tests are adjusted for clustering of students within schools.
† Comparison category.

Table A2.2. Percentage of students in different categories of academic preparation, by sociodemographic and high school characteristics

	AP courses taken in high school				High school GPA quintiles			SAT/ACT performance quintiles		
	0	1 or 2	3 or 4	More than 4	top	middle	bottom	top	middle	bottom
Sociodemographic and high school characteristics										
Parents' education: high school or less†	37.00	34.56	18.35	10.09	13.33	51.52	35.15	7.90	51.06	41.03
Parents' education: some college	33.80	40.44	16.70	9.05	17.14	57.06	25.81	7.88	63.43**	28.69**
Parents' education: bachelor's degree	27.22*	33.23	22.56**	16.99**	19.70**	63.58**	16.72**	21.01**	64.53*	14.46**
Parents' education: graduate/professional degree	18.83**	27.51	25.79**	27.87**	24.39**	62.56**	13.05**	34.60**	56.85	8.56**
African-American	44.93**	34.20*	13.62**	7.25**	9.20**	42.24**	48.56**	2.02*	38.90*	59.08**
Asian	19.09	28.63	28.22	24.07	17.50	61.25	21.25	19.25	64.02	16.74
Hispanic	21.77	40.32	19.35	18.55	12.70**	50.00*	37.30*	7.94**	56.35	35.71**
Other racial/ethnic group	23.01	31.86	25.66	19.47	14.04*	61.40	24.56	24.56	54.39*	21.05*
White†	25.00	32.80	22.65	19.56	23.79	64.88	11.33	26.69	64.52	8.79

Male	26.57	33.06	20.30	20.07	17.97*	59.22	22.81*	24.31*	59.79	15.90
Female†	27.40	32.85	22.77	16.98	21.01	60.67	18.32	19.19	59.63	21.19
Non-English home language	25.78	34.15	21.25	18.82	15.12	56.70	28.18	14.48	59.66	25.86
English home language†	27.27	32.76	21.94	18.03	20.55	60.62	18.83	22.05	59.69	18.25
High school 70% or more non-white	24.50	35.23	25.84	14.43	13.04**	47.49**	39.46**	8.42*	48.48*	43.10**
High school less than 70% non-white†	26.33	32.79	21.84	19.05	21.89	61.80	16.31	22.78	61.56	15.66
All students	27.09	32.93	21.85	18.13	19.87	60.13	20.00	21.20	59.69	19.21

*p < .05, **p < .01 (differences from comparison category). Significance tests are adjusted for clustering of students within schools.
† Comparison category.
Note: Percentages of students in different categories of academic preparation are calculated separately for each sociodemographic/high school group.

Table A2.3. Predicted 2007 CLA score gaps across groups, adjusted for different characteristics (selected results)

	Predicted 2007 CLA score gaps		
	Adjusted for 2005 CLA score	Adjusted for 2005 CLA score and social background	Adjusted for 2005 CLA score, social background, and academic preparation
Sociodemographic and high school characteristics			
Parents' education: high school or less[†]			
Parents' education: some college	4.28	5.31	−3.05
Parents' education: bachelor's degree	32.00*	18.29	−5.24
Parents' education: graduate/professional degree	58.47**	42.10*	1.35
African-American	−135.69 **	−105.52 **	−47.06*
Asian	−43.88**	−31.40*	−22.58[t]
Hispanic	−31.03	−8.40	17.92
Other racial/ethnic group	−47.85*	−41.91*	−27.79
White[†]			
Male	5.01	−0.75	−8.82
Female[†]			
Non-English home language	−30.29[t]	−28.92*	−19.40
English home language[†]			
High school 70% or more non-white	−64.65**	−29.19*	−17.72
High school less than 70% non-white[†]			
Academic preparation			
Took 0 AP courses[†]			
Took 1 AP course	13.59		
Took 2 AP courses	16.60		
Took 3 AP courses	23.20		

	Predicted 2007 CLA score gaps		
	Adjusted for 2005 CLA score	Adjusted for 2005 CLA score and social background	Adjusted for 2005 CLA score, social background, and academic preparation
Took more than 4 AP courses	96.14**		
Top quintile HS GPA	98.94**		
Middle (3) quintiles HS GPA	65.56**		
Bottom quintile HS GPA[†]			
Top quintile SAT/ACT performance	231.38**		
Middle (3) quintiles SAT/ACT performance	108.57**		
Bottom quintile SAT/ ACT performance[†]			

[†]$p < .10$, *$p < .05$, **$p < .01$ (differences from comparison category).

[†] Comparison category.

Note: Results are based on regression models predicting 2007 CLA scores, run separately for each measure of socio-demographic/high school characteristics and academic preparation. Social background variables include sociodemographic characteristics (gender, race/ethnicity, parental education and occupation, non-English home language, two-parent household, and number of siblings) and high school characteristics (region, urbanicity, and high school 70% or more non-white). Academic preparation includes SAT/ACT scores, number of AP courses taken, and high school GPA. Analyses are adjusted for clustering of students within schools.

Table A2.4. Percentages of students attending different college institutional contexts

| | Institutional context | | |
	Highly selective	Selective	Less selective
Sociodemographic and high school characteristics			
Parents' education: high school or less[†]	7.62	49.01	43.38
Parents' education: some college	9.62	52.57	37.81
Parents' education: bachelor's degree	21.23*	56.89	21.88**
Parents' education: graduate/professional degree	44.19**	45.21	10.60**
African-American	4.23*	29.31	66.47**
Asian	18.53	53.45	28.02
Hispanic	23.53	39.50	36.97
Other racial/ethnic group	27.36	45.28	27.36
White[†]	31.43	56.70	11.87
Non-English home language	26.95	40.43	32.62
English home language[†]	24.96	52.16	22.88
Male	24.42	50.43	25.15
Female[†]	25.71	50.75	23.54
High school 70% or more non-white	5.99*	35.92	58.10*
High school less than 70% non-white[†]	26.32	54.43	19.25
Academic preparation			
Took 0 AP courses[†]	12.61	48.65	38.74
Took 1 AP course	13.06	56.97	29.97
Took 2 AP courses	20.22	55.34	24.44*
Took 3 AP courses	23.08	58.97	17.95*
Took 4 AP courses	35.05*	53.27	11.68*
Took more than 4 AP courses	52.58**	37.59	9.83*
Top quintile HS GPA	35.07*	57.69	7.24**
Middle (3) quintiles HS GPA	28.30*	53.75	17.94**
Bottom quintile HS GPA[†]	6.53	34.68	58.78
Top quintile SAT/ACT performance	65.42**	31.25	3.33**
Middle (3) quintiles SAT/ACT performance	18.01	63.73*	18.25**
Bottom quintile SAT/ACT performance[†]	0.48	34.05	65.48
All students	25.22	50.63	24.15

*p < .05, **p < .01 (differences from comparison category).
† Comparison category.
Note: Percentages of students in different college institutional contexts are calculated separately for each sociode-mographic/high school characteristic and academic preparation category.
Significance tests are based on regression models estimating entry into different institutional types, with "less selective" serving as a reference category, and are adjusted for clustering of students within schools.

Table A3.1. Students' perceptions of and interactions with faculty

	Faculty are approachable[†††]	Faculty have high standards[†††]	Faculty have high expectations[†††]	Number of times met with faculty	Never met with faculty
Sociodemographic and high school characteristics					
African-American	−0.24**	−0.13*	−0.12**	3.50	0.10
	(1.17)	(1.13)	(1.17)	(2.40)	
Asian	−0.20*	−0.20**	−0.29**	3.37	0.14*
	(1.12)	(1.06)	(1.18)	(2.51)	
Hispanic	−0.06	−0.11	−0.11**	3.10	0.13
	(1.01)	(1.02)	(1.14)	(2.39)	
White[†]	0.10	0.08	0.09	3.67	0.07
	(0.91)	(0.94)	(0.89)	(2.36)	
Other racial/ethnic group	−0.14	−0.08	−0.05	3.75	0.09
	(1.11)	(1.05)	(1.06)	(2.50)	
Parents' education: high school or less[†]	−0.21	−0.23	−0.17	2.94	0.14
	(1.09)	(1.10)	(1.11)	(2.24)	
Parents' education: some college	−0.05	−0.08	−0.05	3.21	0.10
	(0.95)	(0.98)	(0.99)	(2.25)	
Parents' education: bachelor's degree	0.02**	0.02**	0.01*	3.55**	0.09
	(0.99)	(0.98)	(0.97)	(2.40)	
Parents' education: graduate/professional degree	0.10**	0.12**	0.09**	4.11**	0.05**
	(0.98)	(0.97)	(0.98)	(2.43)	

English home language†	0.02 (0.97)	0.02 (0.99)	0.04 (0.96)	3.62 (2.38)	0.08
Non-English home language	−0.13 (1.16)	−0.16 (1.06)	−0.27** (1.22)	3.34 (2.49)	0.12
Male	0.04 (1.03)	−0.04 (1.00)	−0.02 (1.01)	3.71 (2.47)	0.09
Female†	−0.02 (0.98)	0.03 (1.00)	0.01 (0.99)	3.51 (2.35)	0.09
High school less than 70% non-white†	0.03 (0.97)	0.03 (0.98)	0.04 (0.95)	3.63 (2.37)	0.08
High school 70% or more non-white	−0.23** (1.10)	−0.17 (1.07)	−0.18* (1.17)	3.15 (2.36)	0.11
Academic preparation					
Top quintile SAT/ACT performance	0.24** (0.86)	0.13 (0.92)	0.19** (0.85)	4.03* (2.33)	0.05*
Middle (3) quintiles SAT/ACT performance	−0.01* (0.98)	0.02* (0.97)	0.01** (0.97)	3.56 (2.43)	0.09
Bottom quintile SAT/ACT performance†	−0.22 (1.11)	−0.18 (1.11)	−0.23 (1.15)	3.14 (2.25)	0.12
College institutional context					
Highly selective college	0.20 (0.93)	0.26 (0.93)	0.16 (0.92)	4.28* (2.29)	0.02**

	Faculty are approachable[†††]	Faculty have high standards[†††]	Faculty have high expectations[†††]	Number of times met with faculty	Never met with faculty
Selective college	0.01*	−0.03*	−0.01	3.46	0.10
	(0.97)	(0.96)	(0.98)	(2.40)	
Less selective college[†]	−0.24	−0.21	−0.13	3.15	0.13
	(1.10)	(1.09)	(1.12)	(2.34)	
All students	0.00	0.00	0.00	3.58	0.09
	(1.00)	(1.00)	(1.00)	(2.40)	
Proportion variance across schools (intercept model)	0.104	0.136	0.080	0.116	0.041
Proportion variance across schools (w/ covariates)[††]	0.072	0.153	0.063	0.086	0.029
Proportion variance across schools (w/ selectivity and covariates)	0.064	0.090	0.060	0.068	0.020
R-squared w/ covariates[††]	0.073	0.062	0.059	0.064	0.026
R-squared w/ covariates and school fixed effects	0.133	0.156	0.113	0.128	0.055

*$p < .05$, **$p < .01$ (differences from comparison category). Significance tests are adjusted for clustering of students within schools.

[†] Comparison category.

[††] Covariates include sociodemographic characteristics (gender, race/ethnicity, parental education and occupation, non-English home language, two-parent household, and number of siblings), high school characteristics (region, urbanicity, and high school 70% or more non-white), and academic preparation (SAT/ACT scores, number of AP courses taken, and high school GPA).

[†††] Variables are standardized with a mean of 0 and standard deviation of 1.

Table A3.2. Students' perceptions of and interactions with peers

	Students have high expectations[†††]	Students help others succeed[†††]	Students work hard to succeed[†††]	Percentage of time studying with peers
Sociodemographic and high school characteristics				
African-American	−0.13	−0.12	−0.02	0.30
	(1.01)	(1.11)	(1.04)	(0.22)
Asian	−0.09	0.01	−0.10	0.29
	(1.04)	(0.94)	(1.06)	(0.20)
Hispanic	0.01	−0.19*	0.07	0.26
	(1.05)	(1.16)	(1.08)	(0.22)
White[†]	0.05	0.06	0.02	0.27
	(0.99)	(0.96)	(0.98)	(0.21)
Other racial/ethnic group	−0.12	−0.19**	−0.07	0.27
	(0.95)	(1.07)	(0.95)	(0.19)
Parents' education: high school or less[†]	−0.19	−0.21	−0.11	0.27
	(1.01)	(1.05)	(1.01)	(0.21)
Parents' education: some college	−0.11	−0.04*	−0.09	0.29
	(0.96)	(1.00)	(0.98)	(0.22)
Parents' education: bachelor's degree	0.00*	0.05**	0.00	0.28
	(0.99)	(0.95)	(0.95)	(0.21)
Parents' education: graduate/professional degree	0.14*	0.06**	0.09	0.28
	(1.02)	(1.01)	(1.04)	(0.20)

	(1)	(2)	(3)	(4)
English home language†	0.00	0.02	−0.01	0.28
	(1.00)	(0.99)	(1.00)	(0.21)
Non-English home language	0.03	−0.17*	0.06	0.28
	(1.03)	(1.06)	(1.03)	(0.22)
Male	−0.07	0.05	−0.03	0.29
	(1.03)	(1.01)	(0.98)	(0.22)
Female†	0.04	−0.03	0.02	0.27
	(0.98)	(1.00)	(1.01)	(0.20)
High school less than 70% non-white†	0.01	0.04	0.01	0.28
	(1.00)	(0.99)	(0.98)	(0.20)
High school 70% or more non-white	−0.13	−0.15	−0.04	0.26
	(1.02)	(1.06)	(1.05)	(0.22)
Academic preparation				
Top quintile SAT/ACT performance	0.23	0.14	0.12	0.25**
	(0.99)	(1.01)	(0.96)	(0.20)
Middle (3) quintiles SAT/ACT performance	−0.02	−0.01	−0.03	0.28
	(0.99)	(0.97)	(1.00)	(0.21)
Bottom quintile SAT/ACT performance†	−0.17	−0.10	−0.01	0.31
	(0.97)	(1.06)	(1.01)	(0.22)
College institutional context				
Highly selective college	0.48*	0.10	0.31	0.26
	(0.92)	(1.02)	(0.96)	(0.19)

	Students have high expectations[†††]	Students help others succeed[†††]	Students work hard to succeed[†††]	Percentage of time studying with peers
Selective college	-0.09	-0.01	-0.07	0.28
	(0.97)	(0.97)	(0.97)	(0.21)
Less selective college[†]	-0.28	-0.07	-0.15	0.29
	(0.99)	(1.05)	(1.05)	(0.22)
All students	0.00	0.00	0.00	0.28
	(1.00)	(1.00)	(1.00)	(0.21)
Proportion variance across schools (intercept model)	0.208	0.073	0.152	0.018
Proportion variance across schools (w/ covariates)[††]	0.248	0.058	0.217	0.043
Proportion variance across schools (w/ selectivity and covariates)	0.116	0.054	0.110	0.011
R-squared w/ covariates[††]	0.076	0.057	0.046	0.025
R-squared w/ covariates and school fixed effects	0.224	0.111	0.188	0.042

*p < .05, **p < .01 (differences from comparison category). Significance tests are adjusted for clustering of students within schools.

[†] Comparison category.

[††] Covariates include sociodemographic characteristics (gender, race/ethnicity, parental education and occupation, non-English home language, two-parent household, and number of siblings), high school characteristics (region, urbanicity, and high school 70% or more non-white), and academic preparation. (SAT/ACT scores, number of AP courses taken, and high school GPA).

[†††] Variables are standardized with a mean of 0 and standard deviation of 1.

Table A3.3. Students' self-reported reading/writing course requirements and time spent studying

	Hours per week studying	Took course with more than 20 pages of writing	Took course with more than 40 pages of reading per week	Took course(s) with both requirements	Took course(s) with neither requirement
Sociodemographic and high school characteristics					
African-American	10.54* (7.46)	0.42*	0.56*	0.32**	0.34*
Asian	12.99 (8.00)	0.44	0.64	0.39	0.30
Hispanic	11.40 (7.50)	0.46	0.70	0.40	0.24
White†	12.35 (7.42)	0.54	0.71	0.46	0.22
Other racial/ethnic group	13.52 (9.19)	0.48	0.74	0.45	0.23
Parents' education: high school or less†	11.34 (7.05)	0.40	0.58	0.33	0.35
Parents' education: some college	10.51 (7.33)	0.45	0.57	0.36	0.34
Parents' education: bachelor's degree	12.04 (7.61)	0.50*	0.69**	0.42*	0.23*
Parents' education: graduate/professional degree	13.58** (7.79)	0.58**	0.78**	0.53**	0.16**

English home language[†]	11.99 (7.45)	0.51	0.68	0.43	0.24
Non-English home language	13.25* (8.65)	0.47	0.66	0.43	0.30
Male	11.79 (7.46)	0.53	0.66	0.45	0.26
Female[†]	12.36 (7.71)	0.49	0.69	0.42	0.24
High school less than 70% non-white[†]	12.24 (7.52)	0.51	0.68	0.43	0.24
High school 70% or more non-white	11.27 (8.40)	0.40**	0.59	0.33*	0.34*
Academic preparation					
Top quintile SAT/ACT performance	13.91** (7.67)	0.62**	0.85**	0.60**	0.13**
Middle (3) quintiles SAT/ACT performance	12.02** (7.56)	0.49	0.67**	0.41*	0.25*
Bottom quintile SAT/ACT performance[†]	10.55 (7.34)	0.42	0.53	0.31	0.36
College institutional context					
Highly selective college	15.20** (7.78)	0.71**	0.92**	0.68**	0.05**

	Hours per week studying	Took course with more than 20 pages of writing	Took course with more than 40 pages of reading per week	Took course(s) with both requirements	Took course(s) with neither requirement
Selective college	11.48 (7.27)	0.46	0.62	0.37	0.29
Less selective college[†]	10.57 (7.42)	0.39	0.56	0.31	0.35
All students	12.15 (7.62)	0.50	0.68	0.43	0.25
Proportion variance across schools (intercept model)	0.106	0.086	0.133	0.110	0.106
Proportion variance across schools (w/ covariates)[††]	0.100	0.082	0.092	0.090	0.082
Proportion variance across schools (w/ selectivity and covariates)	0.048	0.046	0.051	0.050	0.040
R-squared w/ covariates[††]	0.074	0.054	0.097	0.077	0.078
R-squared w/ covariates and school fixed effects	0.138	0.113	0.163	0.141	0.134

$*p < .05, **p < .01$ (differences from comparison category). Significance tests are adjusted for clustering of students within schools.

[†] Comparison category.

[††] Covariates include sociodemographic characteristics (gender, race/ethnicity, parental education and occupation, non-English home language, two-parent household, and number of siblings), high school characteristics (region, urbanicity, and high school 70% or more non-white), and academic preparation (SAT/ACT scores, number of AP courses taken, and high school GPA).

Table A3.4. Students' transcript-identified college GPA and course-taking patterns (percentages of courses through sophomore year)

	College GPA	Business	Education and social work	Engineering and computer science	Communications	Health	Science and mathematics	Humanities and social sciences
Sociodemographic and high school characteristics								
African-American	2.91**	0.03	0.05	0.03	0.04	0.03	0.23	0.46
	(0.51)	(0.09)	(0.09)	(0.07)	(0.07)	(0.07)	(0.21)	(0.22)
Asian	3.22	0.05	0.01**	0.06	0.03	0.02	0.33**	0.41
	(0.42)	(0.12)	(0.04)	(0.14)	(0.07)	(0.04)	(0.22)	(0.25)
Hispanic	3.03**	0.04	0.03	0.05	0.03	0.01	0.23	0.53
	(0.43)	(0.11)	(0.06)	(0.12)	(0.04)	(0.06)	(0.20)	(0.25)
White[†]	3.29	0.04	0.03	0.05	0.03	0.03	0.23	0.49
	(0.45)	(0.10)	(0.08)	(0.11)	(0.07)	(0.07)	(0.18)	(0.24)
Other racial/ethnic group	3.22	0.04	0.02	0.05	0.03	0.01*	0.22	0.53
	(0.45)	(0.08)	(0.06)	(0.13)	(0.07)	(0.03)	(0.21)	(0.26)
Parents' education: high school or less[†]	3.07	0.05	0.04	0.05	0.03	0.03	0.25	0.45
	(0.49)	(0.11)	(0.09)	(0.12)	(0.07)	(0.07)	(0.19)	(0.23)
Parents' education: some college	3.08	0.05	0.05*	0.04	0.04	0.03	0.23	0.45
	(0.49)	(0.11)	(0.10)	(0.11)	(0.07)	(0.07)	(0.19)	(0.23)
Parents' education: bachelor's degree	3.23**	0.04	0.03	0.05	0.03	0.03	0.25	0.47
	(0.47)	(0.09)	(0.06)	(0.12)	(0.08)	(0.07)	(0.21)	(0.24)
Parents' education: graduate/professional degree	3.31**	0.04	0.02	0.04	0.03	0.02	0.24	0.53*
	(0.45)	(0.09)	(0.07)	(0.11)	(0.07)	(0.05)	(0.19)	(0.24)

English home language†	3.21 (0.48)	0.04 (0.10)	0.03 (0.08)	0.04 (0.11)	0.03 (0.07)	0.03 (0.07)	0.24 (0.19)	0.49 (0.23)
Non-English home language	3.19 (0.43)	0.04 (0.11)	0.02* (0.06)	0.07 (0.15)	0.02* (0.04)	0.01* (0.05)	0.23 (0.20)	0.48 (0.28)
Male	3.15* (0.49)	0.05** (0.11)	0.02** (0.05)	0.08** (0.15)	0.03 (0.06)	0.01** (0.04)	0.26** (0.19)	0.45** (0.24)
Female†	3.23 (0.47)	0.03 (0.09)	0.04 (0.09)	0.02 (0.08)	0.03 (0.08)	0.03 (0.07)	0.23 (0.20)	0.51 (0.24)
High school less than 70% non-white†	3.23 (0.47)	0.04 (0.10)	0.03 (0.08)	0.04 (0.11)	0.03 (0.07)	0.03 (0.07)	0.24 (0.19)	0.48 (0.24)
High school 70% or more non-white	2.99** (0.48)	0.04 (0.11)	0.03 (0.07)	0.05 (0.11)	0.03 (0.04)	0.02 (0.06)	0.29* (0.23)	0.45 (0.24)
Academic preparation								
Top quintile SAT/ACT performance	3.51** (0.37)	0.02 (0.07)	0.01** (0.03)	0.04 (0.11)	0.02* (0.05)	0.01 (0.04)	0.24 (0.18)	0.57* (0.24)
Middle (3) quintiles SAT/ACT performance	3.20** (0.44)	0.05 (0.11)	0.03 (0.08)	0.05 (0.12)	0.03 (0.07)	0.03 (0.07)	0.25* (0.21)	0.46 (0.24)
Bottom quintile SAT/ACT performance†	2.88 (0.47)	0.05 (0.11)	0.05 (0.10)	0.04 (0.09)	0.04 (0.08)	0.03 (0.07)	0.21 (0.18)	0.46 (0.21)
College institutional context								
Highly selective college	3.43** (0.38)	0.02 (0.06)	0.01 (0.04)	0.01 (0.04)	0.01* (0.05)	0.01 (0.03)	0.20 (0.17)	0.66** (0.19)

	College GPA	Business	Education and social work	Engineering and computer science	Communications	Health	Science and mathematics	Humanities and social sciences
Selective college	3.18	0.05	0.03	0.06	0.03	0.03	0.27	0.43
	(0.47)	(0.10)	(0.08)	(0.13)	(0.08)	(0.07)	(0.20)	(0.23)
Less selective college[†]	3.01	0.05	0.05	0.05	0.04	0.03	0.23	0.41
	(0.50)	(0.12)	(0.09)	(0.12)	(0.07)	(0.06)	(0.21)	(0.22)
All students	3.20	0.04	0.03	0.04	0.03	0.02	0.24	0.48
	(0.48)	(0.10)	(0.08)	(0.11)	(0.07)	(0.06)	(0.20)	(0.24)
Proportion variance across schools (intercept model)	0.134	0.077	0.153	0.138	0.084	0.111	0.076	0.255
Proportion variance across schools (w/ covariates)[††]	0.116	0.060	0.116	0.160	0.081	0.114	0.072	0.257
Proportion variance across schools (w/ selectivity and covariates)	0.074	0.056	0.116	0.115	0.066	0.117	0.064	0.150
R-squared w/ covariates[††]	0.316	0.050	0.097	0.109	0.048	0.064	0.068	0.147
R-squared w/ covariates and school fixed effects	0.341	0.099	0.151	0.212	0.100	0.154	0.137	0.310

*$p < .05$, **$p < .01$ (differences from comparison category). Significance tests are adjusted for clustering of students within schools.

[†] Comparison category.

[††] Covariates include sociodemographic characteristics (gender, race/ethnicity, parental education and occupation, non-English home language, two-parent household, and number of siblings), high school characteristics (region, urbanicity, and high school 70% or more non-white), and academic preparation (SAT/ACT scores, number of AP courses taken, and high school GPA).

Table A3.5. Students' self-reported number of times met with faculty, time spent studying, and reading/writing course requirements, by course subject concentration

	Number of times met with faculty	Hours per week spent studying	Took course with more than 20 pages of writing	Took course with more than 40 pages of reading per week	Took course(s) with both requirements	Took course(s) with neither requirement
Business courses						
Concentrator (> 13.6% courses)	3.34 (2.44)	9.55** (5.66)	0.47	0.58**	0.38	0.33*
Non-concentrator†	3.65 (2.39)	12.44 (7.74)	0.52	0.69	0.44	0.24
Education and social work courses						
Concentrator (> 10.6% courses)	3.35 (2.35)	10.64** (7.27)	0.45	0.61	0.38	0.33*
Non-concentrator†	3.60 (2.40)	12.28 (7.60)	0.52	0.68	0.44	0.24
Engineering and computer science courses						
Concentrator (> 15.1% courses)	3.74 (2.59)	12.69 (8.11)	0.34**	0.45**	0.26**	0.48**
Non-concentrator†	3.65 (2.37)	12.04 (7.52)	0.53	0.70	0.45	0.23
Communications courses						
Concentrator (> 9.7% courses)	3.20 (2.36)	10.51* (6.98)	0.57	0.67	0.47	0.23

Non-concentrator[†]	3.65 (2.39)	12.23 (7.61)	0.51	0.67	0.43	0.25
Health courses						
Concentrator (> 8.4% courses)	2.90** (2.01)	13.17 (8.00)	0.39	0.55**	0.25**	0.31
Non-concentrator[†]	3.69 (2.42)	12.00 (7.53)	0.52	0.68	0.45	0.25
Social science and humanities courses						
Concentrator (> 71.1% courses)	3.71 (2.31)	12.44 (7.75)	0.68**	0.88**	0.64**	0.08**
Non-concentrator[†]	3.59 (2.42)	12.01 (7.53)	0.47	0.62	0.38	0.30
Science and mathematics courses						
Concentrator (> 42.7% courses)	4.03* (2.47)	14.70** (8.23)	0.43	0.62	0.35*	0.31
Non-concentrator[†]	3.52 (2.37)	11.49 (7.28)	0.53	0.69	0.46	0.24

*$p < .05$, **$p < .01$ (differences from comparison category). Significance tests are adjusted for clustering of students within schools.
[†] Comparison category.
Note: Course concentration is defined as greater than one standard deviation above the mean percentage of courses taken in the specific subject area.

Table A3.6. Students' dormitory residence and time spent in extracurricular activities

	Dormitory residence	Hours in fraternity/sorority	Hours in student clubs	Hours volunteering
Sociodemographic and high school characteristics				
African-American	0.70	0.64**	3.04	2.59
		(2.73)	(4.52)	(3.75)
Asian	0.58	1.56	3.02*	2.55
		(4.08)	(4.61)	(4.19)
Hispanic	0.49	0.68**	3.22	2.15
		(2.24)	(4.62)	(3.61)
White[†]	0.73	1.98	3.94	2.15
		(5.08)	(4.97)	(3.14)
Other racial/ethnic group	0.67	1.45	4.69	2.65
		(4.31)	(5.65)	(3.63)
Parents' education: high school or less[†]	0.55	1.02	2.42	2.06
		(3.55)	(3.91)	(3.06)
Parents' education: some college	0.65	1.45	3.39**	2.23
		(4.44)	(5.06)	(3.34)
Parents' education: bachelor's degree	0.67	1.66	3.55**	2.29
		(4.59)	(4.72)	(3.49)
Parents' education: graduate/professional degree	0.80**	1.98*	4.55**	2.40
		(4.94)	(5.17)	(3.52)

English home language†	0.71	1.68 (4.64)	3.77 (4.97)	2.25 (3.37)
Non-English home language	0.57	1.31 (4.02)	3.28 (4.43)	2.53 (3.66)
Male	0.66	1.73 (4.83)	4.12** (5.62)	2.16 (3.56)
Female†	0.72	1.58 (4.40)	3.46 (4.40)	2.36 (3.32)
High school less than 70% non-white†	0.72	1.83 (4.88)	3.82 (4.94)	2.24 (3.29)
High school 70% or more non-white	0.55	0.93* (3.10)	2.93 (4.89)	2.33 (3.92)
Academic preparation				
Top quintile SAT/ACT performance	0.89**	1.18 (3.76)	4.70** (4.96)	2.03 (3.03)
Middle (3) quintiles SAT/ACT performance	0.66	1.92 (4.97)	3.58* (4.88)	2.30 (3.39)
Bottom quintile SAT/ACT performance†	0.58	1.25 (3.99)	3.02 (4.78)	2.52 (3.83)
College institutional context				
Highly selective college	0.99**	1.24 (3.97)	5.11** (5.06)	2.34 (3.27)

		Hours in		
	Dormitory residence	fraternity/sorority	Hours in student clubs	Hours volunteering
Selective college	0.62	2.17	3.51*	2.15
		(5.24)**	(4.90)	(3.21)
Less selective college[†]	0.57	0.76	2.72	2.54
		(2.93)	(4.40)	(3.97)
All students	0.69	1.64	3.71	2.28
		(4.57)	(4.90)	(3.41)
Proportion variance across schools (intercept model)	0.338	0.065	0.046	0.023
Proportion variance across schools (w/ covariates)[††]	0.325	0.060	0.032	0.020
Proportion variance across schools (w/ selectivity and covariates)	0.256	0.060	0.025	0.021
R-squared w/ covariates[††]	0.129	0.042	0.054	0.034
R-squared w/ covariates and school fixed effects	0.368	0.096	0.085	0.059

*$p < .05$, **$p < .01$ (differences from comparison category). Significance tests are adjusted for clustering of students within schools.

[†] signifies comparison category

[††] Covariates include sociodemographic characteristics (gender, race/ethnicity, parental education and occupation, non-English home language, two-parent household, and number of siblings), high school characteristics (region, urbanicity, and high school 70% or more non-white), and academic preparation (SAT/ACT scores, number of AP courses taken, and high school GPA).

Table A3.7. Students' self-reported employment and college financing

	Not working for pay	Hours (per week) working for pay[†††]	Percentage of college costs covered by loans	Percentage of college costs covered by grants/scholarships
Sociodemographic and high school characteristics				
African-American	0.34	14.88**	26.99**	41.05*
		(7.68)	(20.43)	(25.23)
Asian	0.43	12.55	13.80*	39.21
		(7.33)	(15.91)	(27.93)
Hispanic	0.26	15.82**	16.67	43.05*
		(7.02)	(18.30)	(28.83)
White[†]	0.36	11.54	19.66	32.57
		(6.93)	(20.01)	(22.87)
Other racial/ethnic group	0.27	12.85*	18.12	44.04**
		(7.13)	(20.62)	(24.80)
Parents' education: high school or less[†]	0.31	14.60	23.87	43.15
		(7.40)	(21.48)	(26.07)
Parents' education: some college	0.31	13.60	24.93	38.62*
		(6.85)	(20.82)	(23.87)
Parents' education: bachelor's degree	0.35	11.71**	19.53	33.35**
		(7.32)	(20.05)	(24.46)
Parents' education: graduate/professional degree	0.40	11.45**	15.59**	32.46**
		(7.09)	(17.45).	(23.60)

English home language†	0.36	12.37	20.88	34.25
		(7.24)	(20.31)	(23.78)
Non-English home language	0.31	13.30	13.31**	45.85**
		(7.28)	(15.44)	(27.82)
Male	0.41**	12.13	18.10**	35.96
		(6.93)	(18.80)	(25.14)
Female†	0.32	12.67	21.05	35.49
		(7.40)	(20.49)	(24.28)
High school less than 70% non-white†	0.36	12.09	20.59	34.18
		(7.04)	(20.28)	(23.73)
High school 70% or more non-white	0.37	14.84*	18.89	42.23**
		(7.99)	(18.89)	(27.19)
Academic preparation				
Top quintile SAT/ACT performance	0.33	9.85**	14.08**	39.53
		(5.65)	(15.54)	(24.23)
Middle (3) quintiles SAT/ACT performance	0.36	12.73*	20.07*	33.81
		(7.35)	(20.00)	(24.30)
Bottom quintile SAT/ACT performance†	0.38	14.99	26.10	36.95
		(7.65)	(22.05)	(25.33)
College institutional context				
Highly selective college	0.25**	10.21*	15.67	36.69
		(6.17)	(15.44)	(23.30)

	Not working for pay	Hours (per week) working for pay[†††]	Percentage of college costs covered by loans	Percentage of college costs covered by grants/scholarships
Selective college	0.38	12.74	20.48	35.49
		(7.46)	(20.48)	(24.77)
Less selective college[†]	0.40	14.62	23.17	35.04
		(7.23)	(21.92)	(25.47)
All students	0.35	12.48	19.97	35.67
		(7.25)	(19.94)	(24.60)
Proportion variance across schools (intercept model)	0.058	0.131	0.136	0.077
Proportion variance across schools (w/ covariates)[††]	0.065	0.048	0.078	0.088
Proportion variance across schools (w/ selectivity and covariates)	0.046	0.050	0.083	0.091
R-squared w/ covariates[††]	0.050	0.067	0.120	0.154
R-squared w/ covariates and school fixed effects	0.102	0.114	0.173	0.223

*p < .05, **p < .01 (differences from comparison category). Significance tests are adjusted for clustering of students within schools.

[†] Comparison category.

[††] Covariates include sociodemographic characteristics (gender, race/ethnicity, parental education and occupation, non-English home language, two-parent household, and number of siblings), high school characteristics (region, urbanicity, and high school 70% or more non-white), and academic preparation (SAT/ACT scores, number of AP courses taken, and high school GPA).

[†††] Analysis of hours worked conducted only for students reporting that they worked for pay.

Table A4.1. Predicted 2007 CLA scores by students' perceptions of faculty and peers, self-reported interactions with faculty, and reading/writing course requirements

	Predicted 2007 CLA score		
	Adjusted for 2005 CLA score	Adjusted for 2005 CLA score, social background, and academic preparation	Adjusted for 2005 CLA score, social background, academic preparation, and institutions attended (fixed-effects model)
Faculty are approachable			
High	1188.30**	1181.48	1168.14
Medium	1164.17*	1163.42	1158.11
Low†	1118.88	1152.96	1145.43
Faculty have high standards			
High	1180.36*	1170.93	1154.23
Medium	1168.91*	1168.33	1161.65
Low†	1128.49	1146.10	1144.76
Faculty have high expectations			
High	1186.96**	1180.20*	1167.06*
Medium	1162.23**	1161.19	1155.09
Low†	1126.34	1143.10	1140.50
Met with faculty (outside of class)			
Never†	1150.62	1165.13	1163.01
At least once	1167.74	1166.45	1159.46
Reading/writing course requirements			
Neither	1138.19	1154.24	1155.01
Either†	1155.06	1155.23	1155.65
Both	1190.81**	1179.86**	1178.26**
Students have high expectations			
High	1201.29	1180.61	1159.66
Medium	1160.83	1161.96	1157.93
Low†	1151.06	1167.13	1168.25
Students help others succeed			
High	1178.07	1170.38	1154.84
Medium	1167.28	1165.98	1160.26
Low†	1142.74	1158.60	1162.80

		Predicted 2007 CLA score	
	Adjusted for 2005 CLA score	Adjusted for 2005 CLA score, social background, and academic preparation	Adjusted for 2005 CLA score, social background, academic preparation, and institutions attended (fixed-effects model)
Students work hard to succeed			
High	1182.95	1177.64	1158.82
Medium	1164.41	1163.37	1159.26
Low[†]	1156.16	1163.75	1163.89

*p < .05, **p < .01 (differences from the comparison category).

[†] Comparison category.

Note: Results are based on regression models predicting 2007 CLA scores. Each faculty and student characteristic is examined separately. Student reports are divided into three groups (low, medium, and high), based on the proportion of cases falling 1 standard deviation above the mean (high) and 1 standard deviation below the mean (low). Since the original variables were based on a 1–7 scale and were not normally distributed, the three categories contain varying proportions of cases.

Social and academic background variables include sociodemographic characteristics (gender, race/ethnicity, parental education and occupation, non-English home language, two-parent household, and number of siblings), high school characteristics (region, urbanicity, and high school 70% or more non-white), and academic preparation (SAT/ACT scores, number of AP courses taken, and high school GPA). Predicted 2007 scores are calculated at the mean of continuous variables (2005 CLA score, high school GPA, and SAT/ACT), and for a reference group of categorical variables.

N = 2,322. Analyses are adjusted for clustering of students within schools.

Table A4.2. Selected results from regression models identifying relationships between student time use and 2007 CLA scores

	Adjusted for 2005 CLA score	Adjusted for 2005 CLA score, social background, and academic preparation	Adjusted for 2005 CLA score, social background, academic preparation, and institutions attended (fixed-effects model)
Model 1			
Studying	2.183*	0.760	−0.094
	(0.856)	(0.498)	(0.431)
Extracurricular	−1.236**	−1.214**	−0.908**
activities	(0.300)	(0.271)	(0.227)
Model 2			
Studying alone	4.034**	2.388**	1.560*
	(0.879)	(0.603)	(0.635)
Studying with	−3.250*	−3.114*	−3.492*
peers	(1.348)	(1.334)	(1.338)
Working on	7.853*	3.393^t	1.636
campus	(2.951)	(1.822)	(2.017)
Working on cam-	−0.432*	−0.215^t	−0.105
pus squared	(0.175)	(0.107)	(0.109)
Working off	−1.971**	−1.010*	−0.385
campus	(0.596)	(0.438)	(0.448)
Volunteering	−2.604*	−0.547	−1.068
	(1.191)	(1.299)	(1.165)
Student clubs	0.963	−0.364	−0.430
	(1.203)	(1.024)	(0.950)
Fraternity/	−2.467*	−3.522**	−2.580**
sorority	(1.132)	(0.911)	(0.683)

$^t p < .10$, $^*p < .05$, $^{**}p < .01$.

Note: Social and academic background variables include sociodemographic characteristics (gender, race/ethnicity, parental education and occupation, non-English home language, two-parent household, and number of siblings), high school characteristics (region, urbanicity, and high school 70% or more non-white), and academic preparation (SAT/ACT scores, number of AP courses taken, and high school GPA).

N = 2,322. Analyses are adjusted for clustering of students within schools.

Table A4.3. Selected results from regression models identifying relationships between self-reported college majors and 2007 CLA scores

	Adjusted for 2005 CLA score	Adjusted for 2005 CLA score, reading/ writing course requirements, and time spent studying	Adjusted for 2005 CLA score, reading/ writing course requirements, time spent studying, social background, and academic preparation	Adjusted for 2005 CLA score, reading/ writing course requirements, time spent studying, social background, academic preparation, and institutions attended (fixed-effects model)
College major [reference: business]				
Education/ social work	4.518 (23.148)	0.654 (22.158)	13.953 (12.410)	2.674 (13.180)
Engineering/ computer science	35.265^t (17.405)	38.077^t (19.605)	35.838^t (17.582)	18.935 (17.715)
Communications	25.237 (17.245)	15.224 (16.374)	28.256 (16.901)	23.217 (15.560)
Health	24.919^t (13.822)	23.702^t (12.810)	35.389** (10.602)	34.741** (9.741)
Social science/ humanities	68.899** (19.765)	55.211** (16.253)	33.489* (12.420)	28.218* (10.071)
Science/ mathematics	77.027** (26.934)	70.179** (23.972)	46.506** (16.987)	25.984^t (13.211)
Other	38.127^t (19.554)	28.291 (17.327)	15.236 (13.383)	15.565 (13.254)

$^t p < .10$, $^* p < .05$, $^{**} p < .01$.

Note: Social and academic background variables include sociodemographic characteristics (gender, race/ethnicity, parental education and occupation, non-English home language, two-parent household, and number of siblings), high school characteristics (region, urbanicity, and high school 70% or more non-white), and academic preparation (SAT/ACT scores, number of AP courses taken, and high school GPA).

N = 2,322. Analyses are adjusted for clustering of students within schools.

Table A4.4. Selected results from regression models identifying relationships between college financing strategies and 2007 CLA scores

	Adjusted for 2005 CLA score, social background, and academic preparation	Adjusted for 2005 CLA score, social background, academic preparation, and institutions attended (fixed-effects model)
Model 1		
Percentage of college costs covered by grants/scholarships	0.377* (0.161)	0.446* (0.169)
Percentage of college costs covered by loans	−0.287 (0.259)	−0.212 (0.250)
Model 2		
Percentage of college costs covered by grants/scholarships	0.311^{t} (0.170)	0.432* (0.172)
Percentage of college costs covered by loans	−0.311 (0.256)	−0.210 (0.258)
Working on campus	2.868 (2.021)	0.757 (2.057)
Working on campus squared	−0.191 (0.121)	−0.069 (0.117)
Working off campus	−0.999* (0.460)	−0.368 (0.425)

$^{t}p < .10$, *$p < .05$, **$p < .01$.

Note: Social and academic background variables include sociodemographic characteristics (gender, race/ethnicity, parental education and occupation, non-English home language, two-parent household, and number of siblings), high school characteristics (region, urban city, and high school 70% or more non-white), and academic preparation (SAT/ACT scores, number of AP courses taken, and high school GPA).

N = 2,322. Analyses are adjusted for clustering of students within schools.

Table A4.5. Regression models predicting 2007 CLA scores

	Model 1	Model 2	Model 3	Model 4
2005 CLA Score	0.387**	0.221**	0.199**	0.169**
	(0.035)	(0.029)	(0.029)	(0.030)
College: Academic and social experiences[††]				
Faculty expectations and requirements				
Faculty expectations			11.288*	9.610*
			(4.861)	(3.683)
Reading and writing			23.464**	22.444**
requirements			(6.098)	(6.347)
Time use				
Hours spent studying alone			1.650**	0.931[†]
			(0.529)	(0.555)
Hours spent studying with			−3.772*	−4.004**
peers			(1.358)	(1.363)
Hours spent in fraternities/			−3.284**	−2.541**
sororities			(0.774)	(0.591)
College major (reference: business)				
Education/social work			11.313	1.073
			(13.233)	(14.127)
Engineering/computer science			31.497[t]	15.010
			(17.310)	(18.213)
Communications			28.584	22.308
			(16.813)	(15.551)
Health			32.916**	33.676**
			(11.187)	(10.421)
Social science/humanities			29.753*	25.703*
			(13.178)	(11.036)
Science/mathematics			39.155*	21.002
			(15.385)	(13.627)
Other			13.406	14.082
			(14.320)	(13.884)
College financing				
Percentage of college costs cov-			0.335*	0.420*
ered by grants/scholarships			(0.153)	(0.159)
Academic Preparation				
SAT/ACT		0.406**	0.372**	0.369**
		(0.068)	(0.061)	(0.059)
High school GPA		−3.096	−8.885	3.307
		(9.174)	(9.287)	(8.111)

	Model 1	Model 2	Model 3	Model 4
Took AP courses (reference: 0 AP)				
Took 1 AP course		−0.783	1.019	−0.182
		(11.199)	(11.297)	(10.884)
Took 2 AP courses		−2.555	−3.150	−3.334
		(12.504)	(11.944)	(11.477)
Took 3 AP courses		−10.336	−10.949	−7.329
		(13.949)	(12.771)	(12.827)
Took 4 AP courses		11.866	12.915	12.639
		(18.212)	(15.787)	(15.044)
Took 5 or more AP courses		31.802^t	27.570^t	28.603*
		(15.821)	(13.573)	(13.280)

Sociodemographic characteristics

	Model 1	Model 2	Model 3	Model 4
Parental education (reference: high school or less)				
Some college	5.306	−3.046	1.493	4.692
	(12.128)	(11.349)	(11.064)	(9.969)
Bachelor's degree	18.293	−5.237	−1.613	−1.196
	(13.119)	(11.514)	(11.453)	(9.782)
Graduate/professional degree	42.101*	1.354	3.553	4.059
	(15.208)	(13.518)	(13.088)	(10.335)
Parental occupation (reference: skilled manual)				
Professional/managerial	7.400	0.188	2.544	−1.427
	(13.257)	(11.472)	(10.539)	(10.272)
Routine non-manual	10.713	4.659	5.639	3.745
	(13.296)	(11.866)	(11.025)	(10.066)
Petty bourgeoisie	−14.560	−9.037	−7.276	−5.148
	(25.629)	(22.170)	(20.659)	(20.831)
Unskilled	17.724	19.861	17.332	14.702
	(22.950)	(21.271)	(20.602)	(20.268)
Race/ethnicity (reference: white)				
African-American	−105.523**	−47.060*	−58.735**	−49.876**
	(19.965)	(17.073)	(17.164)	(14.684)
Asian	−31.397*	−22.577^t	−23.263*	−26.785*
	(12.965)	(10.963)	(9.976)	(10.880)
Hispanic	−8.400	17.920	8.214	8.392
	(22.794)	(21.255)	(20.159)	(21.022)
Other racial/ethnic group	−41.905*	−27.792	−32.024	−34.814
	(19.724)	(19.961)	(19.803)	(20.548)
Male	−0.749	−8.815	−5.507	−5.843
	(8.717)	(8.253)	(8.805)	(8.678)
Non-English home language	−28.915*	−19.401	−22.283	−31.779*
	(13.839)	(13.746)	(14.748)	(12.730)

	Model 1	Model 2	Model 3	Model 4
Two-parent household	0.743	−6.453	−3.940	−2.046
	(11.261)	(11.825)	(11.577)	(12.097)
Number of siblings	−0.857	3.662	5.062	5.076
	(4.713)	(3.659)	(3.461)	(3.334)
High school characteristics				
70% or more non-white	−29.186*	−17.722	−21.507ᵗ	−31.368*
	(14.025)	(12.732)	(11.695)	(12.613)
Urban	13.726	4.307	0.681	0.285
	(11.083)	(10.941)	(10.015)	(8.740)
Rural	−2.076	5.498	0.017	−5.322
	(11.931)	(11.056)	(10.926)	(10.869)
Midwest	17.096	31.935	28.745	16.168
	(25.924)	(33.403)	(27.708)	(18.127)
South	−34.181	−17.481	−14.670	14.225
	(25.296)	(32.296)	(26.694)	(20.696)
West	19.311	23.461	29.402	52.158**
	(22.841)	(33.238)	(28.351)	(17.158)
Intercept	727.414**	461.373**	499.330**	490.829**
	(44.946)	(72.390)	(69.284)	(61.455)
Fixed effects	no	no	no	yes
R-squared	0.270	0.352	0.374	0.415

ᵗ$p < .10$, *$p < .05$, **$p < .01$.

ᵗᵗ Only college experiences found to be statistically significant in preceding analyses are included.

N = 2,322. Analyses are adjusted for clustering of students within schools.

CLA Student Questionnaire

Part I: College experiences

1. Which years have you attended this school (select all that apply)?
    A. Freshman
    B. Sophomore
    C. Junior
    D. Senior

2. Which of the following best describes your current academic classification in college?
    A. Freshman/first year
    B. Sophomore
    C. Junior
    D. Senior
    E. Unclassified
    F. Other

3. Which of these fields of study best describes your major(s) or expected major(s)? Mark only one in each column. If you do not have a secondary major or minor field of study, mark "N/A (not applicable)."
    1. Agriculture
    2. Anthropology
    3. Architecture
    4. Biological/life sciences (biology, biochemistry, botany, zoology, etc.)
    5. Business (accounting, business administration, marketing, management, etc.)
    6. Communications (speech, journalism, television/radio, etc.)
    7. Computer and information sciences
    8. Economics
    9. Engineering and technology
    10. Education
    11. English and literature
    12. Ethnic, cultural studies, and area studies
    13. Foreign languages and literature (French, Spanish, Chinese etc.)
    14. Health-related fields (nursing, physical therapy, health technology, etc.)
    15. History
    16. Home economics and vocational home economics
    17. Law enforcement
    18. Liberal/general studies

19. Mathematics
20. Multi/interdisciplinary studies (international relations, ecology, environmental studies, etc.)
21. Nursing and physical therapy
22. Parks, recreation, leisure studies, sports management
23. Philosophy
24. Physical education
25. Physical sciences (physics, chemistry, astronomy, earth sciences, etc)
26. Political Science
27. Psychology
28. Religion
29. Public administration (city management, law enforcement, etc.)
30. Sociology
31. Visual and performing arts (art, music, theater, etc.)
32. Undecided
33. Other
34. NA

4. How many credits have you completed at this institution, including those you are completing this semester?
   A. 1–12
   B. 13–24
   C. 25–36
   D. 37–48
   E. over 48

5. Of the total number of credits you have completed at this institution, including those you are completing this semester, how many are in each of the following:

	0	1–4	5–8	9–12	over 12
A. English					
B. Math					
C. Natural or Physical Science					
D. Social Science					
E. Humanities					
F. Your major or intended major					

6. Where do you live?
   A. University housing (on or off campus)
   B. Non-university housing, with family
   C. Non-university housing, independent

7. During the previous semester (Fall 2006), how many times have you done each of the following:

	0	1–2	3–4	5–6	more than 6

Met with a faculty member
  outside of class

Discussed course selection and
  program requirements
  with faculty or staff

Worked with faculty members
  on activities other than coursework
  (e.g., research projects, academic clubs, etc.)

Went to the writing center or attended
  a writing workshop

Met with a tutor

Wrote a research paper

Took a writing-intensive course
  (wrote more than 20 pages over the course of the semester)

Took a reading-intensive course
  (read more than 40 pages a week)

8. How many hours in a typical week do you spend doing each of the following:

	0	1–5	6–10	11–15	16–20	more than 20

Attending classes/labs

Studying alone

Studying with peers

Using computer for schoolwork

Volunteering

Spending time in a fraternity/sorority

Participating in student clubs

Working on campus

Working off-campus

  If you are working on or off campus, is your job related to your field of study or career goals?

  [pull-down menu]

    A. Yes

    B. No

  If you are working on or off campus, are you earning money to pay any tuition costs of attending college?

  [pull-down menu]

    A. Yes

    B. No

If you are working on or off campus, are you earning money to send
home to your family?
[pull-down menu]
  A. Yes
  B. No

9. Approximately what percentage of your college costs (including tuition and
fees, books, and room and board) this semester are covered by each of the
following?

	0–9%	10–39%	40–59%	60–89%	90–100%
Parents/family					
Scholarships					
Grants					
Loans					
On-campus work					
Off-campus work					

10. Please rate the following statements:
Faculty members at my institution are approachable, helpful, and understanding.

                7   6   5   4   3   2   1
Strongly agree   Strongly disagree

Students at my institutions have high academic aspirations.

                7   6   5   4   3   2   1
Strongly agree   Strongly disagree

Faculty members at my institution hold students to high standards.

                7   6   5   4   3   2   1
Strongly agree   Strongly disagree

Students at my institution help each other succeed.

                7   6   5   4   3   2   1
Strongly agree   Strongly disagree

Faculty members at my institution have high expectations for student
like me.

                7   6   5   4   3   2   1
Strongly agree   Strongly disagree

Students at my institution work hard to succeed academically.

                7   6   5   4   3   2   1
Strongly agree   Strongly disagree

My institution has a strong tradition of success for students like myself.

                7   6   5   4   3   2   1
Strongly agree   Strongly disagree

Part II: Background information

11. What is your sex:
    A. Female
    B. Male

12. Which of the following categories best describes your racial/ethnic group?
    A. Black, non-Hispanic
    B. American Indian/Alaska Native
    C. Asian/Pacific Islander
    D. Hispanic
    E. White, non-Hispanic
    F. Other

13. Was English the primary language spoken in your home when you were growing up?
    A. No
    B. Yes

14. What is your citizenship?
    A. U.S. citizen
    B. Permanent U.S. resident
    C. Immigrant (e.g., student visa, employment visa, etc.)

15. In years, how old are you? _____

16. What is the highest degree you expect to attain?
    A. Bachelor's
    B. Master's (e.g., MA, MS, MBA)
    C. Doctorate
    D. Professional (e.g., medical, law, architecture)

17. What is the highest level of education completed by either of your parents?
    A. Less than high school
    B. High school
    C. Some college, less than a bachelor's degree (including associate and technical degrees)
    D. Bachelor's degree
    E. Graduate or professional degree

18. What is your father's or male guardian's current job? _____

19. What is your mother's or female guardian's current job? _____

20. What job do you expect to have six years after completing college? _____
    _____

21. At age 16, were you living with:
    A. Mother and father
    B. Mother and male guardian
    C. Father and female guardian
    D. Mother only
    E. Father only
    F. Other relative or non-relative

22. How many siblings do you have?
    A. 0
    B. 1
    C. 2
    D. 3
    E. more than 3

23. What high school did you attend (if multiple, report the last high school attended)?
    Name _____
    City _____ State_____

24. Describe your grades in high school:
                 English   Math   Science   Social Studies   Overall
    A. Mostly A's
    B. Some A's and Some B's
    C. Mostly B's
    D. Some B's and Some C's
    E. Mostly C's and D's

25. How many AP courses did you take in high school?
    A. 0
    B. 1
    C. 2
    D. 3
    E. 4
    F. more than 4

26. How many college-level courses did you take in high school?
    A. 0
    B. 1
    C. 2
    D. 3
    E. 4
    F. more than 4

Notes

Chapter 1

1. Derek Bok, *Our Underachieving Colleges: A Candid Look at How Much Students Learn and Why They Should Be Learning More* (Princeton, NJ: Princeton University Press, 2006), 8.

2. Bok, *Our Underachieving Colleges*, 109.

3. Claudia Goldin and Lawrence F. Katz, *The Race between Education and Technology* (Cambridge, MA: Belknap Press of Harvard University Press, 2008), 353.

4. Helen Lefkowitz Horowitz, *Campus Life: Undergraduate Cultures from the End of The Eighteenth Century to the Present* (New York: Alfred A. Knopf, 1987), 11–14.

5. James Coleman, *The Adolescent Society* (New York: Free Press, 1961).

6. Barbara Schneider and David Stevenson, *The Ambitious Generation: America's Teenagers Motivated but Directionless* (New Haven: Yale University Press, 1999), 7.

7. Philip Babcock and Mindy Marks, "The Falling Time Cost of College: Evidence from Half a Century of Time Use Data," *Review of Economics and Statistics* (forthcoming).

8. Rebekah Nathan, *My Freshman Year: What a Professor Learned by Becoming a Student* (New York: Penguin Books, 2006), 113. Rebekah Nathan is a pseudonym.

9. Valen E. Johnson, *Grade Inflation: A Crisis in College Education* (New York: Springer-Verlag, 2003), 9.

10. Mary Grigsby, *College Life through the Eyes of Students* (Albany: State University of New York Press, 2009), 117.

11. Arthur G. Powell, Eleanor Farrar, and David K. Cohen, *The Shopping Mall High School: Winners and Losers in the Educational Marketplace* (Boston: Houghton Mifflin Company, 1985), 9, 67–68.

12. George D. Kuh, "What We Are Learning About Student Engagement," *Change* 35 (2003): 28.

13. National Center for Education Statistics (NCES), *Digest of Education Statistics* (Washington, DC: U.S. Department of Education, 2008), table 248.

14. Christopher Jencks and David Riesman, *The Academic Revolution* (New York: Doubleday, 1968), 14.

15. Bok, *Our Underachieving Colleges*, 314.

16. Ernest Boyer, *Scholarship Reconsidered: Priorities of the Professoriate* (Stanford, CA: The Carnegie Foundation for the Advancement of Teaching, 1990), 12.

17. Johnson, *Grade Inflation*, 14.

18. Boyer, *Scholarship Reconsidered*, statistical tables A-5 through A-18.

19. Ibid., 13.

20. Although research orientation is commonly equated with selectivity, the two characteristics represent distinct aspects of higher-education institutions. The correlation between selectivity and research orientation in Astin's study was 0.56, indicating a far-from-perfect relationship. Alexander Astin, *What Matters in College? Four Critical Years Revisited* (San Francisco: Jossey-Bass, 1993), 37.

21. Astin, *What Matters in College*, 337–42.

22. Jeffrey F. Milmen, Joseph B. Berger, and Eric L. Dey, "Faculty Time Allocation: A Study of Change over Twenty Years," *Journal of Higher Education* 17 (2000): 454–75.

23. William F. Massy and Robert Zemsky, "Faculty Discretionary Time: Departments and the Academic Ratchet," *Journal of Higher Education* 65 (1994): 1–22.

24. Jencks and Riesman, *The Academic Revolution*, 14–15.

25. Walter Powell and Jason Owen-Smith, "The New World of Knowledge Production in the Life Sciences," in *The Future of the City of Intellect: The Changing American University*, ed. Steven Brint (Stanford, CA: Stanford University Press, 2002), 115.

26. Derek Bok, *Universities in the Marketplace: The Commercialization of Higher Education* (Princeton, NJ: Princeton University Press, 2003), 9.

27. Powell and Owen-Smith, "The New World of Knowledge Production in the Life Sciences," 117.

28. Steven Brint, "The Rise of the Practical Arts," in *The Future of the City of Intellect: The Changing American University*, ed. Steven Brint (Stanford, CA: Stanford University Press, 2002), 246.

29. Anthony T. Kronman, *Education's End: Why Our Colleges and Universities Have Given Up on the Meaning of Life* (New Haven: Yale University Press, 2007), 111.

30. Derek Bok, *Higher Learning* (Cambridge, MA: Harvard University Press, 1986), 323–24.

31. Gary Rhoades, "The Study of American Professions," in *Sociology of Higher Education: Contributions and their Contexts*, ed. Patricia Gumport (Baltimore: Johns Hopkins University Press, 2007), 128.

32. Ibid., 128–29.

33. Jacqueline E. King, *The American College President 2007 Edition* (Washington, D.C.: American Council on Education, 2007).

34. Reflective of the lack of emphasis on undergraduate learning is also the extent to which many of the highest-paid higher-education employees are now football and basketball coaches, chief financial officers, and doctors working in university hospitals; 88 percent of employees in private colleges and universities making more than $1 million per year were not employed as chief executives or presidents. See Tamar Lewin, "Many Specialists at Private Universities Earn More than Presidents," *New York Times*, February 22, 2009, http://www.nytimes.com/2009/02/23/education/23pay.html.

35. Lewin, "Many Specialists at Private Universities Earn More than Presidents."

36. Brint, "The Rise of the Practical Arts," 243.

37. Mitchell Stevens, *Creating a Class: College Admissions and the Education of Elites* (Cambridge, MA: Harvard University Press, 2007), 264.

38. Ibid., 246, 257.

39. Mitchell Stevens, Elizabeth Armstrong, and Richard Arum, "Sieve, Incubator, Temple, Hub: Empirical and Theoretical Advances in the Sociology of Higher Education," *Annual Review of Sociology* 34 (2008): 127–51.

40. Julie A. Reuben, *The Making of the Modern University: Intellectual Transformation and the Marginalization of Morality* (Chicago: University of Chicago Press, 1996), 4.

41. Clark Kerr, *The Uses of the University* (Cambridge, MA: Harvard University Press, 2001), 31.

42. George Marsden, *The Soul of the American University: From Protestant Establishment to Established Nonbelief* (New York: Oxford University Press, 1994), 423–24.

43. Horowitz, *Campus Life,* 20.

44. Jencks and Riesman, *The Academic Revolution,* 35–39.

45. Donald L. McCabe, Linda Klebe Trevino, and Kenneth D. Butterfield, "Dishonesty in Academic Environments: The Influence of Peer Reporting Requirements," *Journal of Higher Education* 72 (2001): 29–45.

46. Richard Arum, *Judging School Discipline: The Crisis of Moral Authority* (Cambridge, MA: Harvard University Press, 2003).

47. Sheila Slaughter and Larry L. Leslie, *Academic Capitalism: Politics, Policies, and the Entrepreneurial University* (Baltimore: Johns Hopkins University Press, 1997), 72.

48. Ibid., 44.

49. Federal subsidies for college that occur through tax credits established by the 1997 Taxpayer Relief Act have been estimated by Thomas Kane to be larger than federal outlays for Pell grants. See Thomas Kane, *The Price of Admission: Rethinking How Americans Pay for College* (Washington, DC: Brookings Institution Press, 1999), 22.

50. College Board, *Trends in College Pricing* (New York: College Board, 2008), 9.

51. College Board, *Trends in Student Aid* (New York: College Board, 2008), 6.

52. Ibid., 11.

53. Sallie Mae Foundation, *How Undergraduate Students Use Credit Cards: Sallie Mae's National Study of Usage Rates and Trends 2009* (Wilkes-Barre, PA: Sallie Mae Foundation, 2009), 3.

54. Babcock and Marks, "The Falling Time Cost of College."

55. Steven Brint and Matthew Baron Rotondi, "Student Debt, the College Experience and Transitions to Adulthood" (paper presented at the annual meeting for the American Sociological Association, Boston, July 31–August 4, 2008).

56. David Labaree, *How to Succeed in School without Really Learning: The Credentials Race in American Education* (New Haven: Yale University Press, 1997), 259.

57. Ibid., 45.

58. Ibid., 32.

59. U.S. Department of Education, *A Test of Leadership: Charting the Future of U.S. Higher Education* (Washington, DC: U.S. Department of Education, 2006), 3.

60. Ibid., 14.

61. See Robert M. Hauser, et al., eds., *Measuring Literacy: Performance Levels for Adults* (Washington, DC: National Research Council, 2005).

62. U.S. Department of Education, *A Test of Leadership,* 14.

63. The Council for Aid to Education is a national nonprofit organization based in New York City. It was originally established in 1952 by a group of corporate lead-

ers including Alfred Sloan (General Motors), Frank Abrams (Exxon Corporation) and Irving S. Olds (U.S. Steel Corporation) as the Council for Financial Aid to Education to advance corporate support of higher education. When the CLA instrument was developed, the Council for Aid to Education was affiliated with the Rand Corporation (see http://www.cae.org).

64. Since spring 2007 we have continued to follow this cohort of students, collecting additional data including their college transcripts and CLA scores in spring 2009. We also plan to follow them up post-graduation in spring 2010 and spring 2011 to examine their transitions to the labor market or further schooling.

65. Richard Hersch, "Going Naked," *AAC&U Peer Review* 9 (2007): 6.

66. Stephen Klein, Richard Shavelson, and Roger Benjamin, "Setting the Record Straight," *Inside Higher Ed,* February 8, 2007, http://www.insidehighered.com/views/2007/02/08/benjamin.

67. Hersch, "Going Naked," 6.

68. Klein, Shavelson, and Benjamin, "Setting the Record Straight."

69. Richard Shavelson, "The Collegiate Learning Assessment," *Ford Policy Forum 2008: Forum for the Future of Higher Education,* 20, http://net.educause.edu/forum/fp08.asp.

70. Discussed in Shavelson, "The Collegiate Learning Assessment," 20. Prompts reported in posted powerpoints of Richard Benjamin, https://wvhepc.org/resources/RogerPresentation(10.09.03)a.ppt.

71. Council for Aid to Education, *Collegiate Learning Assessment Common Scoring Rubric* (New York: Council for Aid to Education, 2008).

72. Shavelson, "The Collegiate Learning Assessment," 19.

73. Ibid.

74. Ibid., 20.

75. U.S. Department of Education, *A Test of Leadership,* 23.

76. Anne Grosso de León, "The Collegiate Learning Assessment: A Tool for Measuring the Value Added of a Liberal Arts Education," *Carnegie Results,* Fall 2007, 3.

77. James Traub, "No Gr_du_te Left Behind," *New York Times Magazine: The College Issue,* September 30, 2007, 106–9.

78. Doug Lederman, "No College Left Behind?" *Inside Higher Ed,* February 15, 2006, http://www.insidehighered.com/news/2006/02/15/testing.

79. Ibid.

80. Ibid.

81. U.S. Department of Education, *A Test of Leadership,* 23.

82. Organisation for Economic Co-operation and Development (OECD), Directorate for Education, Education Committee, Centre for Educational Research and Innovation (CERI) Governing Board, *PISA for Higher Education* (Paris: Organization for Economic Co-operation and Development, 2006), 3.

83. Organisation for Economic Co-operation and Development, "Assessment of Higher Education Learning Outcomes (AHELO)," http://www.oecd.org/document/41/0,3343,en_2649_35961291_42295209_1_1_1_1,00.html.

84. Catherine Hoffman Breyer, "The Right Way to Measure College Learning: National Standardized Testing Won't Work," *Christian Science Monitor,* April 9, 2007, http://www.csmonitor.com/2007/0409/p09s01-coop.html.

85. Jennifer Epstein, "Questioning College-Wide Assessments," *Inside Higher Ed,* June 21, 2007, http://www.insidehighered.com/news/2007/06/21/assessments.

86. Stephen Klein, Ou Lydia Liu, and James Sconing, *Test Validity Study (TVS) Report,* September 29, 2009, http://www.voluntarysystem.org/docs/reports/TVSReport_Final.pdf.

87. Scott Jaschik, "Does 'Value Added' Add Value?," *Inside Higher Ed,* November 3, 2006, http://www.insidehighered.com/news/2006/11/03/assess.

88. Paul Basken, "Test Touted as 2 Studies Question Its Value: Small Colleges Back Achievement Exam to Measure Accountability," *Chronicle of Higher Education,* June 6, 2008, http://chronicle.com/article/Test-Touted-as-2-Studies/23503/.

89. Robert Frank and Phillip Cook, "It's a Winner Take All Market," *Washington Monthly,* December 1, 1995.

90. For more information on the Wabash National Study of Liberal Arts Education, see http://www.liberalarts.wabash.edu/study-overview/.

91. See, for example, Astin, *What Matters in College,* 199f.

92. William Bowen and Derek Bok, *The Shape of the River* (Princeton, NJ: Princeton University Press, 1998), xxxi.

93. Ibid., 77.

94. James Shulman and William Bowen, *The Game of Life: College Sports and Educational Values* (Princeton, NJ: Princeton University Press, 2001).

95. Camille Charles, et al., *Taming the River: Negotiating the Academic, Financial, and Social Currents in Selective Colleges and Universities* (Princeton, NJ: Princeton University Press, 2009), 2–3. See also Douglas Massey, et al., *The Source of the River: The Social Origins of Freshmen at America's Selective Colleges and Universities* (Princeton, NJ: Princeton University Press, 2003).

96. Charles et al., *Taming the River.*

97. Massey et al., *The Source of The River,* 29.

98. Information for College and Beyond is provided in Bowen and Bok, *The Shape of the River,* Table D3.1. An additional 7 percent of students were estimated to have graduated from institutions other than those in which they had initially enrolled, thus producing the overall graduation rate of 92 percent. National averages vary depending on the dataset and year of entry. For some estimates, see Clifford Adelman, *The Toolbox Revisited* (Washington, DC: U.S. Department of Education, 2006), table 30. Adelman reported that the six-year graduation rate from the same institution for students completing high school in 1992 (which is close to the 1989 cohort included in C&B) and entering four-year colleges and universities was 53 percent. An additional 11 percent of students from this high school cohort graduated within six years from a different four-year institution than where they had started.

Chapter 2

1. Michael Hout, "Politics of Mobility," in *Generating Social Stratification,* ed. Alan C. Kerckhoff (Boulder, CO: Westview Press, 1995), 301–25. Although most of the expansion occurred in public two-year institutions, four-year institutions expanded as well. Enrollments in public four-year institutions as a fraction of the college-age population doubled between 1962 and 1992.

2. National Center for Education Statistics (NCES), *Digest of Education Statistics* (Washington, DC: U.S. Department of Education, 2008), tables 189 and 265.

3. James Rosenbaum, *Beyond College for All: Career Paths for the Forgotten Half* (New York: Russell Sage Foundation, 2001). Also, for increase in expectations over time,

see John Reynolds et al., "Have Adolescents Become Too Ambitious? High School Seniors' Educational and Occupational Plans, 1976 to 2000," *Social Problems* 53 (2006): 186–206.

4. NCES, *Digest of Education Statistics*, table 202. Moreover, this percentage underestimates the ultimate enrollment because more than one-third of college entrants today delay entry by at least one year. See National Center for Education Statistics (NCES), *Waiting to Attend College: Undergraduates Who Delay Their Postsecondary Enrollment*, NCES 2005-152 (Washington, DC: U.S. Department of Education, 2005).

5. Martin Trow, "Reflections on the Transformation from Mass to Universal Higher Education," *Daedalus* 99 (1970): 3–4.

6. Forty-four percent of students who were classified in government reports as marginally qualified or not qualified for college (based on their secondary school GPA, high school rank, test scores, and academic coursework), expected to finish college, and an additional 46 percent expected to attain at least some postsecondary education. National Center for Education Statistics (NCES), *Access to Postsecondary Education for the 1992 High School Graduates*, NCES 98-105 (Washington, DC: U.S. Department of Education, 1997), 21–34.

7. Rosenbaum, *Beyond College for All*, 59–62.

8. Barbara Schneider and David Stevenson, *The Ambitious Generation: America's Teenagers Motivated but Directionless* (New Haven: Yale University Press, 1999), 79–85.

9. Jeffrey Jensen Arnett, *Emerging Adulthood: The Winding Path from the Late Teens through the Twenties* (New York: Oxford University Press, 2004), 125–26.

10. Secretary of Education Margaret Spellings, "Statement on International Education Week 2008," http://www.iew.state.gov/2008/docs/2008sec-ed-statement.pdf. Emphasis added.

11. Statement made by Joan Scott, Harold F. Linder Professor of Social Science at the Institute for Advanced Study in Princeton, on behalf of AAUP, as part of testimony before the Pennsylvania General Assembly's House Select Committee on Student Academic Freedom, November 9, 2005, http://www.aaup.org/AAUP/GR/state/Academic+Bill+of+Rights-State+Level/Scotttestimony.htm.

12. Higher Education Research Institute (HERI), *The American College Teacher: National Norms for 2007–2008* (Los Angeles: HERI, University of California Los Angeles, 2009).

13. This number reflects the difference between CLA performance task score in the fall of 2005 and spring of 2007, divided by the standard deviation of the 2005 score (see table A2.1). Standard error for the 2005 score, adjusted for clustering of students within schools, is 21.11 with a 95-percent confidence interval of [1,090.56, 1,173.32]; standard error for the 2007 score, adjusted for clustering of students within schools, is 23.62 with a 95-percent confidence interval of [1,119.96, 1212.56]. As is discussed in more detail in the methodological appendix, the performance task scores in 2005 were capped at 1,600, while they were allowed to range up to 1,800 in 2007. If we capped the 2007 scores at 1,600, the mean, and consequently the estimated growth, would be slightly lower (the 2007 CLA mean would be 1,162.55, with the growth of 30.61 points or 0.16 standard deviation). Deleting 2007 CLA scores above 1,800 from analysis would decrease the mean, and thus the growth, even further. The limited growth reported in this chapter may thus slightly overstate students' gains during their first two years in college.

14. Ernest T. Pascarella and Patrick T. Terenzini, *How College Affects Students: A Third Decade of Research* (San Francisco: Jossey-Bass, 2005), 156, 205. It is worthwhile to note

that the average improvement of 0.50 standard deviation during college would imply an improvement of 0.06 standard deviation each semester, or 0.18 standard deviation over three semesters, which matches our estimate.

15. This estimate of 45 percent is based on a paired sample t-test of the difference in students' performance between fall 2005 and spring 2007. Specifically, it references the proportion of students who gain less than the upper bound of the 95-percent confidence interval (i.e., 1.96 × standard error of the difference). Other, more conservative estimation strategies would place even more students below the cutoff of significant gains. If we adjusted standard error for clustering of students within schools, the percentage of students demonstrating no significant gains in learning would be slightly higher: 47 percent. Moreover, if we used the standard error of the 2005 CLA score, as opposed to the growth, 53 percent of students would fall below the level of statistically significant gains. If we replicate this final calculation using standard error of the 2005 CLA score and assume constant rates of growth through the senior year, we would still expect 47 percent of students to show no significant gains in critical thinking, analytical reasoning, and written communication by the time they graduate. A test such as the CLA which relies on open-ended prompts may face challenges of reliability, raising the possibility that some of the students showing no gains may actually be learning. However, questions of reliability are likely to pertain to the other half of the distribution as well, meaning that some of the students reporting gains may not actually be learning much.

16. Charles Blaich, "Overview of Findings from the First Year of the Wabash National Study of Liberal Arts Education" (Wabash College, Center for Inquiry in the Liberal Arts, 2007, http://www.liberalarts.wabash.edu/research/). See also a review of previous research in Pascarella and Terenzini, *How College Affects Students*, 155–212.

17. Blaich, "Overview of Findings from the First Year of the Wabash National Study of Liberal Arts Education."

18. Lamont A. Flowers et al., "How Much Do Students Learn in College?" *Journal of Higher Education* 72 (2001): 565–83.

19. National Survey of Student Engagement (NSSE), *Experiences That Matter: Enhancing Student Learning and Success* (Bloomington, IN: Center for Postsecondary Research, Indiana University Bloomington, 2007), 42.

20. George D. Kuh, "What We Are Learning About Student Engagement From NSSE," *Change* 35 (2003): 27.

21. As quoted by David Leonhardt, "The College Dropout Boom," *New York Times*, May 24, 2005, http://www.nytimes.com/2005/05/24/national/class/EDUCATION-FINAL.html?pagewanted=1.

22. Michael Katz, ed., *School Reform Past and Present* (Boston: Little Brown and Company, 1971), 141.

23. Pierre Bourdieu, "Cultural Reproduction and Social Reproduction," in *Knowledge, Education, and Cultural Change*, ed. Richard Brown (London: Tavistock, 1973), 71–112. There are other views of social reproduction, such as those articulated in Samuel Bowles and Herbert Gintis, *Schooling in Capitalist America* (New York: Basic Books, 1976); and Randall Collins, *Credential Society* (New York: Academic Press, 1979).

24. In addition to parental education, we examined the relationship between parental occupation and CLA scores. However, parental occupation was not statistically significant in any of the models examined. We include it as a control in regression analyses, but do not extensively discuss the results.

25. African-American students' 2005 CLA scores were 0.94 standard deviation lower than those of white students. Standard deviations are calculated by dividing the gap between African-American and white students by the standard deviation of the full sample.

26. If we standardized test scores to the 2005 CLA scale, the gap between students whose parents had no college experience and those whose parents held graduate or professional degrees would be 0.64 standard deviation in 2005 and 0.62 standard deviation in 2007.

27. Josipa Roksa et al., "Changes in Higher Education and Social Stratification in the United States" in *Stratification in Higher Education: A Comparative Study*, ed. Yossi Shavit, Richard Arum, and Adam Gamoran (Stanford, CA: Stanford University Press, 2007), 165–91. See also Yossi Shavit and Hans-Peter Blossfeld, *Persistent Inequality: Changing Educational Attainment in Thirteen Countries* (Boulder, CO: Westview Press, 1993).

28. If we standardized test scores to the 2005 CLA scale, the gap of 0.94 standard deviation between African-American and white students from 2005 would increase to 1.12 in 2007.

29. NCES, *Digest of Education Statistics*, tables 188 and 268.

30. Seasonal learning literature indicates that inequality between different groups of students grows particularly during the summer, when students are not in school. For a recent example, see Douglas B. Downey, Paul T. von Hippel, and Beckett A. Broh, "Are Schools the Great Equalizer? Cognitive Inequality during the Summer Months and the School Year," *American Sociological Review* 69 (2004): 613–35.

31. Annette Lareau, *Unequal Childhoods: Class, Race, and Family Life* (Berkeley: University of California Press, 2003), 5.

32. Ibid., 176–77.

33. Samuel R. Lucas, *Tracking Inequality: Stratification and Mobility in American High Schools* (New York: Teachers College Press, 1999).

34. Schneider and Stevenson, *The Ambitious Generation*, 91–96.

35. Annette Lareau and Elliot B. Weininger, "Class and the Transition to Adulthood" in *Social Class: How Does it Work?*, ed. Annette Lareau and Dalton Conley (New York: Russell Sage Foundation, 2008), 127–28.

36. NCES, *Access to Postsecondary Education.*

37. Students could take the SAT or the ACT. Their respective test scores were converted to an SAT equivalent scale.

38. Lareau and Weininger, "Class and the Transition to Adulthood," 127–28, 139.

39. Price quoted by Kaplan for thirty-two hours of tutoring in the Premier Tutoring: SAT Masters Program. http://www.kaptest.com/College/SAT/comparison.html#.

40. As quoted by Julie Bick, "The Long (and Sometimes Expensive) Road to the SAT," May 28, 2006, *New York Times*, http://www.nytimes.com/2006/05/28/business/yourmoney/28test.html?scp=21&sq=SAT%20prep&st=cse.

41. Indeed, in an extensive literature review Adam Gamoran noted: "The most important reason for educational inequality between blacks and whites is socioeconomic." Adam Gamoran, "American Schooling and Educational Inequality: A Forecast for the 21st Century," *Sociology of Education* 75 (2001): 137.

42. We focus the discussion on racial composition of the high school. However, we have also collected information on other high school characteristics, such as the proportion of students receiving free or reduced lunch and school control (public versus private). The free/reduced-price lunch variable was missing in approximately 20 percent of the cases and was not significantly related to CLA scores in regression models.

Consequently, we did not include it in our presented analyses. Private school students were substantially underrepresented in our sample (including only 59 students, or 2.5 percent of the sample). The low number of cases raised questions about the reliability of the private school estimates; school sector was thus excluded from the analyses.

43. James Coleman et al., *Equality of Educational Opportunity* (Washington, DC: U.S. Government Printing Office, 1966).

44. Gary Orfield and Susan E. Eaton, *Dismantling Desegregation: The Quiet Reversal of Brown v. Board of Education* (New York: The New Press, 1996), 53, 64–70.

45. Douglas Massey et al., *The Source of the River: The Social Origins of Freshmen at America's Selective Colleges and Universities* (Princeton, NJ: Princeton University Press, 2003), 93–97.

46. The same finding is reported for a sample of students attending selective colleges and universities in Massey et al., *The Source of the River*, 105.

47. Rosalyn Mickelson, "Segregation and the SAT," *Ohio State Law Journal* 67 (2006): 157–99.

48. For some explanations of the underlying mechanisms and long-lasting consequences of racially segregated environments on college students, see Camille Charles et al., *Taming the River: Negotiating the Academic, Financial, and Social Currents in Selective Colleges and Universities* (Princeton, NJ: Princeton University Press, 2009), 150–71.

49. For a recent review see Min Zhou, "Growing Up American: The Challenge Confronting Immigrant Americans and Children of Immigrants," *Annual Review of Sociology* 23 (1997): 63–95.

50. The difference in CLA performance between students from English-speaking versus non-English-speaking households was statistically significant in 2007 but not in 2005. Moreover, regression analyses predicting 2007 CLA scores while controlling for 2005 CLA scores reveal a statistically significant relationship between English home-language background and learning only in some model specifications (see tables A2.3 and A4.5 in methodolgical appendix). While present, the differences in learning for students from English versus non-English language backgrounds are thus relatively small.

51. Karl L. Alexander and Aaron M. Pallas, "School Sector and Cognitive Performance: When is a Little a Little?," *Sociology of Education* 58 (1985): 120. Emphasis added.

52. For a statistical explanation of why this formulation can be considered to estimate growth between two time points, see Thomas Hoffer, Andrew M. Greeley, and James S. Coleman, "Achievement Growth in Public and Catholic Schools," *Sociology of Education* 58 (1985): 82.

53. If we standardized test scores to the 2005 CLA scale, the African-American-white gap of 136 points would equal almost three-quarters of a standard deviation.

54. The models include sociodemographic characteristics: gender, race/ethnicity, non-English language background, parental education and occupation, household composition (two-parent household and number of siblings), and high school characteristics: region, urbanicity, and 70 percent or more non-white high school.

55. If we standardized test scores to the 2005 CLA scale, the African-American-white gap of 47 points would equal one-quarter of a standard deviation, even after adjusting for family background and academic preparation. This finding is consistent with previous research on the black-white test score gap: social background and academic experiences account for some but not all of the gap between the two groups. See for example, Christopher Jencks and Meredith Phillips, *The Black-White Test Score Gap* (Washing-

ton, DC: Bookings Institution Press, 1998), 1–51. Moreover, it is worthwhile to note that in the final model, after including all of the demographic and academic controls, Asian students have lower growth in critical thinking, complex reasoning, and writing skills than white students. This is due in part to the unique sampling strategy of this study, which relied on institutions as the primary sampling unit. Asian students in our sample are concentrated in four institutions that do not experience the highest gains in CLA. Moreover, although Asian students on average tend to do well academically and have higher high school GPAs and SAT/ACT scores than white students (authors' calculations based on the Beginning Postsecondary Students (BPS) Longitudinal Study, 2003–04 cohort), that is not the case for our sample. The Asian students in our sample are thus not necessarily representative of Asian students attending four-year institutions nationwide.

56. Christopher Jencks, et al., *Inequality: A Reassessment of the Effect of Family and Schooling in America* (New York: Basic Books, 1972), 135.

57. Kevin Carey, *A Matter of Degrees: Improving Graduation Rates in Four-Year College and Universities* (Washington, DC: The Education Trust, 2004), 6–7. See also William G. Bowen, Matthew M. Chingos, and Michael S. McPherson, *Crossing the Finish Line: Completing College at America's Public Universities* (Princeton, NJ: Princeton University Press, 2009).

58. Nicolas Lemann, *The Big Test: The Secret History of the American Meritocracy* (New York: Ferrar Straus and Giroux, 1999).

59. Research on secondary schools suggests that a classroom's intellectual composition affects students' performance, particularly for those of lower ability. See Yehezkel Dar and Nura Resh, "Classroom Intellectual Composition and Academic Achievement," *American Educational Research Journal* 23 (1986): 357–74. Similarly, extensive research on tracking implies that more flexible and inclusive systems can increase overall achievement as well as decrease gaps across students from different tracks. See for example, Adam Gamoran, "The Variable Effects of High School Tracking," *American Sociological Review* 57 (1992): 812–28.

60. John Bound, Michael Lovenheim, and Sarah E. Turner, "Understanding the Decrease in College Completion Rates and the Increased Time to the Baccalaureate Degree." PSC Research Report No. 07-626 (Population Studies Center, University of Michigan, 2007).

61. Clifford Adelman, *The Toolbox Revisited: Paths to Degree Completion from High School through College* (Washington, DC: U.S. Department of Education, 2006).

62. National Center for Education Statistics (NCES), *Community College Students: Goals, Academic Preparation, and Outcomes*, NCES 2003-164 (Washington, DC: U.S. Department of Education, 2003).

63. Remarks of President Barack Obama, prepared to address the joint session of Congress, February 24, 2009 (Washington, DC: White House Press Office).

64. Rosenbaum, *Beyond College for All*, 99.

65. Ibid., 102.

66. Ibid., 101.

67. Paul Attewell and David Lavin, *Passing the Torch: Does Higher Education for the Disadvantaged Pay Off Across the Generations?* (New York: Russell Sage Foundation, 2007).

68. For a description of the warehousing function of schooling, see Pamela Walters, "The Limits of Growth: School Expansion and School Reform in Historical Perspective"

in *Handbook of the Sociology of Education,* ed. Maureen Hallinan (New York: Springer Publishers, 2006), 247–48.

69. Collins, *The Credential Society.*

70. Samuel Lucas, "Effectively Maintained Inequality: Education Transitions, Track Mobility and Social Background Effects," *American Journal of Sociology* 106 (2001): 1642–90; and Theodore Gerber and Sin Yi Cheung, "Horizontal Stratification in Postsecondary Education: Forms, Explanations, and Implications," *Annual Review of Sociology* 34 (2008): 299–318.

71. As cited by Peter Schmidt, "Former Top Official at Education Dept. Criticizes How it Approached College Access," *The Chronicle of Higher Education,* January 9, 2009, http://chronicle.com/news/article/5767/former-top-official-at-education-dept -criticizes-how-it-approached-college-access.

72. National Center for Education Statistics (NCES), *Descriptive Summary of 2003– 2004 Beginning Postsecondary Students: Three Years Later,* NCES 2008-174 (Washington, DC: U.S. Department of Education, 2008).

73. Josipa Roksa et al., *Policies for Promoting Gatekeeper Course Success for Students Needing Developmental Education in Virginia's Community Colleges* (New York: Community College Research Center, Teachers College, Columbia University, 2009).

74. HERI, *The American College Teacher.*

75. For examples see William Bowen and Derek Bok, *The Shape of the River* (Princeton, NJ: Princeton University Press, 1998); and William Bowen, Matthew Chingos, and Michael McPherson, *Crossing the Finish Line: Completing College at America's Public Universities* (Princeton, NJ: Princeton University Press, 2009).

76. John Bound, Michael Lovenheim, and Sarah E. Turner, "Why Have College Completion Rates Declined? An Analysis of Changing Student Preparation and College Resources." NBER working paper No. 15566 (Cambridge, MA: National Bureau of Economic Research, 2009).

Chapter 3

1. Mary Grigsby, *College Life through the Eyes of Students* (Albany: State University of New York Press, 2009), 54.

2. Ibid., 55.

3. Chapter 4 provides an extended discussion of students' time use.

4. Alexander Astin, *What Matters in College? Four Critical Years Revisited* (San Francisco: Jossey-Bass, 1993), 398.

5. Vincent Tinto, *Leaving College: Rethinking the Causes and Cures of Student Attrition* (Chicago: University of Chicago Press, 1993), 50.

6. Astin, *What Matters in College,* 410.

7. Tinto, *Leaving College,* 210.

8. For a recent example, see George D. Kuh et al., *Student Success in College: Creating Conditions that Matter* (San Francisco: Jossey-Bass, 2005); and George D. Kuh et al., *Assessing Conditions to Enhance Educational Effectiveness: The Inventory for Student Engagement and Success* (San Francisco: Jossey-Bass, 2005). Moreover, see the discussion of project DEEP (Documenting Effective Educational Practice) at: http://nsse.iub.edu/ institute/?view=deep/index.

9. Tinto, *Leaving College,* 132.

10. Astin, *What Matters in College,* 226–28.

11. James Coleman, *The Adolescent Society* (New York: Free Press, 1961).

12. Mizuko Ito et al., *Living and Learning with New Media: Summary of Findings from the Digital Youth Project* (Chicago: John D. and Catherine T. MacArthur Foundation, 2008), 2.

13. Loren Pope, *Colleges that Change Lives: 40 Schools that will Change the Way You Think about Colleges* (New York: Penguin Books, 2006), 3.

14. Ibid., 6.

15. Ibid., 255.

16. Ibid., 228.

17. Tim Clydesdale, *The First Year Out: Understanding American Teens after High School* (Chicago: University of Chicago Press, 2007), 162.

18. In the presented analyses, these measures are standardized with a mean of zero and a standard deviation of one.

19. See Astin, *What Matters in College*; and Tinto, *Leaving College*.

20. National Center for Education Statistics (NCES), *Descriptive Summary of 2003–04 Beginning Postsecondary Students: Three Years Later*, NCES 2008-174 (Washington, DC: U.S. Department of Education, 2008), 83–84.

21. Young K. Kim and Linda J. Sax, "Student-Faculty Interaction in Research Universities: Differences by Student Gender, Race, Social Class, and First-Generation Status," *Research in Higher Education* 50 (2009): 437–59; and George D. Kuh and Shouping Hu, "The Effects of Student-Faculty Interaction in the 1990s," *Review of Higher Education* 24 (2001): 309–32.

22. For an argument on the imperative of focusing on the highest ability students under one's charge, see W. E. B. Du Bois, "The Talented Tenth" in *The Negro Problem: A Series of Articles by Representative Negroes of To-day*, ed. Booker T. Washington (New York: J. Pott & Company, 1903), 31–74.

23. Specifically, our analyses control for students' gender, race/ethnicity, parental education, parental occupation, two-parent home, sibling size, region, urbanicity, high school racial composition, and academic preparation (including high school GPA, number of AP courses taken, and SAT/ACT scores).

24. Mark Davies and Denise B. Kandel, "Parental and Peer Influences on Adolescents' Educational Plans: Some Further Evidence," *American Journal of Sociology* 87 (1981): 363–87. Citing a review by Kenneth Spenner and David Featherman, "Achievement Ambition," *Annual Review of Sociology* 4 (1978): 373–420.

25. Maureen T. Hallinan and Richard A. Williams, "Students' Characteristics and the Peer-Influence Process," *Sociology of Education* 63 (1990): 122–32.

26. Barbara J. Banks, Ricky L. Slavings, and Bruce J. Biddle, "Effects of Peer, Faculty, and Parental Influences on Students' Persistence," *Sociology of Education* 63 (1990): 208–25.

27. Hallinan and Williams, "Students' Characteristics and the Peer-Influence Process," 123.

28. Students were asked whether they agreed or disagreed (on a seven-point scale) with the statements. In the presented analyses, student responses are standardized to a scale with a mean of zero and a standard deviation of one.

29. Specifically, students from families with parents who had a graduate education had 0.34 standard deviation higher reports of peer expectations and 0.27 standard deviation higher reports of peer support than students from families with only high-school-educated parents.

30. The R-squared of a model predicting reports of peer high expectations increases from 0.076 to 0.224 when institutional-level fixed effects are added; the R-squared on a model predicting reports of peer support increases from 0.046 to 0.188 when institutional-level fixed effects are included.

31. Rebekah Nathan, *My Freshman Year: What a Professor Learned by Becoming a Student* (New York: Penguin Books, 2006), 101. Rebekah Nathan is a pseudonym.

32. See also, Steven Brint and Allison M. Cantwell, "Undergraduate Time Use and Academic Outcomes: Results from UCUES 2006." Research and Occasional Paper Series (Center for Studies in Higher Education, University of California, Berkeley, 2008); and National Survey of Student Engagement (NSSE), *Experiences that Matter: Enhancing Student Learning and Success* (Bloomington, IN: Center for Postsecondary Research, Indiana University Bloomington, 2007).

33. Grigsby, *College Life through the Eyes of Students*, 116.

34. Nathan, *My Freshman Year*, 112–13.

35. Ibid., 119.

36. The R-squared increased from 0.074 to 0.138 when school-level fixed effects were added.

37. NSSE, *Experiences that Matter*, 42.

38. Ernest L. Boyer, *College: The Undergraduate Experience in America* (New York: Harper and Row, 1987), 85.

39. Ibid., 85.

40. Ibid., 84.

41. Grigsby, *College Life through the Eyes of Students*, 112.

42. See for example, Juan Carlos Calcagno and Bridget Terry Long, "The Impact of Postsecondary Remediation Using a Regression Discontinuity Approach: Addressing Endogenous Sorting and Noncompliance." NBER Working Paper Series no.14194 (Cambridge, MA: National Bureau of Economic Research, 2008).

43. Alexander Astin, "The Changing American College Student: Thirty Year Trends, 1966–1996," *Review of Higher Education* 21 (1998): 115–35.

44. Sarah E. Turner and William Bowen, "The Flight from the Arts and Sciences: Trends in Degrees Conferred," *Science* 250 (1990): 517–21.

45. Steven Brint, "The Rise of the Practical Arts" in *The Future of the City of Intellect: The Changing American University*, ed. Steven Brint (Stanford, CA: Stanford University Press, 2002), 222.

46. Turner and Bowen, "The Flight from the Arts and Sciences," 517.

47. William Damon, *The Path to Purpose: How Young People Find Their Calling in Life* (New York: Free Press, 2008), 5.

48. Ibid., 9.

49. Barbara Schneider and David Stevenson, *The Ambitious Generation: America's Teenagers Motivated but Directionless* (New Haven: Yale University Press, 1999).

50. Nathan, *My Freshman Year*, 114.

51. Clydesdale, *The First Year Out*, 163–64.

52. Valen E. Johnson, *Grade Inflation: A Crisis in College Education* (New York: Springer-Verlag, 2003), 2–3.

53. Noel Perrin, "How Students at Dartmouth Came to Deserve Better Grades," *Chronicle of Higher Education*, October 9, 1998, 68; as cited in Johnson, *Grade Inflation*, 5.

54. Johnson, *Grade Inflation*, 188f.

55. For racial/ethnic differences in course-taking among a recent cohort of students attending selective institutions, see Camille Charles et al., *Taming the River: Negotiating the Academic, Financial, and Social Currents in Selective Colleges and Universities* (Princeton, NJ: Princeton University Press, 2009), 24–33.

56. The R-squared increases from 0.147 to 0.310 when institutional-level fixed effects are added to the model.

57. Damon, *The Path to Purpose*, 8

58. Grigsby, *College Life through the Eyes of Students*, 56.

59. Nathan, *My Freshman Year*, 100.

60. Stephanie A. Clemons, David McKelfresh, and James Banning, "Importance of Sense of Place and Sense of Self in Residence Hall Room Design: A Qualitative Study of First-Year Students," *Journal of the First-Year Experience* 17 (2005): 73–86.

61. George D. Kuh, Robert M. Gonyea, and Megan Palmer, "The Disengaged Commuter Student: Fact or Fiction?" *Commuter Perspectives* 27 (2001): 2–5; Ernest T. Pascarella et al., "Cognitive Effects of Greek affiliation During the First Year of College," *NASPA Journal* 33 (1996): 242–59; and Ernest T. Pascarella et al., "Cognitive Impacts of Living on Campus versus Commuting to College" (University Park, PA: National Center on Postsecondary Teaching, Learning and Assessment, 1992).

62. Pascarella et al., "Cognitive Impacts of Living on Campus," 11.

63. Nathan, *My Freshman Year,* 80.

64. Grigsby, *College Life through the Eyes of Students*, 60.

65. Nathan, *My Freshman Year,* 48.

66. Steven Brint and Mathew Baron Rotondi, "Student Debt, the College Experience, and Transitions to Adulthood" (paper presented at the annual meeting for the American Sociological Association, Boston, July 31–August 4, 2008).

67. Jenny Stuber, "Class, Culture, and Participation in the Collegiate Extra-Curriculum," *Sociological Forum* 24 (2009): 889.

68. Ibid.

69. Susan R. Jones and Kathleen E. Hill, "Understanding Patterns of Commitment: Student Motivation for Community Service Involvement," *Journal of Higher Education* 74 (2003): 516–39; and Helen M. Marks and Susan R. Jones, "Community Service in the Transition: Shifts and Continuities in Participation from High School to College," *Journal of Higher Education* 75 (2004): 307–39.

70. Alexander Astin et al., "How Service Learning Affects Students" (Higher Education Research Institute, University of California Los Angeles, 2000).

71. Brint and Rotondi, "Student Debt."

72. Labor market participation in our sample is lower than the national average, but reasonably comparable to that of traditional-age students in four-year institutions (see table A1.3 in methodological appendix). However, students in our sample are working fewer hours, which would be expected given that we are relying on volunteers who were willing to dedicate a considerable amount of time to the CLA assessment.

73. American Council on Education, "Missed Opportunities Revisited: New Information on Students Who Do Not Apply for Financial Aid." American Council on Education Issue Brief (Washington, DC: American Council on Education, Center for Policy Analysis, 2006).

74. Jacqueline E. King, "Crucial Choice: How Students' Financial Decisions Affect Their Academic Success" (Washington, DC: American Council on Education, Center for Policy Analysis, 2002).

75. Kevin Dougherty, "Financing Higher Education in the United States: Structure, Trends, and Issues." Address to the Institute of Economics of Education, Peking University, May 25, 2004, 21, http://www.tc.columbia.edu/centers/coce/pdf_files/c9.pdf.

76. Brint and Rotondi, "Student Debt," 5.

77. Ibid.

78. Ibid., 15.

79. Robert D. Manning, "Living With Debt: A Life Stage Analysis of Changing Attitudes and Behaviors" (Rochester, NY: Rochester Institute of Technology, 2005), 32.

80. Brint and Rotondi, "Student Debt," 7.

81. Anya Kamenetz, *Generation Debt: How Our Future Was Sold Out for Student Loans, Bad Jobs, No Benefits, and Tax Cuts for Rich Geezers—And How to Fight Back* (New York: Riverhead Books, 2006), 16.

82. Manning, "Living with Debt," 34.

83. Charles F. Manski, "Identification of Endogenous Social Effects: The Reflection Problem," *Review of Economic Studies* 60 (1993): 531–42.

Chapter 4

1. See for example, Charles Murray, *Real Education: Four Simple Truths for Bringing American Schools Back to Reality* (New York: Crown Publishing House, 2008).

2. Pitrim Sorokin, *Social and Cultural Mobility* (New York: Free Press, 1959), 188–89.

3. Lowell C. Rose and Alec M. Gallup, *The 35th Annual Phi Delta Kappa/Gallup Poll of the Public's Attitudes toward the Public Schools* (Bloomington, IN: Phi Delta Kappa International, 2003).

4. Adam Liptak, "On the Bench and Off: The Eminently Quotable Justice Scalia," *New York Times*, May 11, 2009, http://www.nytimes.com/2009/05/12/us/12bar.html.

5. William Bowen and Derek Bok, *The Shape of the River* (Princeton, NJ: Princeton University Press, 1998); William Bowen, Matthew M. Chingos, and Michael S. McPherson, *Crossing the Finish Line: Completing College at America's Public Universities* (Princeton, NJ: Princeton University Press, 2009); and Kevin Carey, *A Matter of Degrees: Improving Graduation Rates in Four-Year Colleges and Universities* (Washington, DC: The Education Trust, 2004).

6. For recent reviews see, George D. Kuh et al., *What Matters to Student Success: A Review of the Literature* (Washington, DC: National Postsecondary Education Cooperative, 2006); and George D. Kuh et al., *Student Success in College: Creating Conditions that Matter* (San Francisco: Jossey-Bass, 2005).

7. Ernest T. Pascarella and Patrick T. Terenzini, *How College Affects Students: A Third Decade of Research* (San Francisco: Jossey-Bass, 2005), 602.

8. For an extensive recent review of the previous literature on the factors associated with development of general skills in higher education, see Pascarella and Terenzini, *How College Affects Students*, 155–212.

9. For clarity of presentation in this section, faculty and peer-climate variables are divided into three categories: "high," which represents one or more standard deviations above the mean; "low," which indicates one or more standard deviations below the mean, and "medium," which represents values in between. Since the original variables were based on a 1–7 scale and were not normally distributed, the three categories contain varying proportions of cases. All models predict 2007 CLA scores while controlling

for 2005 CLA scores, and thus in effect estimate the relationship between different variables of interest and growth in learning over time. As indicated, some models also control for students' sociodemographic/high school characteristics, academic preparation, and institutions attended (fixed-effects model).

10. The correlation between students' perceptions of faculty expectations and standards is 0.637, $p < 0.01$, and between students' perceptions of faculty expectations and being approachable is 0.523, $p < 0.01$.

11. William Sewell, Archibald Haller, and Alejandro Portes, "The Educational and Early Occupational Attainment Process," *American Sociological Review* 34 (1969): 82–92.

12. Alexander Astin, *What Matters in College? Four Critical Years Revisited* (San Francisco: Jossey-Bass, 1993), 217.

13. See for example, Robert M. Carini, George D. Kuh, and Stephen P. Klein, "Student Engagement and Student Learning: Testing the Linkages," *Research in Higher Education* 47 (2006): 1–32.

14. The two variables (faculty expectations and reading/writing requirements) are related, but far from perfectly so. Even if both are entered in the model simultaneously (as will be the case in the final model), they remain statistically significant and of similar magnitude.

15. Alexander Astin, *What Matters in College? Four Critical Years Revisited* (San Francisco: Jossey-Bass, 1993); Vincent Tinto, *Leaving College: Rethinking the Causes and Cures of Student Attrition* (Chicago: University of Chicago Press, 1993).

16. National Survey of Student Engagement (NSSE), *Experiences that Matter: Enhancing Student Learning and Success* (Bloomington, IN: Center for Postsecondary Research, Indiana University Bloomington, 2007), 46.

17. National Center for Education Statistics (NCES), *Descriptive Summary of 2003– 2004 Beginning Postsecondary Students: Three Years Later,* NCES 2008-174. (Washington, DC: U.S. Department of Education, 2008), table 3.1.

18. Carini, Kuh, and Klein, "Student Engagement and Student Learning," table 2.

19. The three measures of peer climates are reasonably highly correlated, with Cronbach's alpha of 0.74. A summary measure combining the three questions is also not related to learning.

20. For a recent study illuminating which peer interactions have positive relationships with learning, see Elizabeth J. Whitt et al., "Interactions with Peers and Objective and Self-Reported Cognitive Outcomes across 3 Years of College," *Journal of College Student Development* 40 (1999): 61–78.

21. Camille Charles et al., *Taming the River: Negotiating the Academic, Financial, and Social Currents in Selective Colleges and Universities* (Princeton, NJ: Princeton University Press, 2009), 82–90.

22. Ibid., 84.

23. Steven Brint and Allison M. Cantwell, "Undergraduate Time Use and Academic Outcomes: Results from UCUES 2006." Research and Occasional Paper Series (Center for Students in Higher Education, University of California, Berkeley, 2008).

24. Victor B. Saenz and Douglas S. Barrera, *Findings from the 2005 College Student Survey (CSS): National Aggregates* (Los Angeles: Higher Education Research Institute, 2007), 6, 10.

25. NSSE, *Experiences that Matter,* 13.

26. To answer this question, we estimate several regression models that predict 2007 CLA scores while controlling for 2005 CLA scores. Some models also control for students' sociodemographic/high school characteristics, academic preparation, and institutions attended (fixed-effects model), as indicated in the text.

27. Astin, *What Matters in College*, 376. For some recent examples of studies examining the relationship between studying and GPA, see Brint and Cantwell "Undergraduate Time Use and Academic Outcomes"; Charles et al., *Taming the River*; and Ralph Stinebrickner and Rodd R. Stinebrickner, "Time-Use and College Outcomes," *Journal of Econometrics* 121 (2003): 243–69.

28. There is no direct tradeoff between studying and participation in extracurricular activities. The two measures are actually slightly positively correlated ($r = 0.120$, $p < 0.01$), indicating that some students are more engaged, both in their studies and in other activities, while other students are less engaged in both domains.

29. For a review of research on the relationship between out-of-class experiences and learning, see Patrick T. Terenzini, Ernest T. Pascarella, and Gregory S. Blimling, "Students' Out-of-Class Experiences and Their Influence on Learning and Cognitive Development: A Literature Review," *Journal of College Student Development* 40 (1999): 610–23.

30. Astin, *What Matters in College*; Tinto, *Leaving College*.

31. Studies in the 1980s were mostly consistent in showing positive effects of on-campus work and negative effects of off-campus work, although recent studies have produced a more mixed set of results (see Pascarella and Terenzini, *How College Affects Students*, 1991; 2005).

32. There is a positive relationship between the two forms of studying: students who spend more time studying alone also spend more time studying with peers ($r = 0.263$, $p < 0.01$).

33. NCES, *Descriptive Summary of 2003–04 Beginning Postsecondary Students*, table 3.11.

34. Robert B. Barr and John Tagg, "From Teaching to Learning: A New Paradigm for Undergraduate Education," *Change* 27 (1995): 12–25.

35. National Science Foundation (NSF), *Shaping the Future: New Expectations for Undergraduate Education in Science, Mathematics, Engineering, and Technology* (Washington, DC: NSF, 1996), http://www.nsf.gov/pubs/stis1996/nsf96139/nsf96139.txt.

36. Small-group learning can appear under the heading of either "cooperative" or "collaborative" learning, which are related but have distinct theoretical bases. For review of recent research, see Leonard Spring, Mary Elizabeth Stanne, and Samuel S. Donovan, "Effects of Small-Group Learning on Undergraduates in Science, Mathematics, Engineering, and Technology: A Meta-Analysis," *Review of Educational Research* 69 (1999): 21–51. See also David W. Johnson, Roger T. Johnson, and Karl A. Smith, "Cooperative Learning Returns to College: What Evidence is There That It Works?" *Change* 30 (1998): 27–35. More recently, a broader definition of active/collaborative learning has been used to represent students' engagement with the learning process, including a range of activities from asking questions and participating in class discussion to working on projects and assignments with peers inside and outside the classroom. See for example, National Survey of Student Engagement (NSSE), *National Benchmarks of Effective Educational Practice* (Bloomington, IN: Center for Postsecondary Research, Indiana University Bloomington, 2000).

37. Carol L. Colbeck, Susan E. Campbell, and Stefani A. Bjorklund, "Grouping in the Dark: What College Students Learn from Group Projects," *Journal of Higher Education* 71 (2000): 61.

38. For example, see William Rau and Barbara Sherman Heyl, "Humanizing the College Classroom: Collaborative Learning and Social Organization among Students," *Teaching Sociology* 18 (1990): 141–55.

39. We include a square term for on-campus employment due to findings from previous research which indicate that work has a positive relationship to student outcomes up to a certain threshold. Indeed, the square term is statistically significant. We have also tested a square term for hours spent working off campus. However, this second square term was not statistically significant and is thus not included in the models.

40. Our results for employment may be weaker than expected because students in our sample work less than the national average. This is not surprising given that we are relying on volunteers who are willing to spend a substantial amount of time completing the CLA assessment and associated surveys. Indeed, very few students in our sample work more than twenty hours per week, and virtually none of them work full-time (i.e., thirty-five or more hours per week). In national samples, 13 percent of employed traditional-age students who entered four-year institutions report working full-time (authors' calculations based on the 2006 survey of the 2003–04 cohort of the Beginning Postsecondary Students (BPS) Longitudinal Study). However, students in our sample report working more hours than students at selective institutions (see Charles et al., *Taming the River*, 84, 87). For recent national estimates of college-student employment, see National Center for Education Statistics (NCES), *Profile of Undergraduates in U.S. Postsecondary Institutions: 2003–2004*, NCES 2006-184 (Washington, DC: U.S. Department of Education, 2006), table 5.1.

41. See also recent research by Pascarella and colleagues, who have conducted some of the most extensive analyses of the relationship between employment and direct measures of student learning. Ernest T. Pascarella et al., "Does Work Inhibit Cognitive Development During College?" *Educational Evaluation and Policy Analysis* 20 (1998): 75–93; and Ernest T. Pascarella et al., "Impacts of the On-Campus and Off-Campus Work on First-Year Cognitive Outcomes," *Journal of College Student Development* 35 (1994): 364–70.

42. Gary R. Pike, "The Influence of Fraternity or Sorority Membership on Students' College Experiences and Cognitive Development," *Research in Higher Education* 41 (2000): 117–39. For an example of a study using objective measures of learning, see Ernest T. Pascarella et al., "Cognitive Effects of Greek Affiliation during the First Year of College," *NASPA Journal* 33 (1996): 242–59.

43. In Grigsby's study, for example, students reported that involvement in Greek organizations has provided some of their most valuable experiences in college, and that affiliation with and leadership roles in these organizations have taught them responsibility and organizational skills. Mary Grigsby, *College Life through the Eyes of Students* (Albany: State University of New York Press, 2009).

44. For a recent review of the literature on the relationship between college major and cognitive development, see Pascarella and Terenzini, *How College Affects Students*, 174–76.

45. We focus on fields of study for ease of interpretation. Fields of study are highly, although not perfectly, correlated with course concentrations described in the previous chapter.

46. John C. Smart and Paul D. Umbach, "Faculty and Academic Environments: Using Holland's Theory to Explore Differences in How Faculty Structure Undergraduate Courses," *Journal of College Student Development* 48 (2007): 183–95; and Paul D. Umbach, "Faculty Cultures and College Teaching," in *The Scholarship of Teaching and Learning in Higher Education: An Evidence-Based Perspective*, ed. Raymond P. Perry and John C. Smart (New York: Springer, 2007), 263–318.

47. John M. Braxton, Deborah Olsen, and Ada Simmons, "Affinity Disciplines and the Use of Principles of Good Practice for Undergraduate Education," *Research in Higher Education* 39 (1998): 299–318.

48. John L. Holland, *Making Vocational Choices: A Theory of Vocational Personalities and Work Environments* (Odessa, FL: Psychological Assessment Resources, 1997).

49. Steven Brint, Allison M. Cantwell, and Robert A. Hanneman, "The Two Cultures of Undergraduate Academic Engagement," *Research in Higher Education* 49 (2008): 383–402.

50. The correlation between the percentage of costs covered through grants/scholarships and hours worked off campus is −0.080, $p < 0.01$; and the correlation for hours worked on campus is 0.083, $p < 0.01$. The correlation between the percentage of costs covered through loans and hours worked off campus is 0.053, $p < 0.01$, and the correlation for hours worked on campus is 0.050, $p < 0.05$.

51. We find no statistically significant interactions between any of the academic and social activities in college and race/ethnicity. Recent studies that have reported "compensatory effects" include Carini, Kuh and Klein, "Student Engagement and Student Learning"; Kuh et al., *What Matters to Student Success*; and George D. Kuh et al., "Unmasking the Effects of Student Engagement on College Grades and Persistence" (paper presented at the annual meeting for the American Educational Research Association, Chicago, April 9–13, 2007).

52. For a review of issues related to this topic see Christopher Jencks and Meredith Phillips, eds., *The Black-White Test Score Gap* (Washington, DC: Brookings Institution Press, 1998).

53. Signithia Fordham and John U. Ogbu, "Black Student's School Success: Coping with the 'Burden of Acting White,'" *Urban Review* 18 (1986): 176–206.

54. For some recent examples, see Karolyn Tyson, William Darity, and Domini Castellino, "It's Not 'a Black Thing': Understanding the Burden of Acting White and Other Dilemmas of High Achievement," *American Sociological Review* 70 (2005): 582–605; and James Ainsworth-Darnell and Douglas Downey, "Assessing the Oppositional Culture for Racial/Ethnic Differences in School Performance," *American Sociological Review* 63 (1998): 536–53.

55. Ann Swidler, "Culture in Action: Symbols and Strategies," *American Sociological Review* 51 (1986): 273–86.

56. Douglas Downey, "Black/White Differences in School Performance: The Oppositional Culture Explanation," *Annual Review of Sociology* 34 (2008): 121.

57. Claude M. Steele, "A Threat in the Air: How Stereotypes Shape Intellectual Identity and Performance," *American Psychologist* 52 (1997): 613–29.

58. Claude M. Steele and Joshua Aronson, "Stereotype Threat and the Intellectual Test Performance of African-Americans," *Journal of Personality and Social Psychology* 69 (1995): 797–811.

59. Charles et al., *Taming the River*, 173–87.

60. See for example, Carey, *A Matter of Degrees*.

61. Top-performing institutions include four with the highest gains in CLA scores, after adjusting for students' sociodemographic and high school characteristics as well as for academic preparation. Reported differences are statistically significant at $p < 0.05$.

62. Kuh et al., "An Unshakeable Focus on Student Learning," in *Student Success in College*.

63. For a review of research on learning communities, see Kathe Taylor, *Learning Community Research and Assessment: What We Know Now*. National Learning Communities Project Monograph Series (Olympia: Washington Center for Improving the Quality of Undergraduate Education, 2003). Moreover, for a recent study examining the relationship between learning communities and self-reported gains in learning and intellectual development, see Gary R. Pike, "The Effects of Residential Learning Communities and Traditional Residential Living Arrangements on Educational Gains During the First Year of College," *Journal of College Student Development* 40 (1999): 269–84.

64. George D. Kuh, "What We Are Learning About Student Engagement from NSSE," *Change* 35 (2003): 24–32; and National Survey of Student Engagement (NSSE), *Promoting Engagement for All Students: The Imperative to Look Within* (Bloomington, IN: Center for Postsecondary Research, Indiana University Bloomington, 2008).

65. For this analysis, we include only institutions with at least twenty-five students in the sample.

66. Correlation between 2007 CLA scores and college GPA is 0.35l, $p < 0.01$.

67. Students who report having both requirements report studying 2.29 hours more than those not having the requirements ($p < 0.01$).

68. This estimate is based on change in R^2 between model 2 (including 2005 CLA score, background characteristics, and academic preparation) and model 4 (adding measures of students' college experiences and controlling for institutions attended) in table A4.5.

69. This estimate is based on change in R^2 between model 1 (including 2005 CLA score and background characteristics) and model 2 (adding academic preparation) in table A4.5.

70. If our sample were less socioeconomically advantaged, we might have observed more time dedicated to activities such as work, child-rearing, caring for siblings, etc. These time commitments are very distinct from socializing, but they nonetheless take students away from the focus on academics. Whether it is frivolity or necessity, students in higher education have many competing demands. And in this competition, learning seems to often lose out.

71. Brint and Cantwell, "Undergraduate Time Use and Academic Outcomes," 3.

72. As Jenny Stuber pointed out recently, this emerges largely from the middle-class conception of schooling. Jenny Stuber, "Class, Culture, and the Participation in the Collegiate Extra-Curriculum," *Sociological Forum* 24 (2009): 877–900.

Chapter 5

1. Excerpt from an interview transcript of Lee S. Shulman in *Declining by Degrees: Higher Education at Risk* (New York: Public Broadcast System, 2005).

2. Helen Lefkowitz Horowitz, *Campus Life: Undergraduate Cultures from the End of the Eighteenth Century to the Present* (New York: Alfred A. Knopf, 1987), 11.

3. The National Commission on Excellence in Education, *A Nation at Risk: The Imperative for Educational Reform* (Washington, DC: U.S. Department of Education, 1983).

4. Richard Herrnstein and Charles Murray, *The Bell Curve: Intelligence and Class Structure in American Life* (New York: Free Press, 1994). For a critique of Herrnstein and Murray, see Claude Fischer et al., *Inequality by Design: Cracking the Bell Curve Myth* (Princeton, NJ: Princeton University Press, 1996), and Richard Nisbett, *Intelligence and How to Get It* (New York: Norton, 2009).

5. Patrick Callan, *Commentary on Measuring Up 2006 Report* (San Jose, CA: The National Center for Public Policy and Higher Education, 2006).

6. Arthur M. Hauptman and Young Kim, *Cost, Commitment, and Attainment in Higher Education: An International Comparison* (Boston: Jobs for the Future, 2009).

7. U.S. Department of Education, *A Test of Leadership: Charting the Future of U.S. Higher Education* (Washington, DC: U.S. Department of Education, 2006), vii.

8. Alan Wagner, *Measuring Up Internationally: Developing Skills and Knowledge for the Global Knowledge Economy* (San Jose, CA: National Center for Public Policy and Higher Education, 2006). On the federal government's recent decision to participate in this project, see Doug Lederman, "Measuring Student Learning, Globally," *Inside Higher Ed*, January 28, 2010.

9. Claudia Goldin and Lawrence F. Katz, *The Race between Education and Technology* (Cambridge, MA: Belknap Press of Harvard University Press, 2008).

10. Richard Arum, Josipa Roksa, and Michelle Budig, "The Romance of College Attendance: Higher Education Stratification and Mate Selection," *Research in Social Stratification and Mobility* 26 (2008): 107–22.

11. Richard Arum, *Judging School Discipline: The Crisis of Moral Authority* (Cambridge, MA: Harvard University Press, 2003), 2.

12. Clifford Adelman, *The Toolbox Revisited: Paths to Degree Completion From High School Through College* (Washington, DC: U.S. Department of Education, 2006), 5.

13. Ibid., 34.

14. Arum, *Judging School Discipline*.

15. Barbara Schneider and David Stevenson, *The Ambitious Generation: America's Teenagers Motivated but Directionless* (New Haven: Yale University Press, 1999).

16. William Damon, *The Path to Purpose: How Young People Find Their Calling in Life* (New York: Free Press, 2008), 111.

17. George D. Kuh et al., *Student Success in College: Creating Conditions that Matter* (San Francisco: Jossey-Bass, 2005), 272.

18. Ibid., 270.

19. Jillian Kinzie and George D. Kuh, "Going DEEP: Learning from Campuses that Share Responsibility for Student Success," *About Campus* 9 (2004): 2–8; and George D. Kuh et al., "Never Let It Rest: Lessons about Student Success from High-Performing Colleges and Universities," *Change* 37 (2005): 44–51.

20. Julie A. Reuben, *The Making of the Modern University: Intellectual Transformation and the Marginalization of Morality* (Chicago: University of Chicago Press, 1996), 260.

21. Ibid., 260–61.

22. Mary Grigsby, *College Life through the Eyes of Students* (Albany: State University of New York Press, 2009), 58–59.

23. Valerie Lee and Anthony Bryk, "A Multilevel Model of the Social Distribution of High School Achievement," *Sociology of Education* 62 (1989): 172–92; and Meredith Phillips, "What Makes Schools Effective? A Comparison of the Relationships of Communitarian Climate and Academic Climate to Mathematics Achievement and Attendance during Middle School," *American Educational Research Journal* 34 (1997): 633–62.

24. Robert Rosenthal and Lenore Jacobson, "Pygmalion in the Classroom," *Urban Review* 3 (1968): 1–16.

25. Arthur W. Chickering and Zelda F. Gamson, "Seven Principles for Good Practice in Undergraduate Education," *AAHE Bulletin* 39 (1987): 3–7. See also Arthur W. Chickering and Zelda F. Gamson, eds., *Applying the Seven Principles for Good Practice in Undergraduate Education. New Directions for Teaching and Learning, No. 47* (San Francisco: Jossey-Bass, 1991).

26. Kuh et al., *Success in College*. See also National Survey of Student Engagement (NSSE), *National Benchmarks of Effective Educational Practice* (Bloomington, IN: Center for Postsecondary Research, Indiana University Bloomington, 2000).

27. Kuh et al., *Success in College*. See also George D. Kuh et al., "Unmasking the Effects of Student Engagement on College Grades and Persistence" (paper presented at the annual meeting for the American Educational Research Association, Chicago, April 9–13, 2007).

28. Charles Blaich, "Overview of Findings from the First Year of the Wabash National Study of Liberal Arts Education" (Wabash College, Center of Inquiry in the Liberal Arts, 2007, http://www.liberalarts.wabash.edu/research/).

29. George D. Kuh, "What We Are Learning about Student Engagement from NSSE," *Change* 35 (2004): 28.

30. Robert B. Barr and John Tagg, "From Teaching to Learning: A New Paradigm for Undergraduate Education," *Change* 27 (1995): 12–25. For a review of scholarship on higher-education teaching and learning, see Ernest T. Pascarella and Patrick T. Terenzini, *How College Affects Students: A Third Decade of Research* (San Francisco: Jossey-Bass, 2005).

31. Martha Stone Wiske, ed., *Teaching for Understanding: Linking Research with Practice* (San Francisco: Jossey-Bass, 1998), 350. See also website for Harvard Project Zero at http://pzweb.harvard.edu/.

32. National Survey of Student Engagement (NSSE), *Experiences that Matter: Enhancing Student Learning and Success* (Bloomington, IN: Center for Postsecondary Research, Indiana University, Bloomington, 2007), 44.

33. Steven Brint, "The Academic Devolution? Movements to Reform Teaching and Learning in U.S. Colleges and Universities, 1985–2010." Working Paper Series (Center for Studies in Higher Education, University of California, Berkeley, 2009). For the interpretation of the history of Dewey and progressive education, Brint cites Lawrence Cremin, *The Transformation of the School, 1876–1957* (New York: Random House, 1961).

34. NSSE, *Experiences that Matter*, 42, 44.

35. Robert M. Carini, George D. Kuh, and Stephen P. Klein, "Student Engagement and Student Learning: Testing the Linkages," *Research in Higher Education* 47 (2006): 1–32.

36. Victor B. Saenz and Douglas S. Barrera, *Findings from the 2005 College Student Survey (CSS): National Aggregates* (Los Angeles: Higher Education Research Institute, 2007), 6.

37. George D. Kuh et al., *What Matters to Student Success: A Review of the Literature* (Washington, DC: National Postsecondary Education Cooperative, 2006), 68.

38. Chris M. Golde and Timothy M. Dore, *At Cross Purposes: What the Experiences of Today's Graduate Students Reveal about Doctoral Education* (Philadelphia: Pew Charitable Trusts, 2001), 22. It is also important to note that making something available does not

mean that it's taken advantage of; only slightly more than two-thirds of students who had TA training available to them actually participated.

39. Jody D. Nyquist et al., *The Development of Graduate Students as Prospective Teaching Scholars: A Four Year Longitudinal Study, Final Report* (Seattle: University of Washington, 2001).

40. Jody D. Nyguist et al., "On the Road to Becoming a Professor: The Graduate Student Experience." *Change* 31 (1999): 23–24.

41. Golde and Dore, *At Cross Purposes*, 18. See also Lee S. Shulman, "The Doctoral Imperative: Examining the Ends of Erudition." Talk presented at a Conference on Re-examining the PhD, held in Seattle in April 2000. Reprinted in *Teaching as Community Property: Essays on Higher Education* (San Francisco: Jossey-Bass, 2004), 220–32.

42. Chris Golde, "Findings of the Survey of Doctoral Education and Career Preparation: A Report to the Preparing Future Faculty Program" (unpublished manuscript, University of Wisconsin–Madison, 2001). For other evaluations and resources, see the Preparing Future Faculty Program website at http://www.preparing-faculty.org/.

43. For the role of teaching in the academy, see essays by Lee S. Shulman in *Teaching as Community Property* (San Francisco: Jossey-Bass, 2004). See in particular the following essays: "Teaching as Community Property: Putting an End to Pedagogical Solitude," 140–44; "From Minsk to Pinsk: Why a Scholarship of Teaching and Learning?," 156–62, and "The Doctoral Imperative: Examining the Ends of Erudition," 220–32.

44. Vincent Tinto, *Leaving College: Rethinking the Causes and Cures of Student Attrition* (Chicago: University of Chicago Press, 1993), 206. Emphasis added.

45. Alexander Astin, *What Matters in College? Four Critical Years Revisited* (San Francisco: Jossey-Bass, 1993), 196.

46. Camille Charles et al., *Taming the River: Negotiating the Academic, Financial, and Social Currents in Selective Colleges and Universities* (Princeton, NJ: Princeton University Press, 2009), 226. Emphasis in original.

47. Tinto, *Leaving College*, 131.

48. Richard Arum, Adam Gamoran, and Yossi Shavit, "More Inclusion than Diversion: Expansion, Differentiation, and Market Structure in Higher Education" in *Stratification in Higher Education: A Comparative Study*, ed. Yossi Shavit, Richard Arum, and Adam Gamoran (Stanford, CA: Stanford University Press, 2007), 1–38.

49. John Dewey, *The Child and the Curriculum and the School and Society* (Chicago: University of Chicago Press, 1956), 7.

50. U.S. Department of Education, *A Test of Leadership*, 16.

51. Ibid., 13.

52. Ibid.

53. Ibid., 22.

54. Derek Bok, *Our Underachieving Colleges: A Candid Look at How Much Students Learn and Why They Should Be Learning More* (Princeton, NJ: Princeton University Press, 2006), 326–27.

55. Association of American Colleges and Universities and the Council for Higher Education Accreditation, *New Leadership for Student Learning and Accountability: A Statement of Principles, Commitments to Action* (Washington, DC: Association of American Colleges and Universities and the Council for Higher Education Accreditation, 2008).

56. U.S. Department of Education, *A Test of Leadership*, 21.

57. Association of American Colleges and Universities, *Our Students' Best Work: A*

Framework for Accountability Worthy of Our Mission. Statement from the Board of Directors (Washington, DC: Association of American Colleges and Universities, 2008), 8. Cited in Brint, "The Academic Devolution?"

58. Frederick Hess, *Tough Love for Schools: Essays on Competition, Accountability and Excellence* (Washington, DC: American Enterprise Institute, 2006), 78–80.

59. Federal 2009 research budgets, including those of the National Institutes of Health and National Science Foundation, include federal stimulus dollars as reported by the American Association for the Advancement of Science, "September R&D Funding Update" (Washington, DC: American Association for the Advancement of Science, 2009). Support for the Fund for Post-Secondary Improvement was reported by the U.S. Department of Education, "FY 2009 Congressional Action" (Washington, DC: U.S. Department of Education, 2009).

60. A survey of employers conducted on behalf of the Association of American Colleges and Universities by Peter D. Hart Research Associated, Inc., *How Should Colleges Assess and Improve Student Learning? Employers Views on the Accountability Challenge* (Washington DC: Peter D. Hart Research Associated, Inc., 2008).

61. *Are They Really Ready to Work? Employers' Perspectives on the Basic Knowledge and Applied Skills of New Entrants to the 21st Century U.S. Workforce* (The Conference Board, Corporate Voices for Working Families, the Partnership for 21st Century Skills, and the Society of Human Resource Management, 2006, http://www.21stcenturyskills.org/documents/FINAL_REPORT_PDF09–29–06.pdf), 20, 34.

62. Association of American Colleges and Universities, *How Should Colleges Assess and Improve Student Learning*, 4.

63. Pew Research Center, *Pew Research Center Biennial News Consumption Survey* (Washington, DC: Pew Research Center, 2008).

64. President John F. Kennedy, speech given at Rice University, Houston, TX, on September 12, 1962.

Methodological Appendix

1. Judith D. Singer, "Using SAS PROC MIXED to Fit Multilevel Models, Hierarchical Models, and Individual Growth Models." *Journal of Educational and Behavioral Statistics* 23/4 (1998): 323–55.

Bibliography

Adelman, Clifford. *The Toolbox Revisited: Paths to Degree Completion from High School through College.* Washington, DC: U.S. Department of Education, 2006.

Ainsworth-Darnell, James, and Douglas Downey. "Assessing the Oppositional Culture for Racial/Ethnic Differences in School Performance." *American Sociological Review* 63 (1998): 536–53.

Alexander, Karl L., and Aaron M. Pallas. "School Sector and Cognitive Performance: When Is a Little a Little?" *Sociology of Education* 58 (1985): 115–28.

American Association for the Advancement of Science. "September R&D Funding Update." Washington, DC: American Association for the Advancement of Science, 2009.

American Council on Education (ACE). "ACE Issue Brief: Missed Opportunities Revisited: New Information on Students Who Do Not Apply for Financial Aid." Washington, DC: ACE Center for Policy Analysis, 2006.

Are They Really Ready to Work? Employers' Perspectives on the Basic Knowledge and Applied Skills of New Entrants to the 21st Century U.S. Workforce. The Conference Board, Corporate Voices for Working Families, the Partnership for 21st Century Skills, and the Society of Human Resource Management, 2006, http://www.21stcenturyskills.org/documents/FINAL_REPORT_PDF09-29-06.pdf

Arnett, Jeffrey Jensen. *Emerging Adulthood: The Winding Path from the Late Teens through the Twenties.* New York: Oxford University Press, 2004.

Arum, Richard. *Judging School Discipline: The Crisis of Moral Authority.* Cambridge, MA: Harvard University Press, 2003.

Arum, Richard, Adam Gamoran, and Yossi Shavit. "More Inclusion than Diversion: Expansion, Differentiation, and Market Structure in Higher Education." In *Stratification in Higher Education: A Comparative Study,* edited by Yossi Shavit, Richard Arum, and Adam Gamoran, 1–38. Stanford, CA: Stanford University Press, 2007.

Arum, Richard, Josipa Roksa, and Michelle Budig. "The Romance of College Attendance: Higher Education Stratification and Mate Selection." *Research in Social Stratification and Mobility* 26 (2008): 107–22.

Association of American Colleges and Universities. *Statement from the Board of Directors: Our Students' Best Work: A Framework for Accountability Worthy of Our Mission.* Washington, DC: Association of American Colleges and Universities, 2008.

Association of American Colleges and Universities, and the Council for Higher Education Accreditation. *New Leadership for Student Learning and Accountability: A Statement of Principles, Commitments to Action.* Washington, DC: Association of American College and Universities, and the Council for Higher Education Accreditation, 2008.

Astin, Alexander. *What Matters in College? Four Critical Years Revisited.* San Francisco: Jossey-Bass, 1993.

———. "The Changing American College Student: Thirty Year Trends, 1966–1996." *Review of Higher Education* 21 (1998): 115–35.

Astin, Alexander, Lori J. Vogelgesang, Elaine K. Ikeda, and Jennifer A. Yee. "How Service Learning Affects Students." Higher Education Research Institute, University of California Los Angeles, 2000.

Attewell, Paul, and David Lavin. *Passing the Torch: Does Higher Education for the Disadvantaged Pay Off across the Generations?* New York: Russell Sage Foundation, 2007.

Babcock, Philip, and Mindy Marks. "The Falling Time Cost of College: Evidence from Half a Century of Time Use Data." *Review of Economics and Statistics* (forthcoming).

Banks, Barbara J., Ricky L. Slavings, and Bruce J. Biddle. "Effects of Peer, Faculty, and Parental Influences on Students' Persistence." *Sociology of Education* 63 (1990): 208–25.

Barr, Robert B., and John Tagg. "From Teaching to Learning: A New Paradigm for Undergraduate Education." *Change* 27 (1995): 12–25.

Basken, Paul. "Test Touted as 2 Studies Question Its Value: Small Colleges Back Achievement Exam to Measure Accountability." *Chronicle of Higher Education,* June 6, 2008, http://chronicle.com/article/Test-Touted-as-2-Studies/23503/.

Bick, Julie. "The Long (and Sometimes Expensive) Road to the SAT." *New York Times,* May 28, 2006, http://www.nytimes.com/2006/05/28/business/yourmoney/28test .html?scp=21&sq=SAT%20prep&st=cse

Blaich, Charles. "Overview of Findings from the First Year of the Wabash National Study of Liberal Arts Education." Wabash College, Center of Inquiry in the Liberal Arts, 2007, http://www.liberalarts.wabash.edu/research/.

Bok, Derek. *Higher Learning.* Cambridge, MA: Harvard University Press, 1986.

———. *Universities in the Marketplace: The Commercialization of Higher Education.* Princeton, NJ: Princeton University Press, 2003.

———. *Our Underachieving Colleges: A Candid Look at How Much Students Learn and Why They Should Be Learning More.* Princeton, NJ: Princeton University Press, 2006.

Bound, John, Michael Lovenheim, and Sarah E. Turner. "Understanding the Decrease in College Completion Rates and the Increased Time to the Baccalaureate Degree." PSC Research Report No. 07–626. Population Studies Center, University of Michigan, 2007.

———. "Why Have College Completion Rates Declined? An Analysis of Changing Student Preparation and College Resources." NBER Working Paper no. 15566. Cambridge, MA: National Bureau of Economic Research, 2009.

Bourdieu, Pierre. "Cultural Reproduction and Social Reproduction." In *Knowledge, Edu-*

cation, and Cultural Change, edited by Richard Brown, 71–112. London: Tavistock, 1973.

Bowen, William, and Derek Bok. *The Shape of the River: Long-Term Consequences of Considering Race in College and University Admissions*. Princeton, NJ: Princeton University Press, 1998.

Bowen, William G., Matthew M. Chingos, and Michael S. McPherson. *Crossing the Finish Line: Completing College at America's Public Universities*. Princeton, NJ: Princeton University Press, 2009.

Bowles, Samuel, and Herbert Gintis. *Schooling in Capitalist America*. New York: Basic Books, 1976.

Boyer, Ernest L. *College: The Undergraduate Experience in America*. New York: Harper and Row, 1987.

———. *Scholarship Reconsidered: Priorities of the Professoriate*. Stanford, CA: The Carnegie Foundation for the Advancement of Teaching, 1990.

Braxton, John M., Deborah Olsen, and Ada Simmons. "Affinity Disciplines and the Use of Principles of Good Practice for Undergraduate Education." *Research in Higher Education* 39 (1998): 299–318.

Breyer, Catherine Hoffman. "The Right Way to Measure College Learning: National Standardized Testing Won't Work." *Christian Science Monitor,* April 9, 2007, http://www.csmonitor.com/2007/0409/p09s01-coop.html.

Brint, Steven. "The Rise of the Practical Arts." In *The Future of the City of Intellect: The Changing American University*, edited by Steven Brint, 222–59. Stanford, CA: Stanford University Press, 2002.

———. "The Academic Devolution? Movements to Reform Teaching and Learning in U.S. Colleges and Universities, 1985–2010." Working Paper Series. Center for Studies in Higher Education, University of California, Berkeley, 2009.

Brint, Steven, and Allison M. Cantwell. "Undergraduate Time Use and Academic Outcomes: Results From UCUES 2006." Research and Occasional Paper Series. Center for Studies in Higher Education, University of California, Berkeley, 2008.

Brint, Steven, Allison M. Cantwell, and Robert A. Hanneman. "The Two Cultures of Undergraduate Academic Engagement." *Research in Higher Education* 49 (2008): 383–402.

Brint, Steven, and Mathew Baron Rotondi. "Student Debt, the College Experience, and Transitions to Adulthood." Paper presented at the annual meeting for the American Sociological Association, Boston, July 31–August 4, 2008.

Calcagno, Juan Carlos, and Bridget Terry Long. "The Impact of Postsecondary Remediation Using a Regression Discontinuity Approach: Addressing Endogenous Sorting and Noncompliance." NBER Working Paper Series no. 14194. Cambridge, MA: National Bureau of Economic Research, 2008.

Callan, Patrick. *Commentary on Measuring Up 2006 Report*. San Jose, CA: The National Center for Public Policy and Higher Education, 2006.

Carey, Kevin. *A Matter of Degrees: Improving Graduation Rates in Four-Year Colleges and Universities*. Washington, DC: The Education Trust, 2004.

Carini, Robert M., George D. Kuh, and Stephen P. Klein. "Student Engagement and Student Learning: Testing the Linkages." *Research in Higher Education* 47 (2006): 1–32.

Charles, Camille, Mary Fischer, Margarita Mooney, and Douglas Massey. *Taming the River: Negotiating the Academic, Financial, and Social Currents in Selective Colleges and Universities*. Princeton, NJ: Princeton University Press, 2009.

Chickering, Arthur W., and Zelda F. Gamson. "Seven Principles for Good Practice in Undergraduate Education." *AAHE Bulletin* 39 (1987): 3–7.

———, eds. *Applying the Seven Principles for Good Practice in Undergraduate Education. New Directions for Teaching and Learning, No. 47.* San Francisco: Jossey-Bass, 1991.

Clemons, Stephanie A., David McKelfresh, and James Banning. "Importance of Sense of Place and Sense of Self in Residence Hall Room Design: A Qualitative Study of First-Year Students." *Journal of the First-Year Experience* 17 (2005): 73–86.

Clydesdale, Tim. *The First Year Out: Understanding American Teens after High School.* Chicago: University of Chicago Press, 2007.

Colbeck, Carol L., Susan E. Campbell, and Stefani A. Bjorklund. "Grouping in the Dark: What College Students Learn from Group Projects." *Journal of Higher Education* 71 (2000): 60–83.

Coleman, James. *The Adolescent Society.* New York: Free Press, 1961.

Coleman, James, et al. *Equality of Educational Opportunity.* Washington, DC: Government Printing Office, 1966.

College Board. *Trends in College Pricing.* New York: College Board, 2008.

———. *Trends in Student Aid.* New York: College Board, 2008.

Collins, Randall. *Credential Society.* New York: Academic Press, 1979.

Council for Aid to Education. *Collegiate Learning Assessment Common Scoring Rubric.* New York: Council for Aid to Education, 2008.

Cremin, Lawrence Arthur. *The Transformation of the School Progressivism in American Education, 1876–1957.* New York: Knopf, 1961.

Damon, William. *The Path to Purpose: How Young People Find Their Calling in Life.* New York: Free Press, 2008.

Dar, Yehezkel, and Nura Resh. "Classroom Intellectual Composition and Academic Achievement." *American Educational Research Journal* 23 (1986): 357–74.

Davies, Mark, and Denise B. Kandel. "Parental and Peer Influences on Adolescents' Educational Plans: Some Further Evidence." *American Journal of Sociology* 87 (1981): 363–87.

Dewey, John. *The Child and the Curriculum and the School and Society.* Chicago: University of Chicago Press, 1956.

Dougherty, Kevin. "Financing Higher Education in the United States: Structure, Trends, and Issues." Address to the Institute of Economics of Education, Peking University, May 25, 2004, http://www.tc.columbia.edu/centers/coce/pdf_files/c9.pdf.

Downey, Douglas. "Black/White Differences in School Performance: The Oppositional Culture Explanation." *Annual Review of Sociology* 34 (2008): 107–26.

Downey, Douglas B., Paul T. von Hippel, and Beckett A. Broh. "Are Schools the Great Equalizer? Cognitive Inequality during the Summer Months and the School Year." *American Sociological Review* 69 (2004): 613–35.

Du Bois, W.E.B. "The Talented Tenth." In *The Negro Problem: A Series of Articles by Representative Negroes of To-day,* edited by Booker T. Washington, 31–74. New York: James Pott & Company, 1903.

Epstein, Jennifer. "Questioning College-Wide Assessments." *Inside Higher Ed,* June 21, 2007, http://www.insidehighered.com/news/2007/06/21/assessments.

Fischer, Claude S., Michael Hout, Martin Sanchez Jankowksi, Samuel R. Lucas, Ann Swidler, and Kim Vos. *Inequality by Design: Cracking the Bell Curve Myth.* Princeton, NJ: Princeton University Press, 1996.

Flowers, Lamont A., Steven J. Osterlind, Ernest T. Pascarella, and Christopher T.

Pierson. "How Much Do Students Learn in College?" *Journal of Higher Education* 72 (2001): 565–83.

Fordham, Signithia, and John U. Ogbu. "Black Student's School Success: Coping with the 'Burden of Acting White'." *Urban Review* 18 (1986): 176–206.

Frank, Robert, and Phillip Cook. "It's a Winner-Take-All Market." *Washington Monthly*, December 1, 1995.

Gamoran, Adam. "The Variable Effects of High School Tracking." *American Sociological Review* 57 (1992): 812–28.

———. "American Schooling and Educational Inequality: A Forecast for the 21st Century." *Sociology of Education* 75 (2001): 135–53.

Gerber, Theodore P., and Sin Yi Cheung. "Horizontal Stratification in Postsecondary Education: Forms, Explanation, and Implications." *Annual Review of Sociology* 34 (2008): 299–318.

Golde, Chris M. "Findings of the Survey of Doctoral Education and Career Preparation: A Report to the Preparing Future Faculty Program." Unpublished manuscript. University of Wisconsin–Madison, 2001.

Golde, Chris M., and Timothy M. Dore. *At Cross Purposes: What the Experiences of Today's Graduate Students Reveal about Doctoral Education.* Philadelphia: Pew Charitable Trusts, 2001.

Goldin, Claudia, and Lawrence F. Katz. *The Race between Education and Technology.* Cambridge, MA: Belknap Press of Harvard University Press, 2008.

Grigsby, Mary. *College Life through the Eyes of Students.* Albany: State University of New York Press, 2009.

Grosso de León, Anne. "The Collegiate Learning Assessment: A Tool for Measuring the Value Added of a Liberal Arts Education." *Carnegie Results.* New York: Carnegie Corporation of New York, Fall 2007.

Hallinan, Maureen T., and Richard A. Williams. "Students' Characteristics and the Peer-Influence Process." *Sociology of Education* 63 (1990): 122–32.

Hauptman, Arthur M., and Young Kim. *Cost, Commitment, and Attainment in Higher Education: An International Comparison.* Boston: Jobs for the Future, 2009.

Hauser, Robert M., Christopher F. Edley Jr., Judith Anderson Koenig, and Stuart W. Elliott, eds. *Measuring Literacy: Performance Levels for Adults.* Washington, DC: National Research Council, 2005.

Herrnstein, Richard, and Charles Murray. *The Bell Curve: Intelligence and Class Structure in American Life.* New York: Free Press, 1994.

Hersch, Richard. "Going Naked." *AAC&U Peer Review* 9 (2007): 4–8.

Hess, Frederick. *Tough Love for Schools: Essays on Competition, Accountability and Excellence.* Washington, DC: American Enterprise Institute, 2006.

Higher Education Research Institute (HERI). *The American College Teacher: National Norms for 2007–2008.* Los Angeles: HERI, University of California Los Angeles, 2009.

Hoffer, Thomas, Andrew M. Greeley, and James S. Coleman. "Achievement Growth in Public and Catholic Schools." *Sociology of Education* 58 (1985): 74–97.

Holland, John L. *Making Vocational Choices: A Theory of Vocational Personalities and Work Environments.* Odessa, FL: Psychological Assessment Resources, 1997.

Horowitz, Helen Lefkowitz. *Campus Life: Undergraduate Cultures from the End of the Eighteenth Century to the Present.* New York: Alfred A. Knopf, 1987.

Hout, Michael. "Politics of Mobility." In *Generating Social Stratification*, edited by Alan C. Kerckhoff, 301–25. Boulder, CO: Westview Press, 1995.

Ito, Mizuko, Heather Horst, Matteo Bittanti, Danah Botd, Becky Herr-Stephenson, Patricia G. Lange, C. J. Pascoe, and Laura Robinson. *Living and Learning with New Media: Summary of Findings from the Digital Youth Project.* Chicago: John D. and Catherine T. MacArthur Foundation, 2008.

Jaschik, Scott. "Does 'Value Added' Add Value?" *Inside Higher Ed,* November 3, 2006, http://www.insidehighered.com/news/2006/11/03/assess.

Jencks, Christopher, and Meredith Phillips. *The Black-White Test Score Gap.* Washington, DC: Bookings Institution Press, 1998.

Jencks, Christopher, and David Riesman. *The Academic Revolution.* New York: Doubleday, 1968.

Jencks, Christopher, Marshall Smith, Henry Acland, Mary Jo Bane, David Cohen, Herbert Gintis, Barbara Heyns, and Stephan Michelson. *Inequality: A Reassessment of the Effect of Family and Schooling in America.* New York: Basic Books, 1972.

Johnson, David W., Roger T. Johnson, and Karl A. Smith. "Cooperative Learning Returns to College: What Evidence is There That it Works?" *Change* 30 (1998): 27–35.

Johnson, Valen E. *Grade Inflation: A Crisis in College Education.* New York: Springer-Verlag, 2003.

Jones, Susan R., and Kathleen E. Hill. "Understanding Patterns of Commitment; Student Motivation for Community Service Involvement." *Journal of Higher Education* 74 (2003): 516–39.

Kamenetz, Anya. *Generation Debt: How Our Future Was Sold Out for Student Loans, Bad Jobs, No Benefits, and Tax Cuts for Rich Geezers—And How to Fight Back.* New York: Riverhead Books, 2006.

Kane, Thomas. *The Price of Admission: Rethinking How Americans Pay for College.* Washington, DC: Brookings Institution Press, 1999.

Katz, Michael, ed. *School Reform Past and Present.* Boston: Little Brown and Company, 1971.

Kennedy, John F. Speech given at Rice University, Houston, TX, September 12, 1962.

Kerr, Clark. *The Uses of the University.* Cambridge, MA: Harvard University Press, 2001.

Kim, Young K., and Linda J. Sax. "Student-Faculty Interaction in Research Universities: Differences by Student Gender, Race, Social Class, and First-Generation Status." *Research in Higher Education* 50 (2009): 437–59.

King, Jacqueline E. "Crucial Choice: How Students' Financial Decisions Affect Their Academic Success." Washington, DC: American Council on Education, Center for Policy Analysis, 2002.

———. *The American College President 2007 Edition.* Washington, DC: American Council on Education, 2007.

Kinzie, Jillian, and George D. Kuh. "Going DEEP: Learning from Campuses that Share Responsibility for Student Success." *About Campus* 9 (2004): 2–8.

Klein, Stephen, Ou Lydia Liu, and James Sconing. *Test Validity Study (TVS) Report.* September 29, 2009. http://www.voluntarysystem.org/docs/reports/TVSReport _Final.pdf

Klein, Stephen, Richard Shavelson, and Roger Benjamin. "Setting the Record Straight." *Inside Higher Ed,* February 8, 2007, http://www.insidehighered.com/views/2007/ 02/08/benjamin

Kronman, Anthony T. *Education's End: Why Our Colleges and Universities Have Given Up on the Meaning of Life.* New Haven: Yale University Press, 2007.

Kuh, George D. "What we are learning about student engagement from NSSE." *Change* 35 (2003): 24–32.

Kuh, George D., Ty Cruce, Rick Shoup, Jillian Kinzie, and Robert M. Gonyea. "Unmasking the Effects of Student Engagement on College Grades and Persistence." Paper presented at the annual meeting for the American Educational Research Association, Chicago, April 9–13, 2007.

Kuh, George D., Robert M. Gonyea, and Megan Palmer. "The Disengaged Commuter Student: Fact or Fiction?" *Commuter Perspectives* 27 (2001): 2–5.

Kuh, George D. and Shouping Hu. "The Effects of Student-Faculty Interaction in the 1990s." *Review of Higher Education* 24 (2001): 309–32.

Kuh, George D., Jillian Kinzie, Jennifer A. Buckely, Brian K. Bridges, and John C. Hayek. *What Matters to Student Success: A Review of the Literature.* Washington, DC: National Postsecondary Education Cooperative, 2006.

Kuh, George D., Jillian Kinzie, John H. Schuh, and Elizabeth J. Whitt. "Never Let It Rest: Lessons about Student Success from High-Performing Colleges and Universities." *Change* 37 (2005): 44–51.

———. *Assessing Conditions to Enhance Educational Effectiveness: The Inventory for Student Engagement and Success.* San Francisco: Jossey-Bass, 2005.

Kuh, George D., Jillian Kinzie, John H. Schuh, Elizabeth J. Whitt, et al. *Student Success in College: Creating Conditions that Matter.* San Francisco: Jossey-Bass, 2005.

Labaree, David. *How to Succeed in School without Really Learning: The Credentials Race in American Education.* New Haven: Yale University Press, 1997.

Lareau, Annette. *Unequal Childhoods: Class, Race, and Family Life.* Berkeley: University of California Press, 2003.

Lareau, Annette, and Elliot B. Weininger. "Class and the Transition to Adulthood." In *Social Class: How Does it Work?*, edited by Annette Lareau and Dalton Conley, 118–51. New York: Russell Sage Foundation, 2008.

Lederman, Doug. "Measuring Student Learning, Globally." *Inside Higher Ed*, January 28, 2010, http://www.insidehighered.com/news/2010/01/28/oecd.

———. "No College Left Behind?" *Inside Higher Ed*, February 15, 2006, http://www.insidehighered.com/news/2006/02/15/testing.

Lee, Valerie, and Anthony Bryk. "A Multilevel Model of the Social Distribution of High School Achievement." *Sociology of Education* 62 (1989): 172–92.

Lemann, Nicolas. *The Big Test: The Secret History of the American Meritocracy.* New York: Ferrar Straus and Giroux, 1999.

Leonhardt, David. "The College Dropout Boom." *New York Times*, May 24, 2005, http://www.nytimes.com/2005/05/24/national/class/EDUCATION-FINAL.html?pagewanted=1

Lewin, Tamar. "Many Specialists at Private Universities Earn More than Presidents." *New York Times*, February 22, 2009, http://www.nytimes.com/2009/02/23/education/23pay.html

Liptak, Adam. "On the Bench and Off: The Eminently Quotable Justice Scalia." *New York Times*, May 11, 2009, http://www.nytimes.com/2009/05/12/us/12bar.html

Lucas, Samuel R. *Tracking Inequality: Stratification and Mobility in American High Schools.* New York: Teachers College Press, 1999.

———. "Effectively Maintained Inequality: Education Transitions, Track Mobility and Social Background Effects." *American Journal of Sociology* 106 (2001): 1642–90.

Manning, Robert D. "Living With Debt: A Life Stage Analysis of Changing Attitude and Behaviors." Rochester, NY: Rochester Institute of Technology, 2005.

Manski, Charles F. "Identification of Endogenous Social Effects: The Reflection Problem." *Review of Economic Studies* 60 (1993): 531–42.

Marks, Helen M., and Susan R. Jones. "Community Service in the Transition: Shifts and Continuities in Participation from High School to College." *Journal of Higher Education* 75 (2004): 307–39.

Marsden, George. *The Soul of the American University: From Protestant Establishment to Established Nonbelief.* New York: Oxford University Press, 1994.

Massey, Douglas, Camille Charles, Garvey Lundy, and Mary Fischer. *The Source of the River: The Social Origins of Freshmen at America's Selective Colleges and Universities.* Princeton, NJ: Princeton University Press, 2003.

Massy, William F., and Robert Zemsky. "Faculty Discretionary Time: Departments and the Academic Ratchet." *Journal of Higher Education* 65 (1994): 1–22.

McCabe, Donald L., Linda Klebe Trevino, and Kenneth D. Butterfield. "Dishonesty in Academic Environments: The Influence of Peer Reporting Requirements." *Journal of Higher Education* 72 (2001): 29–45.

Mickelson, Rosalyn. "Segregation and the SAT." *Ohio State Law Journal* 67 (2006): 157–99.

Milmen, Jeffrey F., Joseph B. Berger, and Eric L. Dey. "Faculty Time Allocation: A Study of Change over Twenty Years." *Journal of Higher Education* 17 (2000): 454–75.

Murray, Charles. *Real Education: Four Simple Truths for Bringing American Schools Back to Reality.* New York: Crown Publishing House, 2008.

Nathan, Rebekah. *My Freshman Year: What a Professor Learned by Becoming a Student.* New York: Penguin Books, 2006.

National Center for Education Statistics (NCES). *Access to Postsecondary Education for the 1992 High School Graduates, NCES 98–105.* Washington, DC: U.S. Department of Education, 1997.

———. *Community College Students: Goals, Academic Preparation, and Outcomes, NCES 2003-164.* Washington, DC: U.S. Department of Education, 2003.

———. *Waiting to Attend College: Undergraduates Who Delay Their Postsecondary Enrollment, NCES 2005-152.* Washington, DC: U.S. Department of Education, 2005.

———. *Profile of Undergraduates in U.S. Postsecondary Institutions: 2003–2004, NCES 2006-184.* Washington, DC: U.S. Department of Education, 2006.

———. *Descriptive Summary of 2003–04 Beginning Postsecondary Students: Three Years Later, NCES 2008-174.* Washington, DC: U.S. Department of Education, 2008.

———. *Digest of Education Statistics.* Washington, DC: U.S. Department of Education, 2008.

National Commission on Excellence in Education. *A Nation at Risk: The Imperative for Educational Reform.* Washington, DC: U.S. Department of Education, 1983.

National Science Foundation (NSF). *Shaping the Future: New Expectations for Undergraduate Education in Science, Mathematics, Engineering, and Technology.* Washington, DC: NSF, 1996, http://www.nsf.gov/pubs/stis1996/nsf96139.txt

National Survey of Student Engagement (NSSE). *National Benchmarks of Effective Educational Practice.* Bloomington, IN: Center for Postsecondary Research, Indiana University Bloomington, 2000.

———. *Experiences That Matter: Enhancing Student Learning and Success.* Bloomington, IN: Center for Postsecondary Research, Indiana University Bloomington, 2007.

———. *Promoting Engagement for All Students: The Imperative to Look Within.* Blooming-ton, IN: Center for Postsecondary Research, Indiana University Bloomington, 2008.

Nisbett, Richard. *Intelligence and How to Get It.* New York: Norton, 2009.

Nyquist, Jody D., Ann E. Austin, Jo Sprague, and Donald H. Wulff. *The Development of Graduate Students as Prospective Teaching Scholars: A Four-Year Longitudinal Study, Final Report.* Seattle: University of Washington, 2001.

Nyquist, Jody D., Laura Manning, Donald H. Wulff, and Ann E. Austin. "On the Road to Becoming a Professor: The Graduate Student Experience." *Change* 31 (1999): 18–27.

Obama, Barack. Remarks prepared for the Joint Session of Congress, February 24, 2009. Washington, DC: White House Press Office.

Orfield, Gary, and Susan E. Eaton. *Dismantling Desegregation: The Quiet Reversal of Brown v. Board of Education.* New York: The New Press, 1996.

Organisation for Economic Co-operation and Development, Directorate for Educa-tion, Education Committee, Centre for Educational Research and Innovation (Ceri) Governing Board. *PISA for Higher Education.* Paris: Organisation for Economic Co-operation and Development, 2006.

Organisation for Economic Co-operation and Development. "Assessment of Higher Education Learning Outcomes (AHELO)." http://www.oecd.org/document/41/0,3343,en_2649_35961291_42295209_1_1_1_1,00.html

Pascarella, Ernest T., and Patrick T. Terenzini. *How College Affects Students: Findings and Insights from Twenty Years of Research.* San Francisco: Jossey-Bass, 1991.

———. *How College Affects Students: A Third Decade of Research.* San Francisco: Jossey-Bass, 2005.

Pascarella, Ernest T., Louise Bohr, Amaury Nora, Michelle Desler, and Barbara Zusman. "Impacts of the On-Campus and Off-Campus Work on First-Year Cognitive Out-comes." *Journal of College Student Development* 35 (1994): 362–70.

Pascarella, Ernest T., Louise Bohr, Amaury Nora, Barbara Zusman, and Patricia Inman. "Cognitive Impacts of Living on Campus versus Commuting to College." University Park, PA: National Center on Postsecondary Teaching, Learning and Assessment, 1992.

Pascarella, Ernest T., Marcia Edison, Amaury Nora, Linda Serra Hagedorn, and Pat-rick T. Terenzini. "Does Work Inhibit Cognitive Development During College?" *Educational Evaluation and Policy Analysis* 20 (1998): 75–93.

Pascarella, Ernest T., Marcia Edison, Elizabeth J.Whitt, Amaury Nora, Linda Serra Hagedorn, and Patrick T. Terenzini. "Cognitive Effects of Greek Affiliation during the First Year of College." *NASPA Journal* 33 (1996): 242–59.

Pascarella, Ernest T., Lamont Flowers, and Elizabeth J. Whitt. "Cognitive Effects of Greek Affiliation in College: Additional Evidence." *NASPA Journal* 38 (2001): 280–301.

Perrin, Noel. "How Students at Dartmouth Came to Deserve Better Grades." *Chronicle of Higher Education,* October 9, 1998.

Peter D. Hart Research Associated, Inc. *How Should Colleges Assess and Improve Student Learning? Employers Views on the Accountability Challenge.* Washington, DC: Peter D. Hart Research Associated, Inc., 2008.

Pew Research Center. *Pew Research Center Biennial News Consumption Survey.* Washing-ton, DC: Pew Research Center, 2008.

Phillips, Meredith. "What Makes Schools Effective? A Comparison of the Relationships of Communitarian Climate and Academic Climate to Mathematics Achievements and Attendance during Middle School." *American Educational Research Journal* 34 (1997): 633–62.

Pike, Gary R. "The Effects of Residential Learning Communities and Traditional Residential Living Arrangements on Educational Gains during the First Year of College." *Journal of College Student Development* 40 (1999): 269–84.

———. "The Influence of Fraternity or Sorority Membership on Students' College Experiences and Cognitive Development." *Research in Higher Education* 41 (2000): 117–39.

Pope, Loren. *Colleges that Change Lives: 40 Schools That Will Change the Way You Think about Colleges.* New York: Penguin Books, 2006.

Powell, Arthur G., Eleanor Farrar, and David K. Cohen. *The Shopping Mall High School: Winners and Losers in the Educational Marketplace.* Boston: Houghton Mifflin Company, 1985.

Powell, Walter, and Jason Owen-Smith. "The New World of Knowledge Production in the Life Sciences." In *The Future of the City of Intellect: The Changing American University,* edited by Steven Brint, 107–32. Stanford, CA: Stanford University Press, 2002.

Rau, William, and Barbara Sherman Heyl. "Humanizing the College Classroom: Collaborative Learning and Social Organization among Students." *Teaching Sociology* 18 (1990): 141–55.

Reuben, Julie A. *The Making of the Modern University: Intellectual Transformation and the Marginalization of Morality.* Chicago: University of Chicago Press, 1996.

Reynolds, John, Michael Stewart, Ryan MacDonald, and Lacey Sischo. "Have Adolescents Become Too Ambitious? High School Seniors' Educational and Occupational Plans, 1976 to 2000." *Social Problems* 53 (2006): 186–206.

Rhoades, Gary. "The Study of American Professions." In *Sociology of Higher Education: Contributions and their Contexts,* edited by Patricia Gumport, 113–46. Baltimore: Johns Hopkins University Press, 2007.

Roksa, Josipa, Eric Grodsky, Richard Arum, and Adam Gamoran. "Changes in Higher Education and Social Stratification in the United States." In *Stratification in Higher Education: A Comparative Study,* edited by Yossi Shavit, Richard Arum, and Adam Gamoran, 165–91. Stanford, CA: Stanford University Press, 2007.

Roksa, Josipa, Davis Jenkins, Shanna Jaggars, Matthew Zeidenberg, and Sung-Woo Cho. *Policies for Promoting Gatekeeper Course Success for Students Needing Developmental Education in Virginia's Community Colleges.* New York: Community College Research Center, Teachers College, Columbia University, 2009.

Rose, Lowell C., and Alec M. Gallup. *The 35th Annual Phi Delta Kappa/Gallup Poll of the Public's Attitudes toward the Public Schools.* Bloomington, IN: Phi Delta Kappa International, 2003.

Rosenbaum, James. *Beyond College for All: Career Paths for the Forgotten Half.* New York: Russell Sage Foundation, 2001.

Rosenthal, Robert, and Lenore Jacobson. "Pygmalion in the Classroom." *Urban Review* 3 (1968): 1–16.

Saenz, Victor B., and Douglas S. Barrera. *Findings from the 2005 College Student Survey (CSS): National Aggregates.* Los Angeles: Higher Education Research Institute, University of California at Los Angeles, 2007.

Sallie Mae Foundation. *How Undergraduate Students Use Credit Cards: Sallie Mae's National Study of Usage Rates and Trends 2009.* Wilkes-Barre, PA: Sallie Mae Foundation, 2009.

Schmidt, Peter. "Former Top Official at Education Dept. Criticizes How it Approached

College Access." *Chronicle of Higher Education*, January 9, 2009, http://chronicle
.com/news/article/5767/former-top-official-at-education-dept-criticizes-how-it
-approached-college-access

Schneider, Barbara, and David Stevenson. *The Ambitious Generation: America's Teenagers Motivated but Directionless*. New Haven: Yale University Press, 1999.

Scott, Joan. Statement on behalf of AAUP, as part of a Testimony Before the Pennsylvania General Assembly's House Select Committee on Student Academic Freedom, November 9, 2005, http://www.aaup.org/AAUP/GR/state/Academic+Bill+of+Rights+State+Level/Scotttestimony.htm

Sewell, William, Archibald Haller, and Alejandro Portes. "The Educational and Early Occupational Attainment Process." *American Sociological Review* 34 (1969): 82–92.

Shavelson, Richard. "The Collegiate Learning Assessment." *Ford Policy Forum 2008: Forum for the Future of Higher Education*, http://net.educause.edu/forum/fp08.asp

Shavit, Yossi, and Hans-Peter Blossfeld. *Persistent Inequality: Changing Educational Attainment in Thirteen Countries*. Boulder, CO: Westview Press, 1993.

Shulman, James, and William Bowen. *The Game of Life: College Sports and Educational Values*. Princeton, NJ: Princeton University Press, 2001.

Shulman, Lee S. *Teaching as Community Property: Essays on Higher Education*. San Francisco: Jossey-Bass, 2004.

———. Excerpt from transcript of the documentary film *Declining by Degrees: Higher Education at Risk*. New York: Public Broadcast System, 2005, http://www
.decliningbydegrees.org/meet-experts-5.html.

Singer, Judith D. "Using SAC PRO MIXED to Fit Multilevel Models, Hierarchical Models, and Individual Growth Models." *Journal of Educational and Behavioral Statistics* 23/4 (1998): 323–55.

Slaughter, Sheila, and Larry L. Leslie. *Academic Capitalism: Politics, Policies, and the Entrepreneurial University*. Baltimore: Johns Hopkins University Press, 1997.

Smart, John C., and Paul D. Umbach. "Faculty and Academic Environments: Using Holland's Theory to Explore Differences in how Faculty Structure Undergraduate Courses." *Journal of College Student Development* 48 (2007): 183–95.

Sorokin, Pitrim. *Social and Cultural Mobility*. New York: Free Press, 1959.

Spellings, Margaret. "Statement on International Education Week 2008." Washington, DC, 2008, http://www.iew.state.gov/2008/docs/2008sec-ed-statement.pdf

Spenner, Kenneth, and David Featherman. "Achievement Ambition." *Annual Review of Sociology* 4 (1978): 373–420.

Spring, Leonard, Mary Elizabeth Stanne, and Samuel S. Donovan. "Effects of Small-Group Learning in Undergraduates in Science, Mathematics, Engineering, and Technology: A Meta-Analysis." *Review of Educational Research* 69 (1999): 21–51.

Steele, Claude M. "A Threat in the Air: How Stereotypes Shape Intellectual Identity and Performance." *American Psychologist* 52 (1997): 613–29.

Steele, Claude M., and Joshua Aronson. "Stereotype Threat and the Intellectual Test Performance of African-Americans." *Journal of Personality and Social Psychology* 69 (1995): 797–811.

Stevens, Mitchell. *Creating a Class: College Admissions and the Education of Elites*. Cambridge, MA: Harvard University Press, 2007.

Stevens, Mitchell, Elizabeth Armstrong, and Richard Arum. "Sieve, Incubator, Temple, Hub: Empirical and Theoretical Advances in the Sociology of Higher Education." *Annual Review of Sociology* 34 (2008): 127–51.

Stinebrickner, Ralph, and Todd R. Stinebrickner. "Time-Use and College Outcomes." *Journal of Econometrics* 121 (2004): 243–69.

Stuber, Jenny. "Class, Culture, and the Participation in the Collegiate Extra-Curriculum." *Sociological Forum* 24 (2009): 877–900.

Swidler, Ann. "Culture in Action: Symbols and Strategies." *American Sociological Review* 51 (1986): 273–86.

Taylor, Kathe. *Learning Community Research and Assessment: What We Know Now. National Learning Communities Project Monograph Series.* Olympia: Washington Center for Improving the Quality of Undergraduate Education, 2003.

Terenzini, Patrick T., Ernest T. Pascarella, and Gregory S. Blimling. "Students' Out-of-Class Experiences and Their Influence on Learning and Cognitive Development: A Literature Review." *Journal of College Student Development* 40 (1999): 610–23.

Tinto, Vincent. *Leaving College: Rethinking the Causes and Cures of Student Attrition.* Chicago: University of Chicago Press, 1993.

Traub, James. "No Gr_du_te Left Behind." *New York Times Magazine,* September 30, 2007.

Trow, Martin. "Reflections on the Transformation from Mass to Universal Higher Education." *Daedalus* 99 (1970): 1–42.

Turner, Sarah E., and William Bowen. "The Flight from the Arts and Sciences: Trends in Degrees Conferred." *Science* 250 (1990): 517–21.

Tyson, Karolyn, William Darity, and Domini Castellino. "It's Not 'a Black Thing': Understanding the Burden of Acting White and Other Dilemmas of High Achievement." *American Sociological Review* 70 (2005): 582–605.

Umbach, Paul D. "Faculty Cultures and College Teaching." In *The Scholarship of Teaching and Learning in Higher Education: An Evidence-Based Perspective,* edited by Raymond P. Perry and John C. Smart, 263–318. New York: Springer, 2007.

United States Department of Education. *A Test of Leadership: Charting the Future of U.S. Higher Education.* Washington, DC: U.S. Department of Education, 2006.

———. *FY 2009 Congressional Action.* Washington, DC: U.S. Department of Education, 2009.

Wagner, Alan. *Measuring Up Internationally: Developing Skills and Knowledge for the Global Knowledge Economy.* San Jose, CA: National Center for Public Policy and Higher Education, 2006.

Walters, Pamela. "The Limits of Growth: School Expansion and School Reform in Historical Perspective." In *Handbook of the Sociology of Education,* edited by Maureen Hallinan, 241–61. New York: Springer Publishers, 2006.

Whitt, Elizabeth J., Marcia Edison, Ernest T. Pascarella, Amaury Nora, and Patrick T. Terenzini. "Interactions with Peers and Objective and Self-Reported Cognitive Outcomes across 3 Years of College." *Journal of College Student Development* 40 (1999): 61–78.

Wiske, Martha Stone, ed. *Teaching for Understanding: Linking Research with Practice.* San Francisco: Jossey-Bass, 1998.

Zhou, Min. "Growing Up American: The Challenge Confronting Immigrant Americans and Children of Immigrants." *Annual Review of Sociology* 23 (1997): 63–95.

Index